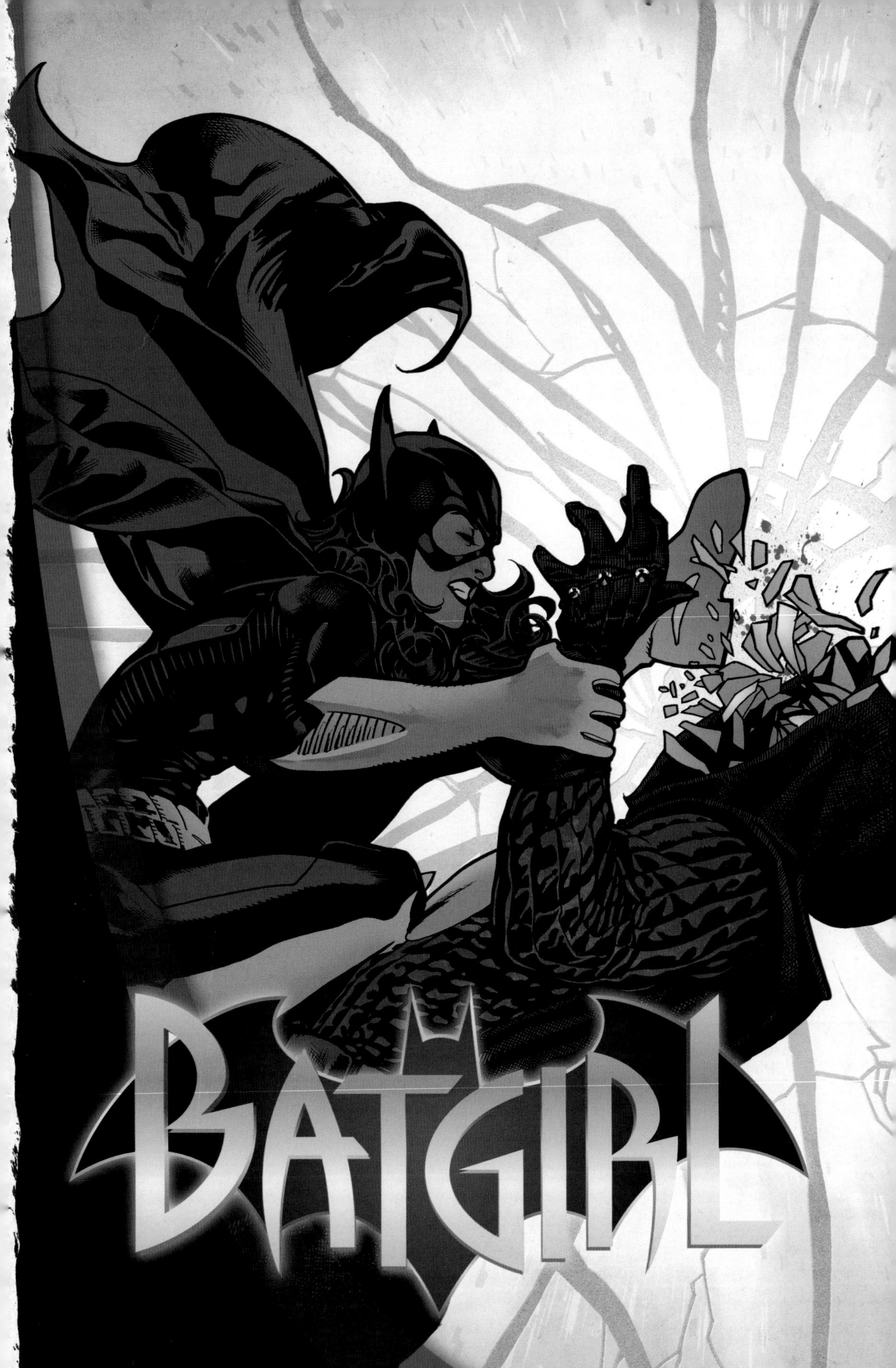
BATGIRL

VOLUME 1 THE DARKEST REFLECTION

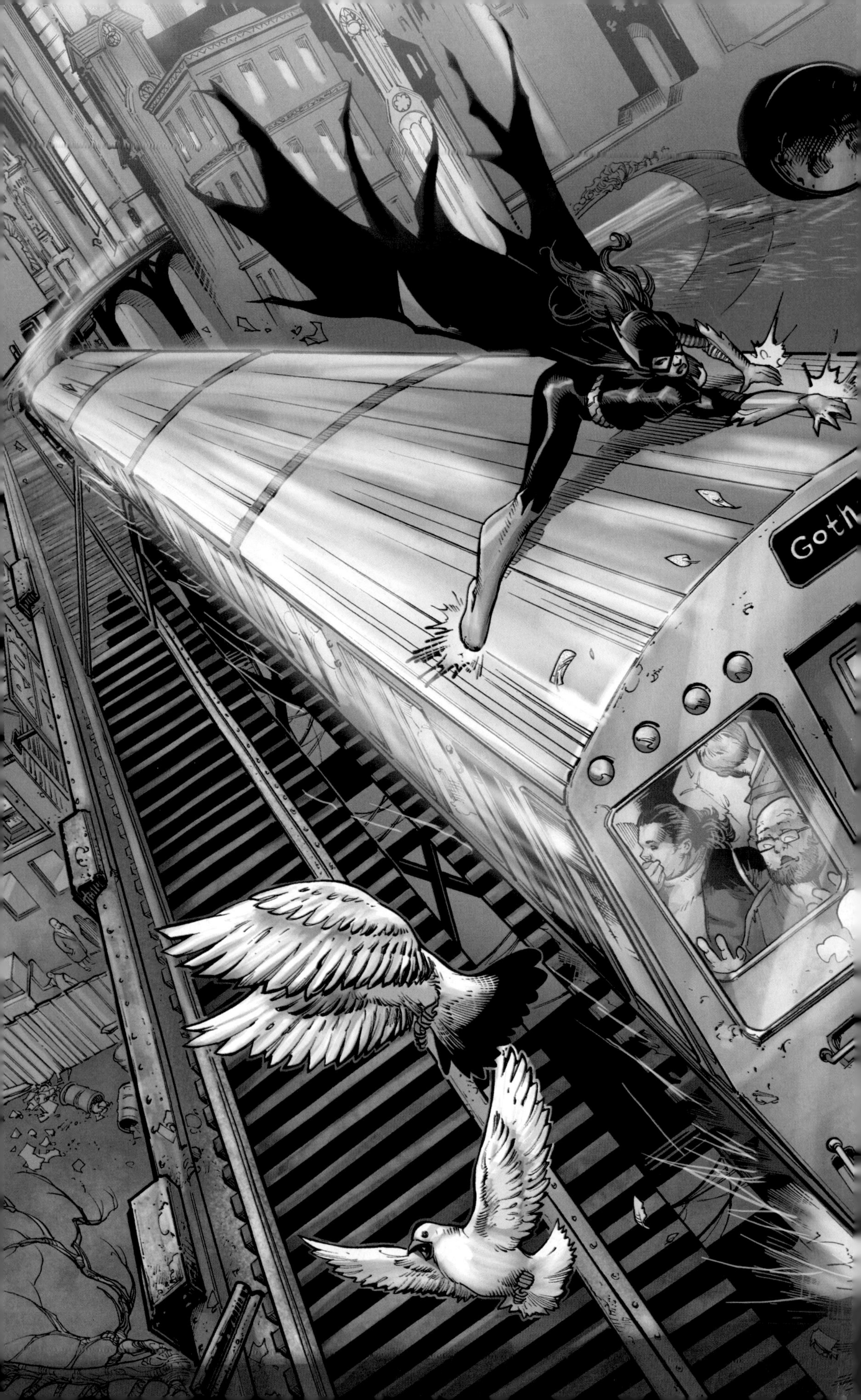
Goth

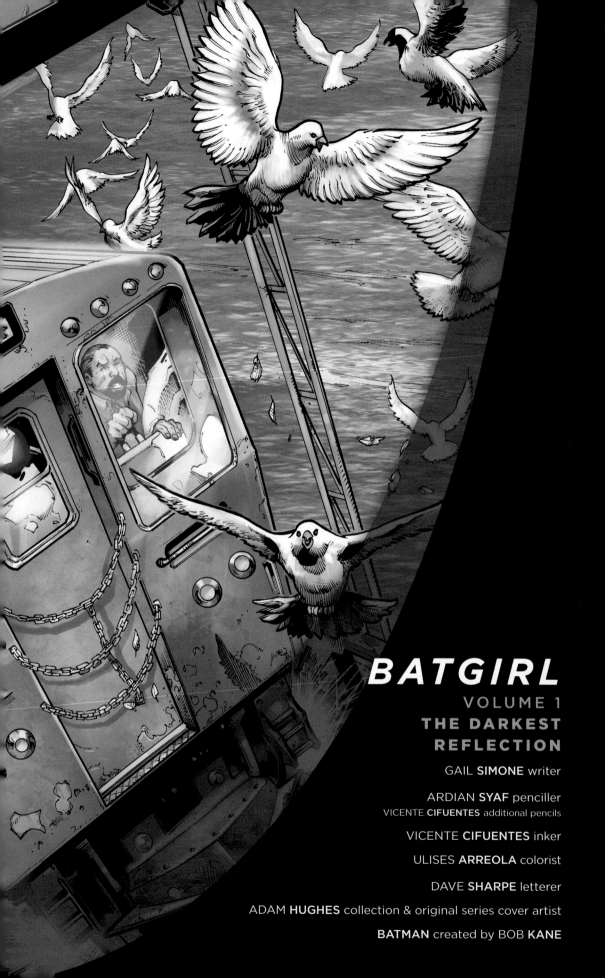

BATGIRL

VOLUME 1
THE DARKEST REFLECTION

GAIL **SIMONE** writer

ARDIAN **SYAF** penciller
VICENTE **CIFUENTES** additional pencils

VICENTE **CIFUENTES** inker

ULISES **ARREOLA** colorist

DAVE **SHARPE** letterer

ADAM **HUGHES** collection & original series cover artist

BATMAN created by BOB **KANE**

BOBBIE CHASE Editor – Original Series KATIE KUBERT Assistant Editor – Original Series PETER HAMBOUSSI Editor
ROBBIN BROSTERMAN Design Director – Books ROBBIE BIEDERMAN Publication Design

BOB HARRAS VP – Editor-in-Chief

DIANE NELSON President DAN DIDIO and JIM LEE Co-Publishers
GEOFF JOHNS Chief Creative Officer
JOHN ROOD Executive VP – Sales, Marketing and Business Development
AMY GENKINS Senior VP – Business and Legal Affairs NAIRI GARDINER Senior VP – Finance
JEFF BOISON VP – Publishing Operations MARK CHIARELLO VP – Art Direction and Design
JOHN CUNNINGHAM VP – Marketing TERRI CUNNINGHAM VP – Talent Relations and Services
ALISON GILL Senior VP – Manufacturing and Operations HANK KANALZ Senior VP – Digital
JAY KOGAN VP – Business and Legal Affairs, Publishing JACK MAHAN VP – Business Affairs, Talent
NICK NAPOLITANO VP – Manufacturing Administration SUE POHJA VP – Book Sales
COURTNEY SIMMONS Senior VP – Publicity BOB WAYNE Senior VP – Sales

BATGIRL VOLUME 1: THE DARKEST REFLECTION

DC Comics, 1700 Broadway, New York, NY 10019
A Warner Bros. Entertainment Company
Printed by RR Donnelley, Salem, VA, USA. 6/8/12. First Printing.

HC ISBN: 978-1-4012-3475-1
SC ISBN: 978-1-4012-3814-8

Library of Congress Cataloging-in-Publication Data

Simone, Gail.
Batgirl. Volume 1, The darkest reflection / Gail Simone, Ardian Syaf, Vicente Cifuentes.
p. cm.
"Originally published in single magazine form in BATGIRL 1-6" _ T.p. verso.
ISBN 978-1-4012-3475-1
1. Graphic novels. I. Syaf, Ardian. II. Cifuentes, Vicente. III. Title. IV. Title: Darkest reflection.
PN6728.B358S56 2012
741.5'973 — dc23
2012010303

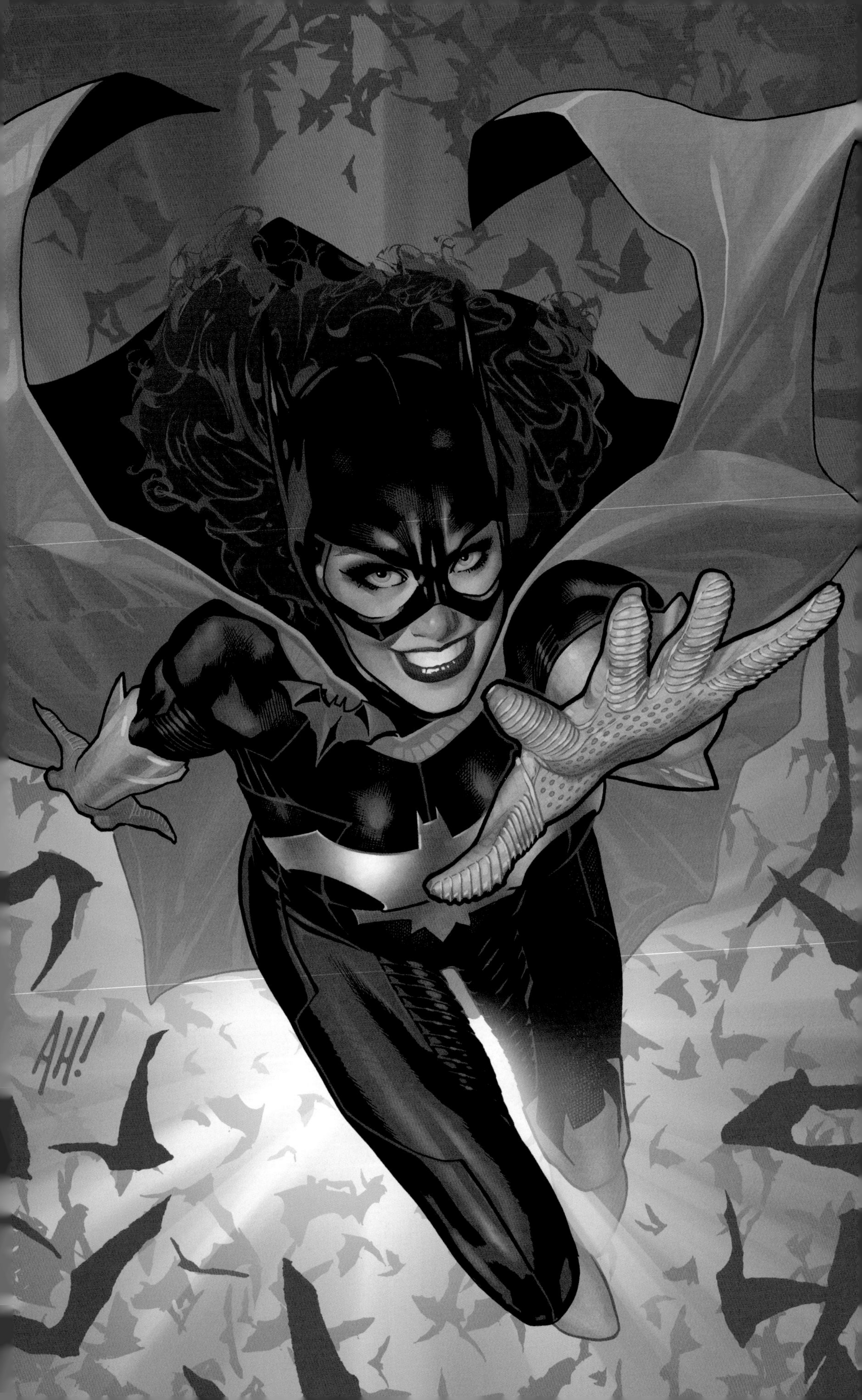
AH!

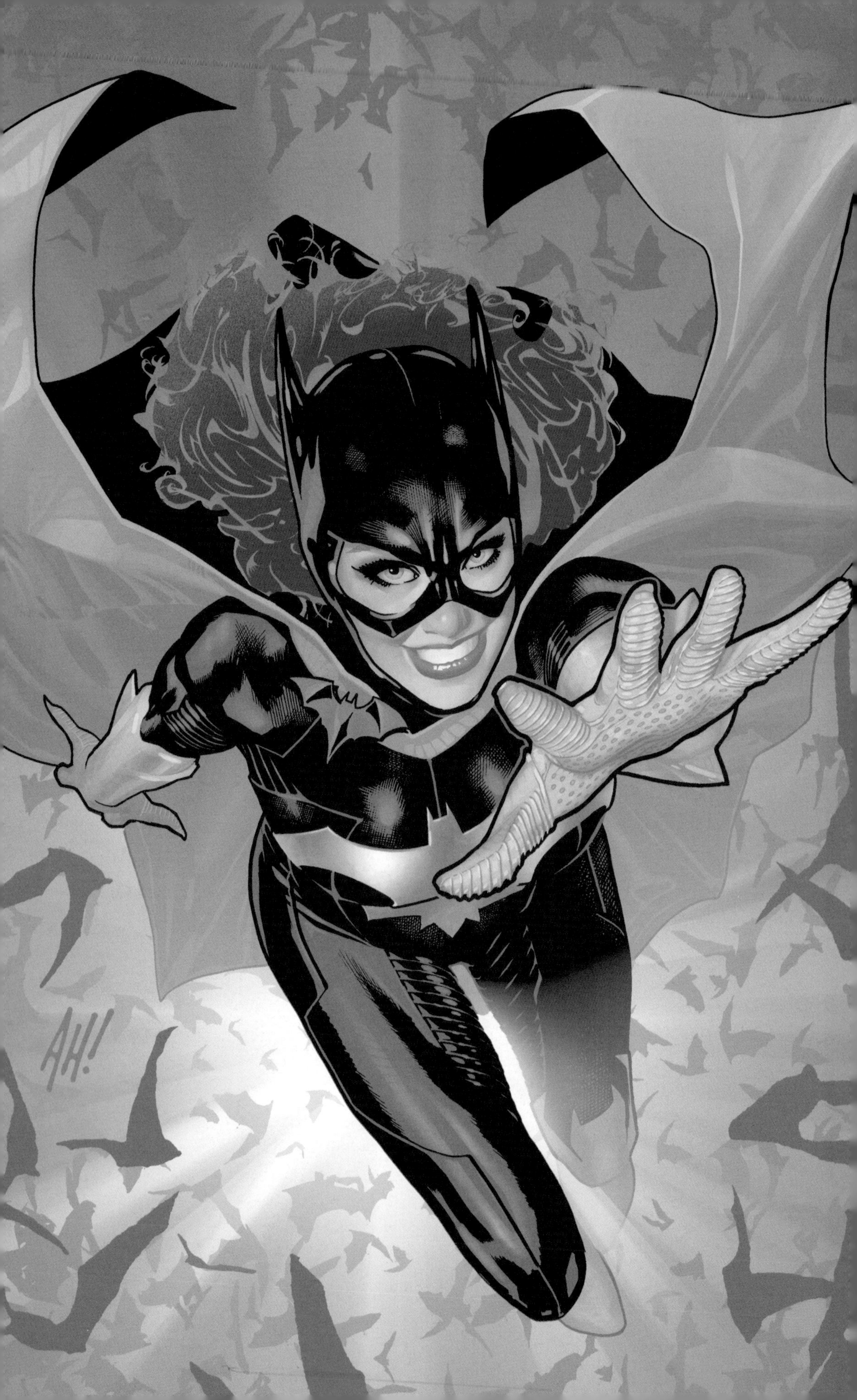
AH!

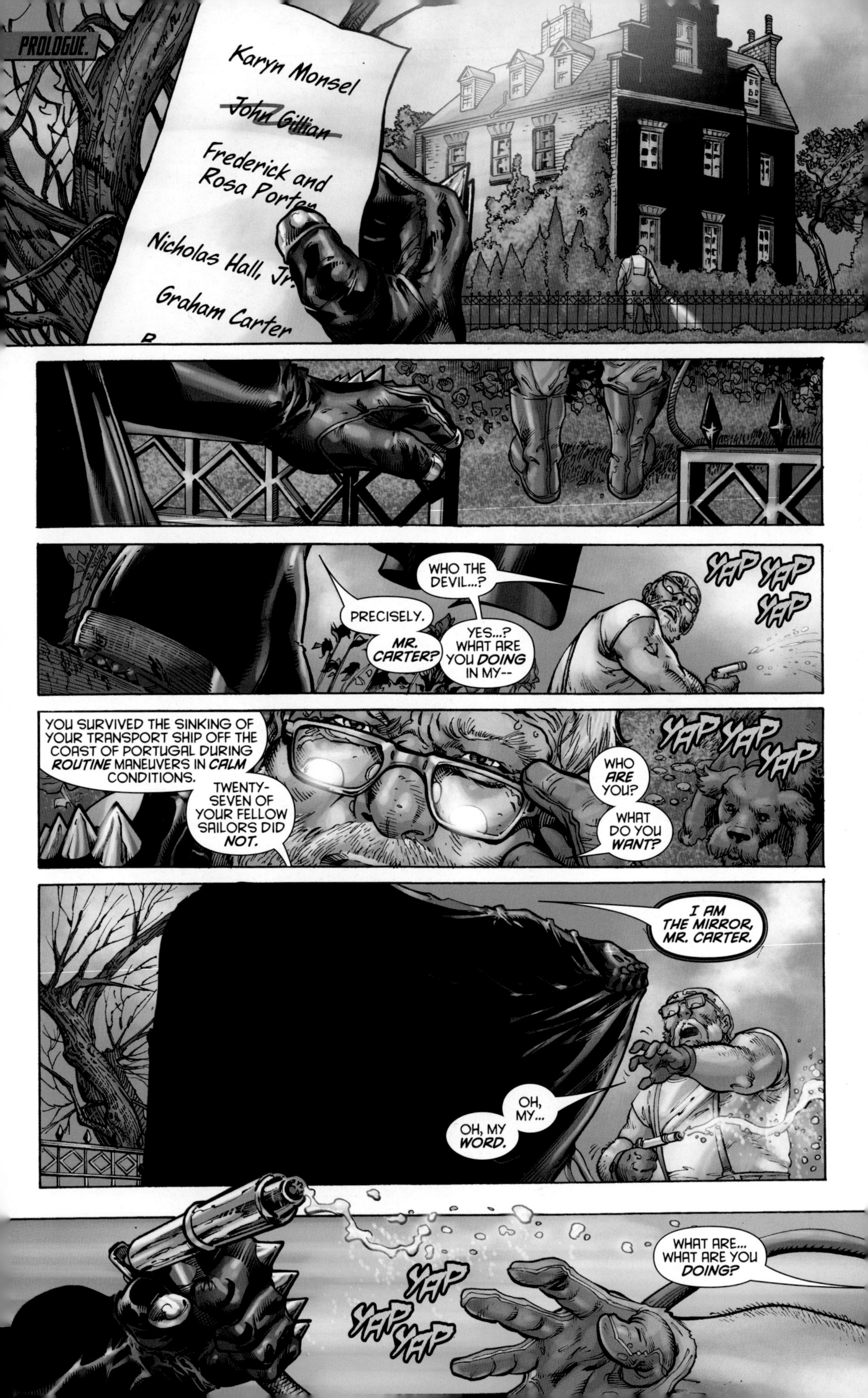

PROLOGUE.
Karyn Monsel
John Gillian
Frederick and Rosa Porter
Nicholas Hall, Jr.
Graham Carter
WHO THE DEVIL...?
PRECISELY.
MR. CARTER?
YES...? WHAT ARE YOU DOING IN MY--
YAP YAP YAP
YOU SURVIVED THE SINKING OF YOUR TRANSPORT SHIP OFF THE COAST OF PORTUGAL DURING ROUTINE MANEUVERS IN CALM CONDITIONS.
TWENTY-SEVEN OF YOUR FELLOW SAILORS DID NOT.
WHO ARE YOU?
WHAT DO YOU WANT?
YAP YAP YAP
I AM THE MIRROR, MR. CARTER.
OH, MY...
OH, MY WORD.
WHAT ARE... WHAT ARE YOU DOING?
YAP YAP YAP

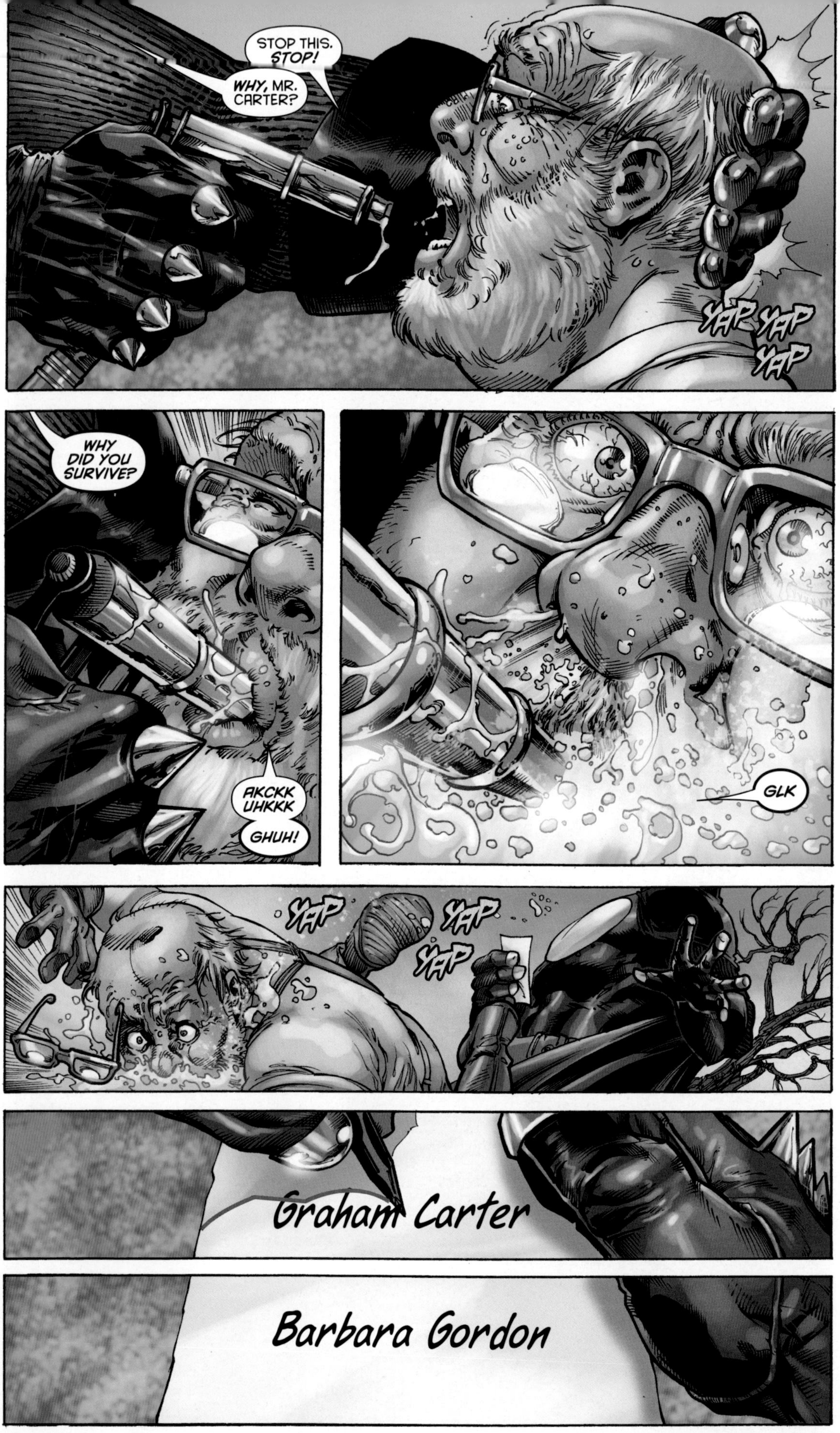
STOP THIS. STOP!
WHY, MR. CARTER?
YAP YAP YAP
WHY DID YOU SURVIVE?
AKCKK UHKKK
GHUH!
GLK
YAP YAP YAP
Graham Carter
Barbara Gordon

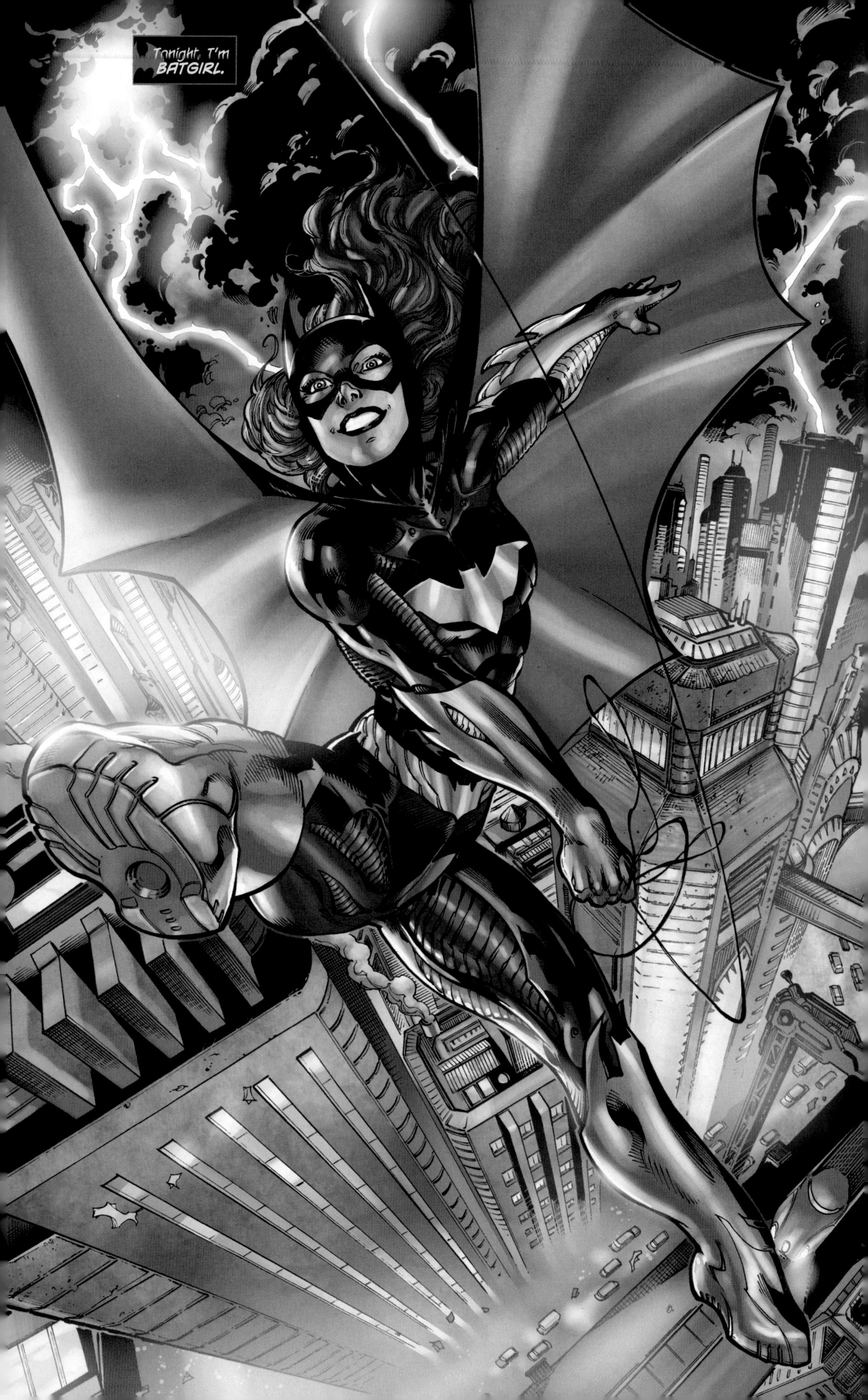
Tonight, I'm BATGIRL.

"HAVE YOU EVER WANTED SOMETHING SO BADLY THAT IT WAS ALL YOU THOUGHT ABOUT, DAY AND NIGHT?"

"TO BE FREE, I MEAN. UNFETTERED. WITHOUT THE CHAINS THAT HOLD US DOWN."

YOU CAN'T CALL IT A DREAM, EVEN. IT'S A NEED. A *NECESSITY*.

SO DEEP, IT'S IN THE BLOOD. IT'S IN THE *BONES*.

THAT'S HOW I FEEL ABOUT *HOME INVASION* AND *MURDER*.

PLEASE. PLEASE, JUST *LEAVE*. WE WON'T...WE WON'T...

WHO *ARE* YOU?

OH. WHERE ARE MY MANNERS?

I'M SORRY, I THOUGHT YOU KNEW.

DANNY, GIVE THE ORTEGAS THE SCRAPBOOK, WOULD YOU?

WE'RE *THE BRISBY KILLERS*.

FAMILY MASSACRE IN GOTHAM SUBURB

Jack Ryder
World Associated Press and Times

Only Surviving Daughter Returns to Gruesome Scene

Tonight, the peaceful Gotham suburb of Brisby is quiet for the most tragic reason possible. Brisby is the retirement community of choice for former members of the Gotham City Police Force, and is run as an area local criminals stay well clear... tragedy managed to find one ...er, ...family even in this quiet, ...in what witnesses say ...d shocking

"BRISBY KILLERS" LIKELY PERPETRATORS IN SECOND BLOODBATH

Breaking News, Central News Desk

In a horrifying scene that alarmed even the most hardened of state troopers, a second family was found killed in the Brisby area outside of Gotham City lines early Thursday morning when neighbors were alerted by the terrified barking of the family's beloved pet dog. The bodies were posed in a grotesque mockery of

(CONT. PAGE TWO)

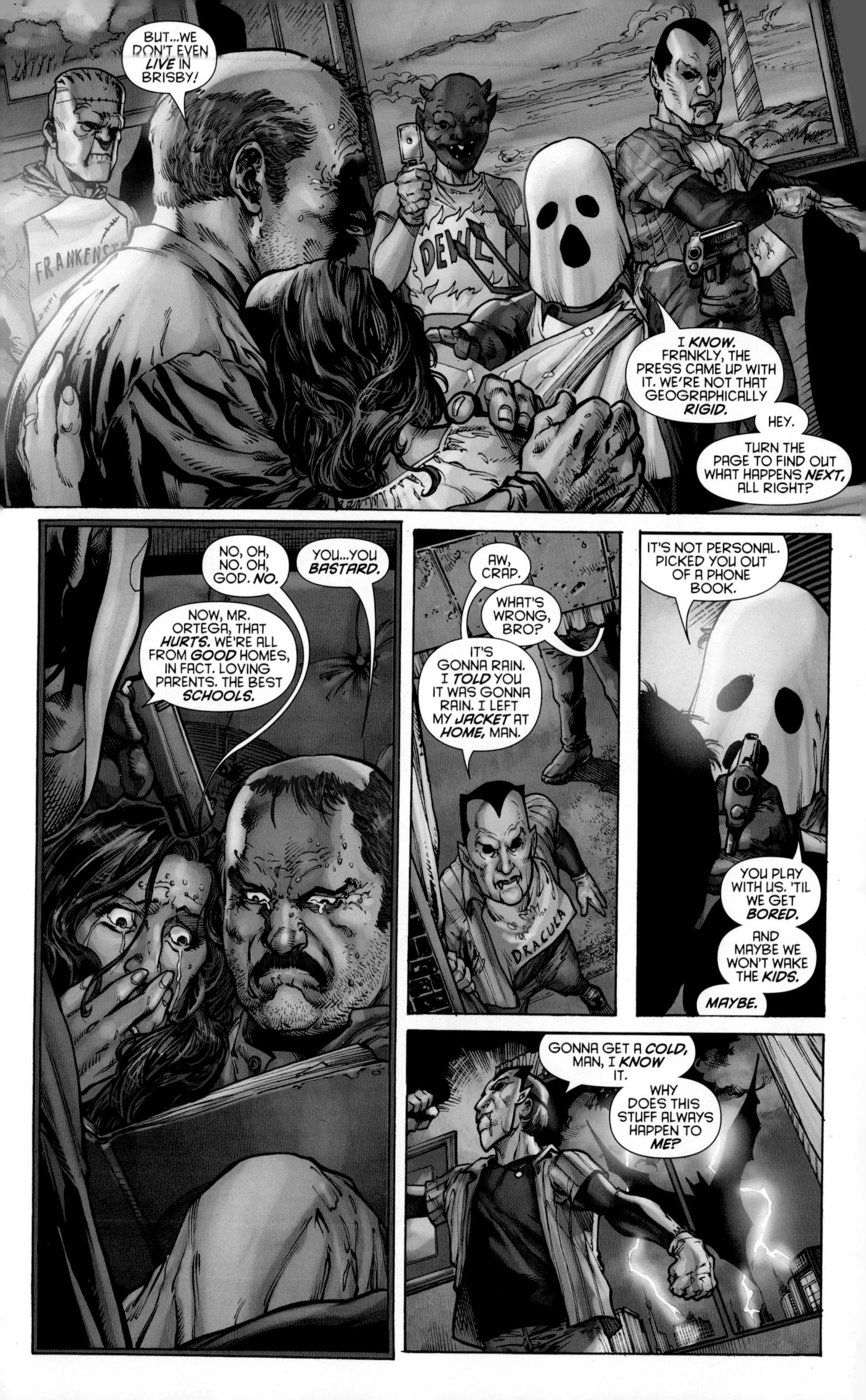
BUT...WE DON'T EVEN LIVE IN BRISBY!
I KNOW. FRANKLY, THE PRESS CAME UP WITH IT. WE'RE NOT THAT GEOGRAPHICALLY RIGID.
HEY.
TURN THE PAGE TO FIND OUT WHAT HAPPENS NEXT, ALL RIGHT?
FRANKENS
DEVIL
NO, OH, NO. OH, GOD. NO.
YOU...YOU BASTARD.
NOW, MR. ORTEGA, THAT HURTS. WE'RE ALL FROM GOOD HOMES, IN FACT. LOVING PARENTS. THE BEST SCHOOLS.
AW, CRAP.
WHAT'S WRONG, BRO?
IT'S GONNA RAIN. I TOLD YOU IT WAS GONNA RAIN. I LEFT MY JACKET AT HOME, MAN.
DRACULA
IT'S NOT PERSONAL. PICKED YOU OUT OF A PHONE BOOK.
YOU PLAY WITH US. 'TIL WE GET BORED.
AND MAYBE WE WON'T WAKE THE KIDS.
MAYBE.
GONNA GET A COLD, MAN, I KNOW IT.
WHY DOES THIS STUFF ALWAYS HAPPEN TO ME?

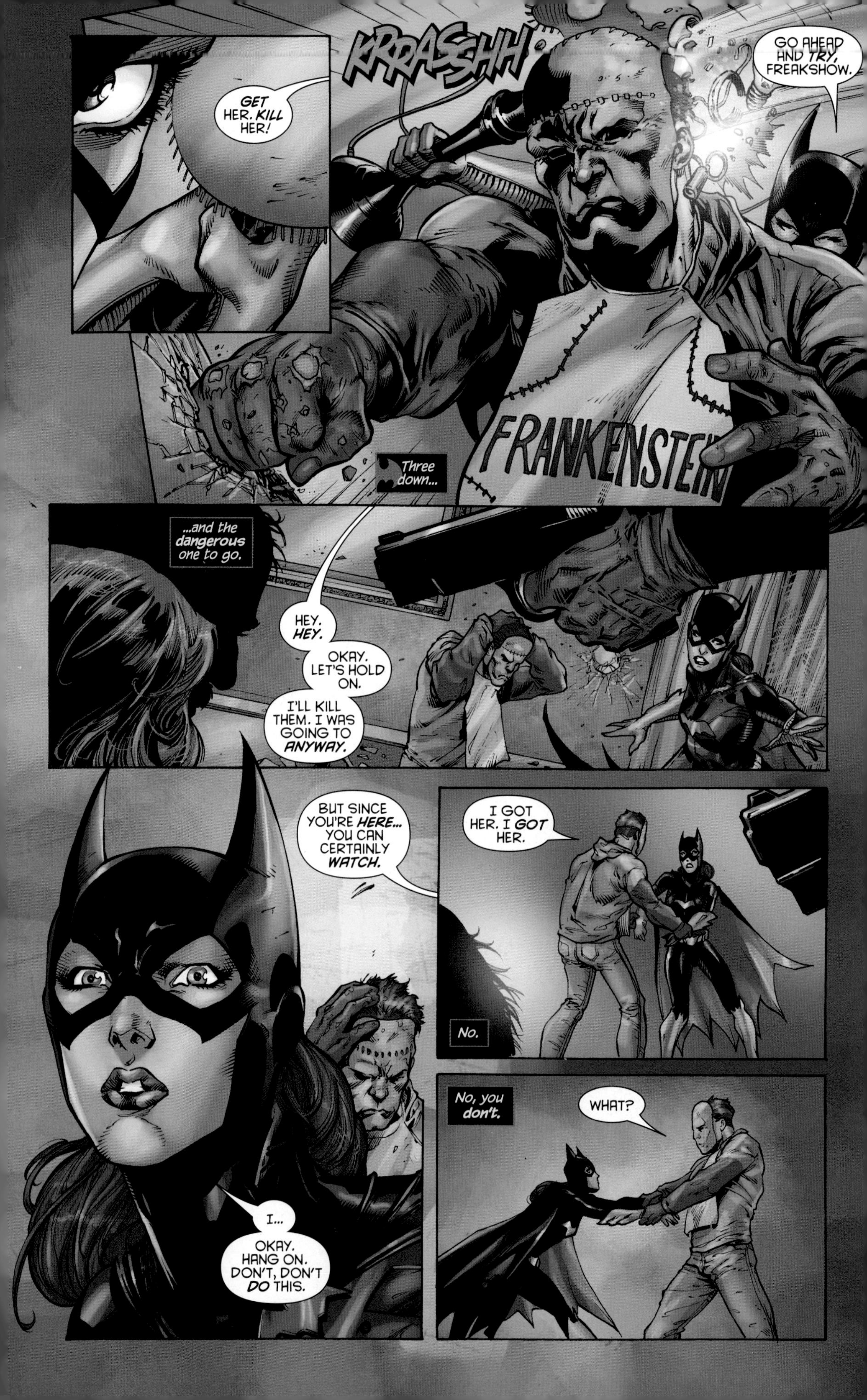
GET HER. KILL HER!
KRRASCHH
GO AHEAD AND TRY, FREAKSHOW.
FRANKENSTEIN
Three down...
...and the dangerous one to go.
HEY. HEY.
OKAY. LET'S HOLD ON.
I'LL KILL THEM. I WAS GOING TO ANYWAY.
BUT SINCE YOU'RE HERE... YOU CAN CERTAINLY WATCH.
I...
OKAY. HANG ON. DON'T, DON'T DO THIS.
I GOT HER. I GOT HER.
No.
No, you don't.
WHAT?

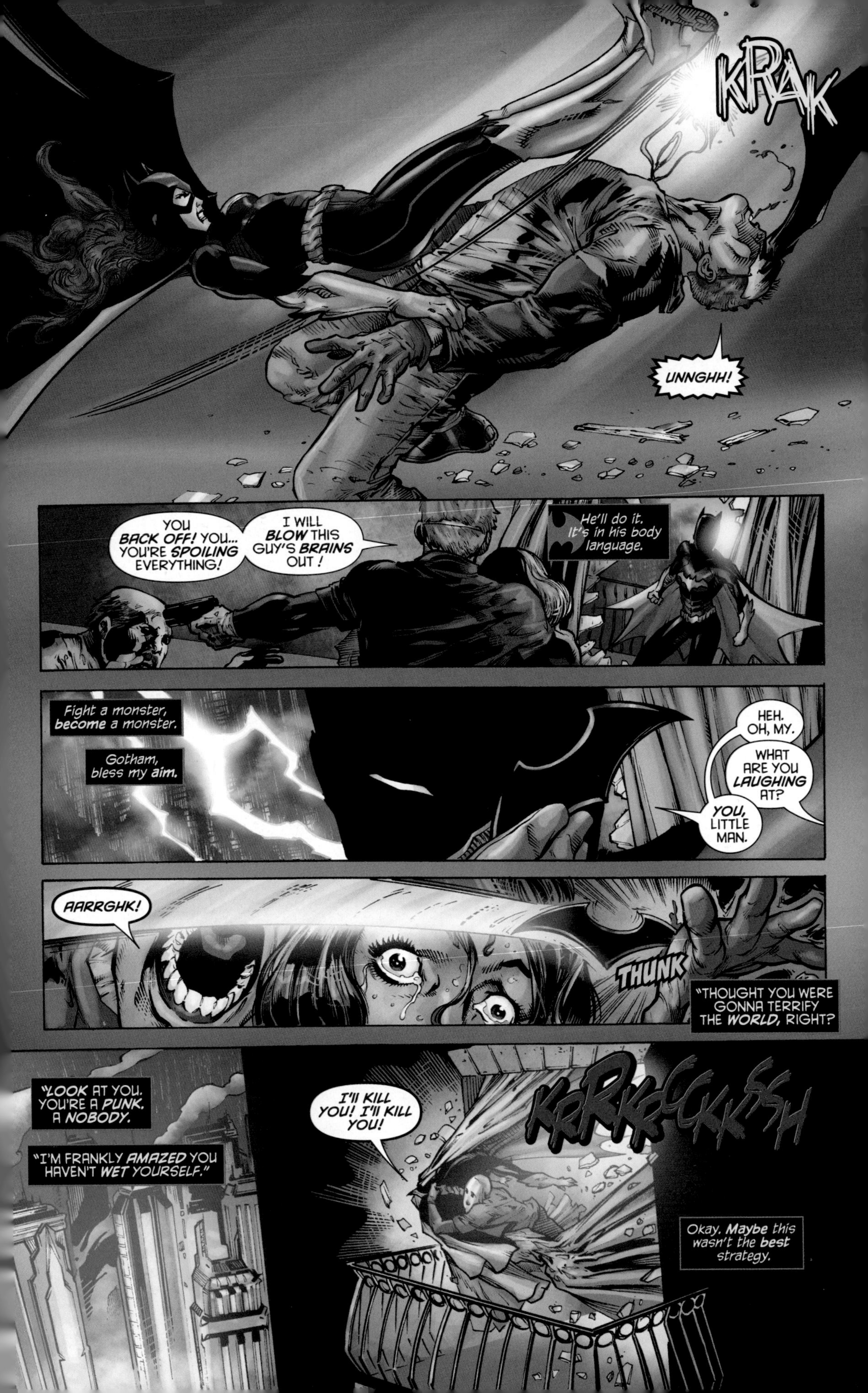
KRAK
UNNGHH!
YOU BACK OFF! YOU... YOU'RE SPOILING EVERYTHING!
I WILL BLOW THIS GUY'S BRAINS OUT !
He'll do it. It's in his body language.
Fight a monster, become a monster.
Gotham, bless my aim.
HEH. OH, MY.
WHAT ARE YOU LAUGHING AT?
YOU, LITTLE MAN.
AARRGHK!
THUNK
"THOUGHT YOU WERE GONNA TERRIFY THE WORLD, RIGHT?
"LOOK AT YOU. YOU'RE A PUNK. A NOBODY.
"I'M FRANKLY AMAZED YOU HAVEN'T WET YOURSELF."
I'LL KILL YOU! I'LL KILL YOU!
KRRKKCKKSSH
Okay. Maybe this wasn't the best strategy.

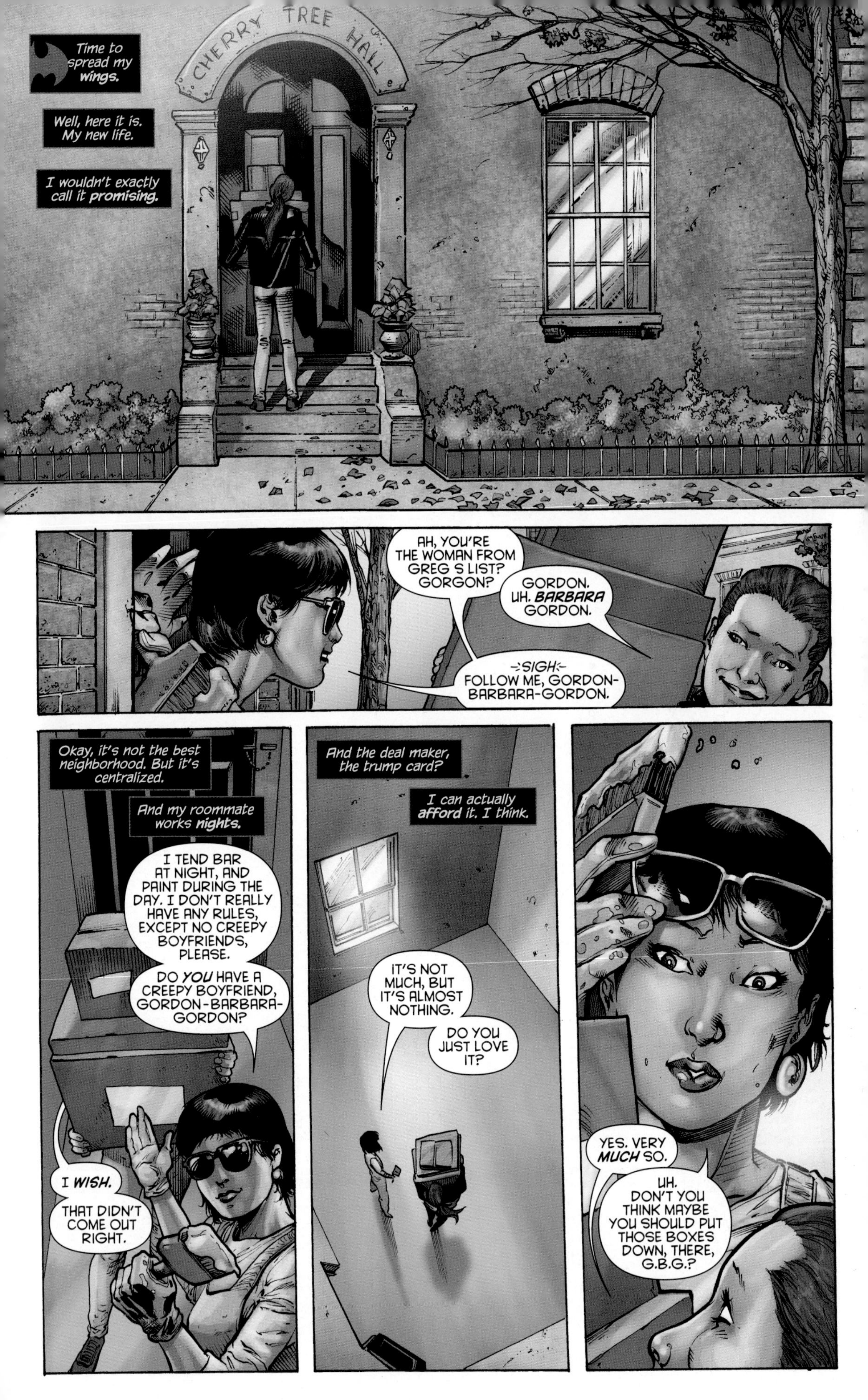
CHERRY TREE HALL
Time to spread my wings.
Well, here it is. My new life.
I wouldn't exactly call it promising.
AH, YOU'RE THE WOMAN FROM GREG S LIST? GORGON?
GORDON. UH. BARBARA GORDON.
SIGH
FOLLOW ME, GORDON-BARBARA-GORDON.
Okay, it's not the best neighborhood. But it's centralized.
And my roommate works nights.
I TEND BAR AT NIGHT, AND PAINT DURING THE DAY. I DON'T REALLY HAVE ANY RULES, EXCEPT NO CREEPY BOYFRIENDS, PLEASE.
DO YOU HAVE A CREEPY BOYFRIEND, GORDON-BARBARA-GORDON?
I WISH.
THAT DIDN'T COME OUT RIGHT.
And the deal maker, the trump card?
I can actually afford it. I think.
IT'S NOT MUCH, BUT IT'S ALMOST NOTHING.
DO YOU JUST LOVE IT?
YES. VERY MUCH SO.
UH. DON'T YOU THINK MAYBE YOU SHOULD PUT THOSE BOXES DOWN, THERE, G.B.G.?

COME ON, I'LL HELP. THEN I'LL MAKE SOME TEA AND WE CAN DISCOVER WHAT THINGS WE BOTH HATE.

REALLY? THAT'D BE... THAT'D BE NICE.

BUT JUST FAIR WARNING, OKAY?

I'M KINDA AN *ACTIVIST*.

ALL GOOD?

FIGHT THE POWER!

It took a while, after the shooting, to let strangers back in.

It'd be *nice* to have someone to have tea with.

WE'RE ALL *GOOD*.

HECTIC, HECTIC DAY.

BUT ALL, ALL *GOOD*.

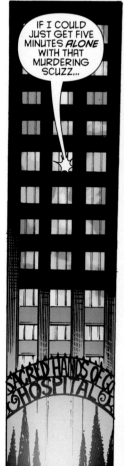

IF I COULD JUST GET FIVE MINUTES *ALONE* WITH THAT MURDERING SCUZZ...

WELL, FIRST, YOU KNOW HE'S ASLEEP, RIGHT?

SECOND, OUR LITTLE THRILL KILLER GOT HIMSELF A SLASHED HAND AND A SNOOTFUL OF *MEDS*.

WAIT 'TIL HIS LAWYER SHOWS, MEL.

SACRED HANDS OF G... HOSPITAL

MY SHIFT STARTS IN TWENTY, BUT I CAN HELP YOU UNPACK. THIS YOUR VAN?

YES. NO. *WAIT*.

I MEAN... UM. I'LL DO IT. GOT SOME FRAGILE STUFF. YOU KNOW.

SUIT YOURSELF.

WHEELCHAIR LIFT, HUH?

SOMEONE IN YOUR FAMILY?

YEAH. SORTA.

THAT'S MY BIGGEST FEAR, BEING TRAPPED IN A CHAIR LIKE THAT. CAN YOU IMAGINE? LIKE PRISON.

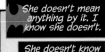

She doesn't mean anything by it, I know she doesn't.

She doesn't know what it's like, what the chair helps you do.

And I guess I don't feel like explaining that to her able-bodied-but-well-intended-self right now.

OKAY, THIS IS GONNA WORK.

SORRY, ROOMIE. I'M A HUGGER.

...OKAY?

HERE TO SEE RANKIN.

THEODORE.

NAME, PLEASE?

HI, I'm HEIDI!

MIRROR.

HI, I'M HEIDI!

WHUMM XPH

HEY. ALL RIGHT, HANG ON, BIG FELLA.

BACK OFF. I MEAN IT!

HALT. I WILL SHOOT YOU!

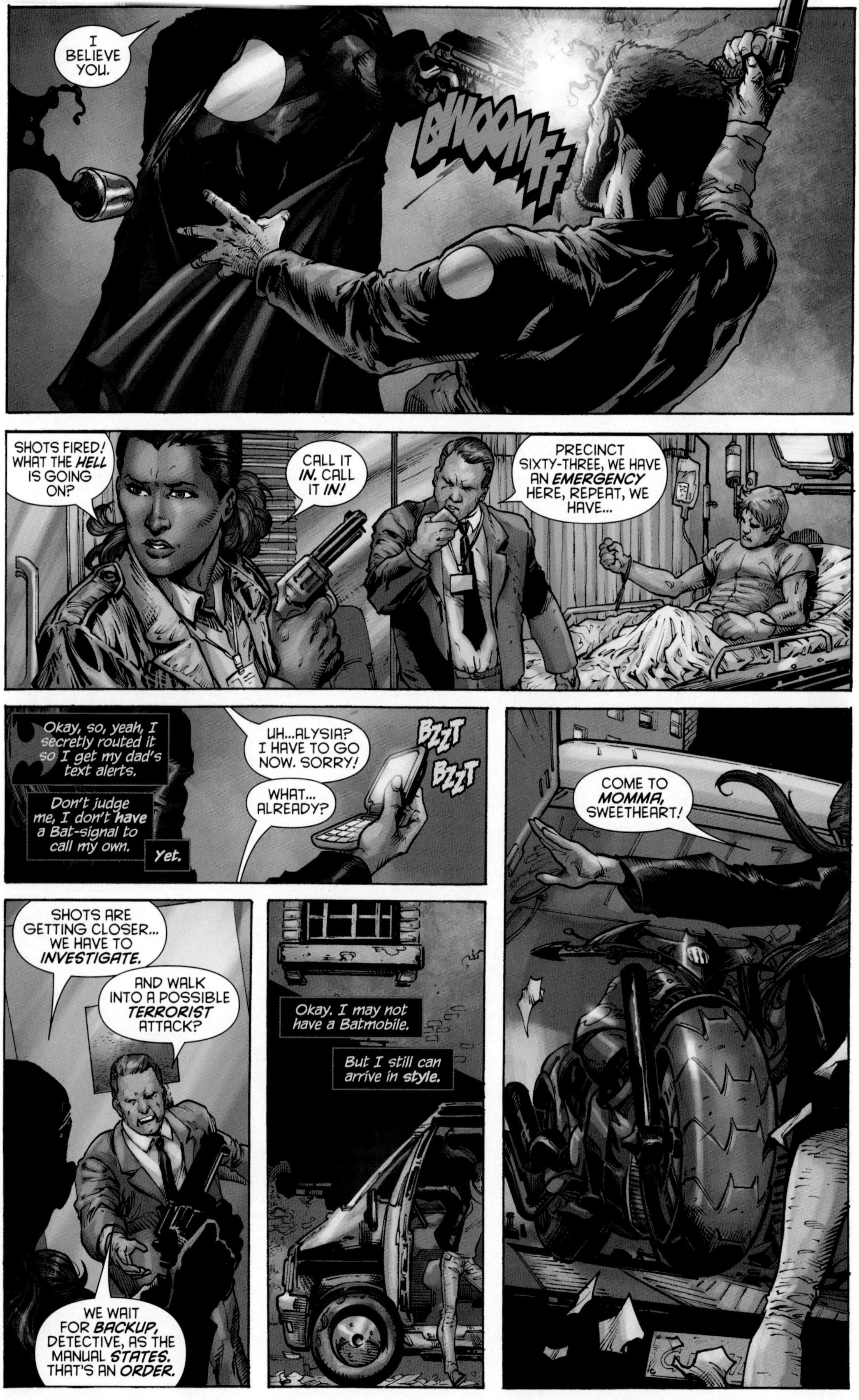
I BELIEVE YOU.
BWOOMFF
SHOTS FIRED! WHAT THE HELL IS GOING ON?
CALL IT IN. CALL IT IN!
PRECINCT SIXTY-THREE, WE HAVE AN EMERGENCY HERE, REPEAT, WE HAVE...
Okay, so, yeah, I secretly routed it so I get my dad's text alerts.
Don't judge me, I don't have a Bat-signal to call my own.
Yet.
UH...ALYSIA? I HAVE TO GO NOW. SORRY!
WHAT... ALREADY?
BZZZT
BZZZT
SHOTS ARE GETTING CLOSER... WE HAVE TO INVESTIGATE.
AND WALK INTO A POSSIBLE TERRORIST ATTACK?
WE WAIT FOR BACKUP, DETECTIVE, AS THE MANUAL STATES. THAT'S AN ORDER.
Okay. I may not have a Batmobile.
But I still can arrive in style.
COME TO MOMMA, SWEETHEART!

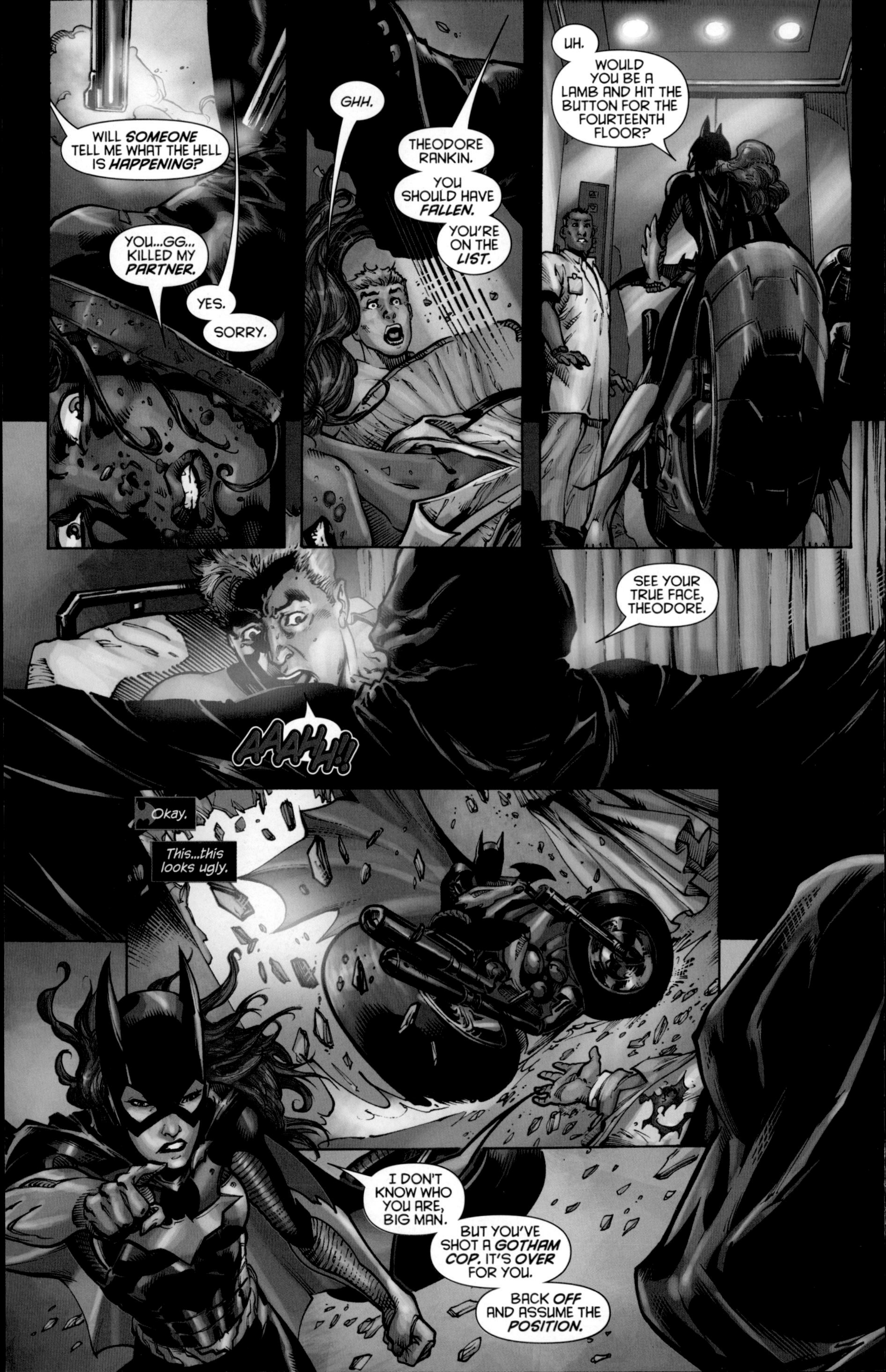
WILL SOMEONE TELL ME WHAT THE HELL IS HAPPENING?
YOU...GG... KILLED MY PARTNER.
YES.
SORRY.
GHH.
THEODORE RANKIN.
YOU SHOULD HAVE FALLEN.
YOU'RE ON THE LIST.
UH.
WOULD YOU BE A LAMB AND HIT THE BUTTON FOR THE FOURTEENTH FLOOR?
SEE YOUR TRUE FACE, THEODORE.
AAAHH!!
Okay.
This...this looks ugly.
I DON'T KNOW WHO YOU ARE, BIG MAN.
BUT YOU'VE SHOT A GOTHAM COP. IT'S OVER FOR YOU.
BACK OFF AND ASSUME THE POSITION.

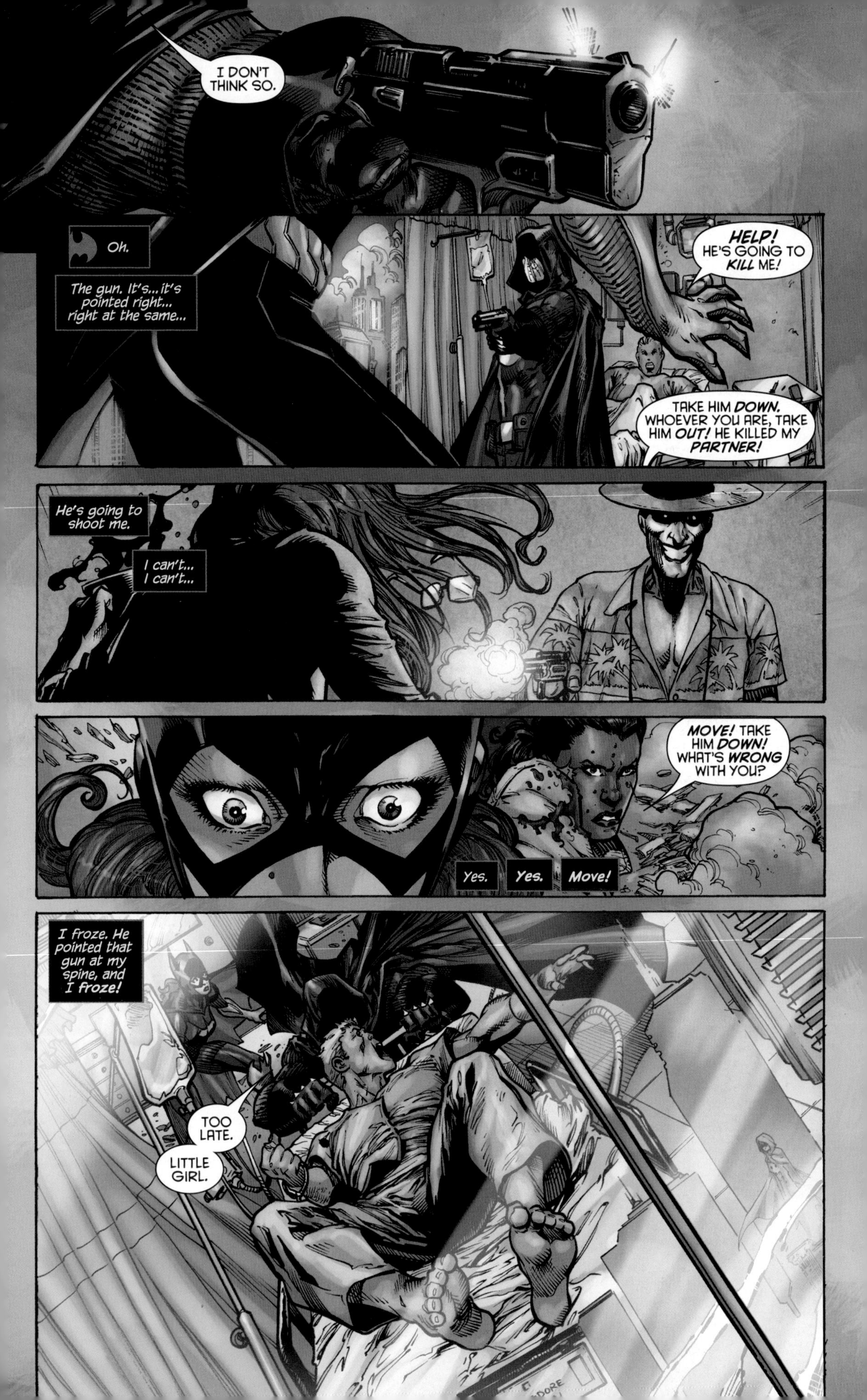
I DON'T THINK SO.
Oh.
The gun. It's... it's pointed right... right at the same...
HELP! HE'S GOING TO KILL ME!
TAKE HIM DOWN. WHOEVER YOU ARE, TAKE HIM OUT! HE KILLED MY PARTNER!
He's going to shoot me.
I can't... I can't...
MOVE! TAKE HIM DOWN! WHAT'S WRONG WITH YOU?
Yes.
Yes.
Move!
I froze. He pointed that gun at my spine, and I froze!
TOO LATE.
LITTLE GIRL.

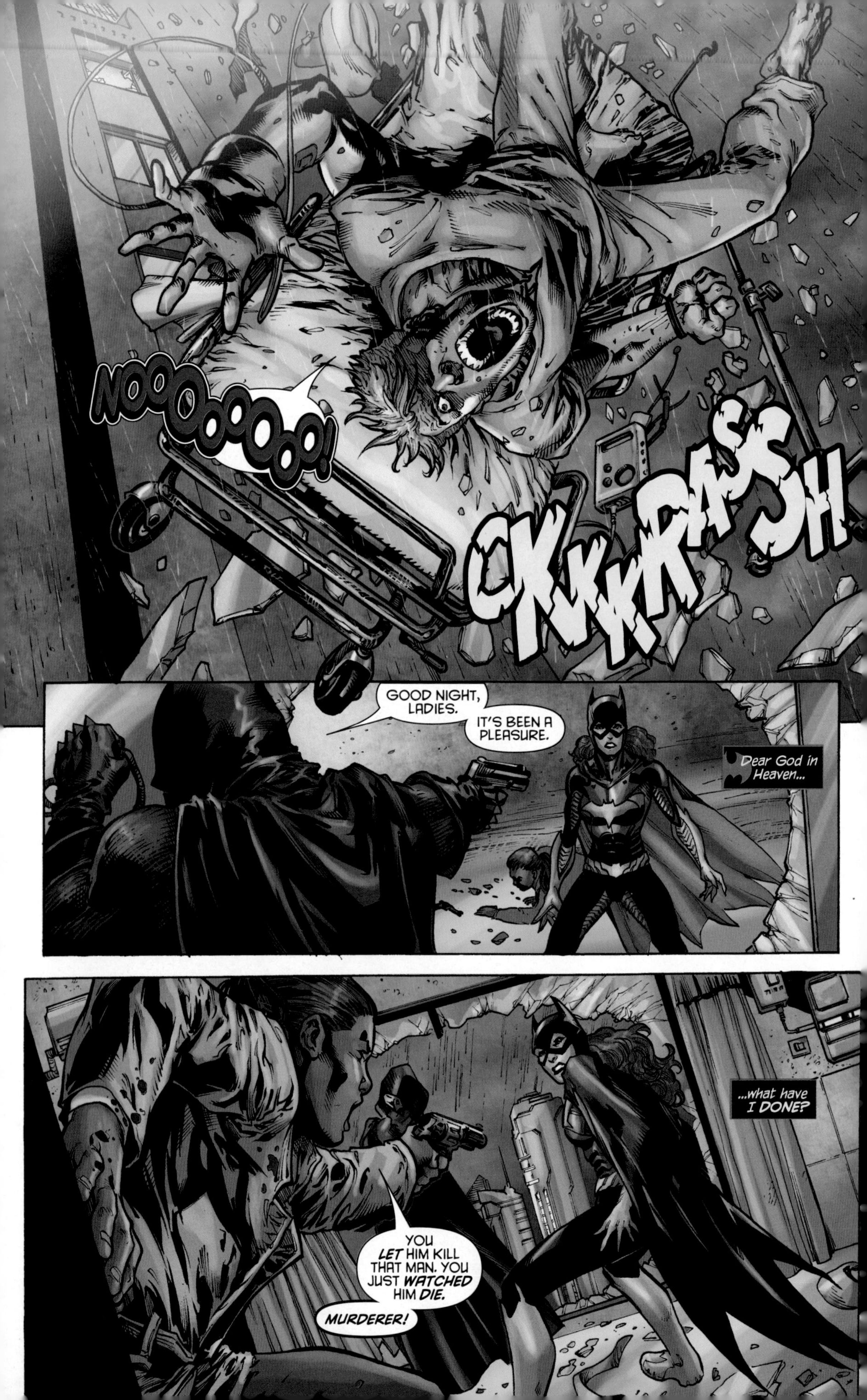
NOOOOOOOOO!
CKKKRASSH
GOOD NIGHT, LADIES.
IT'S BEEN A PLEASURE.
Dear God in Heaven...
...what have I DONE?
YOU LET HIM KILL THAT MAN. YOU JUST WATCHED HIM DIE.
MURDERER!

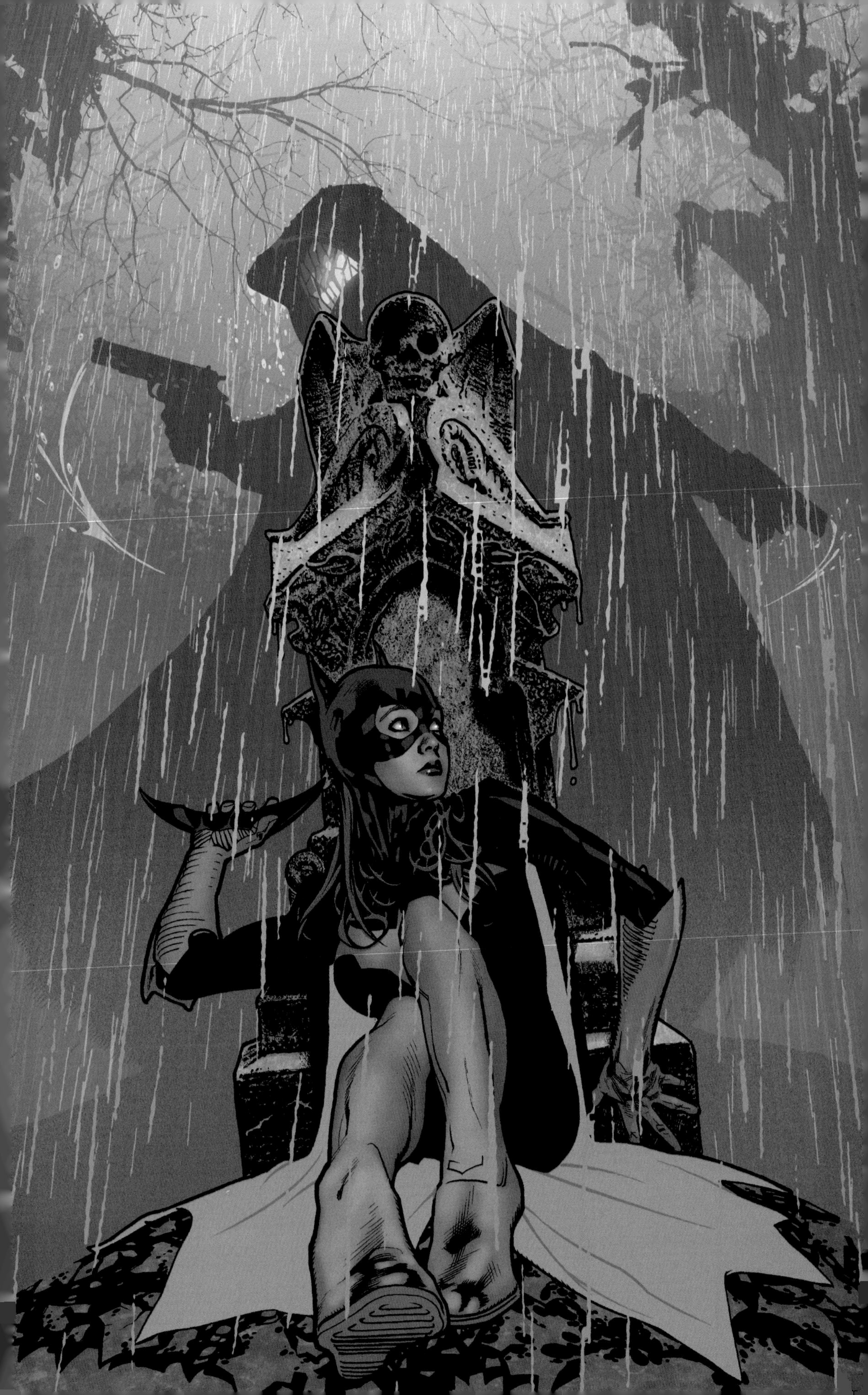

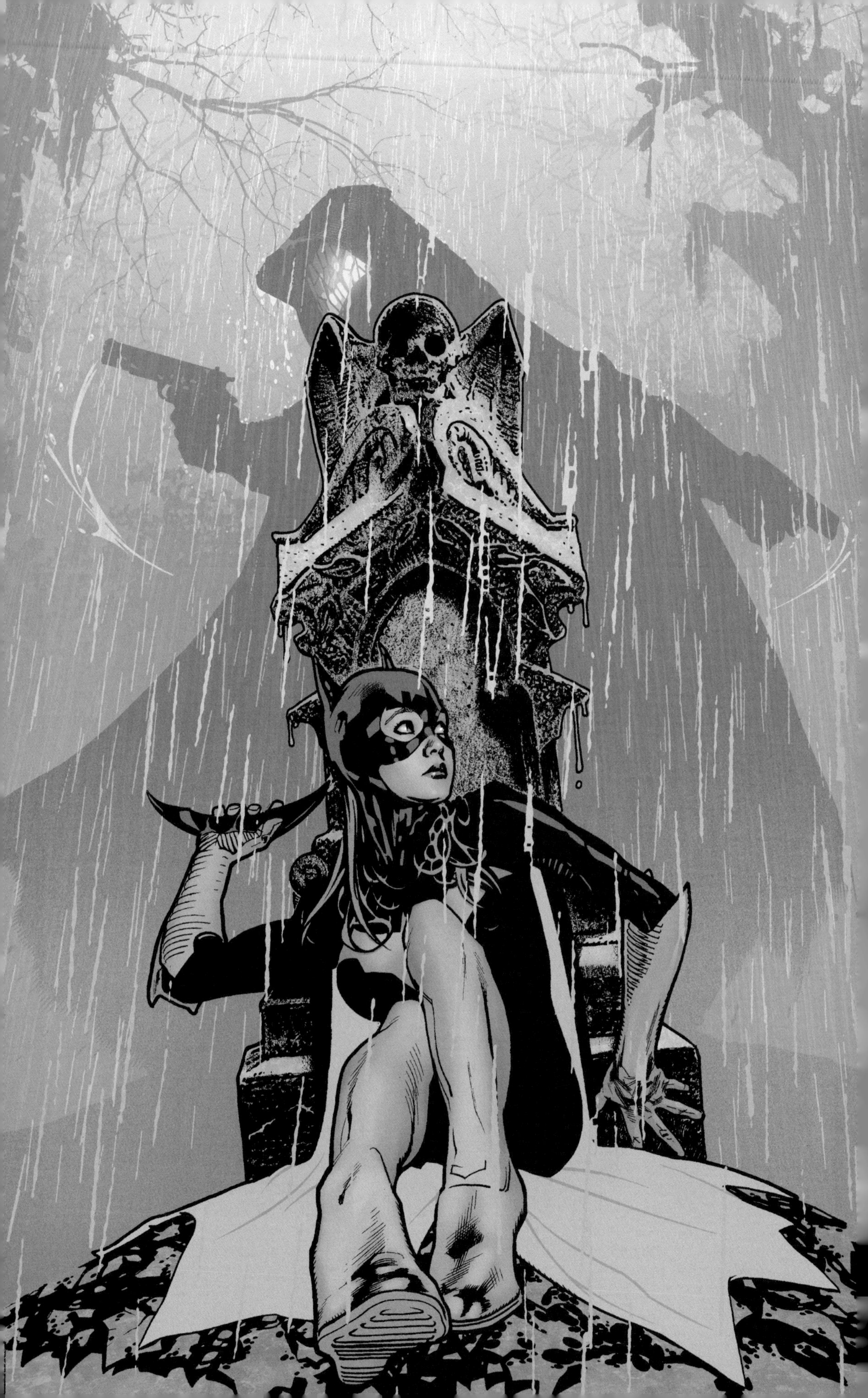

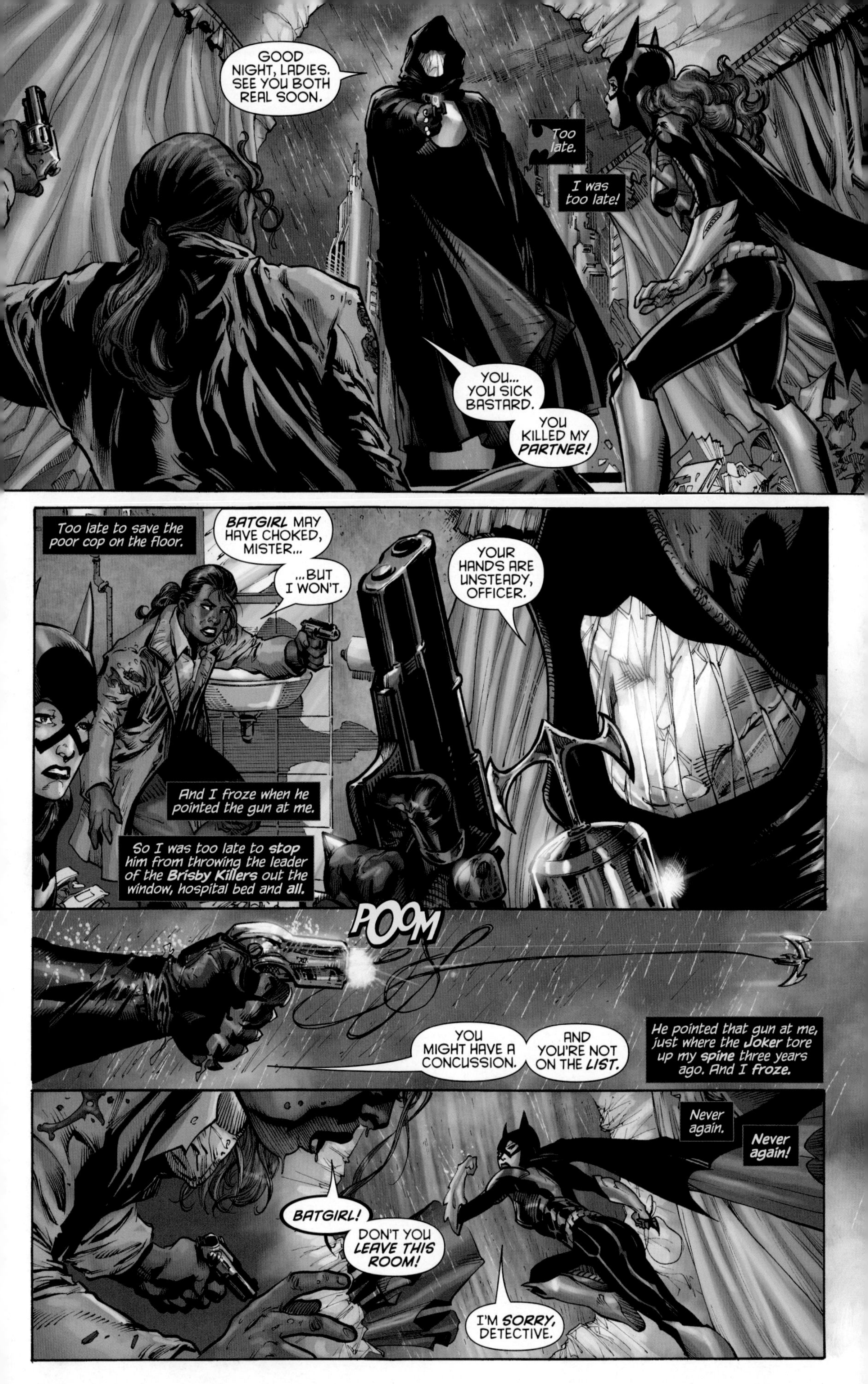
GOOD NIGHT, LADIES. SEE YOU BOTH REAL SOON.
Too late.
I was too late!
YOU... YOU SICK BASTARD.
YOU KILLED MY PARTNER!
Too late to save the poor cop on the floor.
BATGIRL MAY HAVE CHOKED, MISTER...
...BUT I WON'T.
YOUR HANDS ARE UNSTEADY, OFFICER.
And I froze when he pointed the gun at me.
So I was too late to stop him from throwing the leader of the Brisby Killers out the window, hospital bed and all.
POOM
YOU MIGHT HAVE A CONCUSSION.
AND YOU'RE NOT ON THE LIST.
He pointed that gun at me, just where the Joker tore up my spine three years ago. And I froze.
Never again.
Never again!
BATGIRL!
DON'T YOU LEAVE THIS ROOM!
I'M SORRY, DETECTIVE.

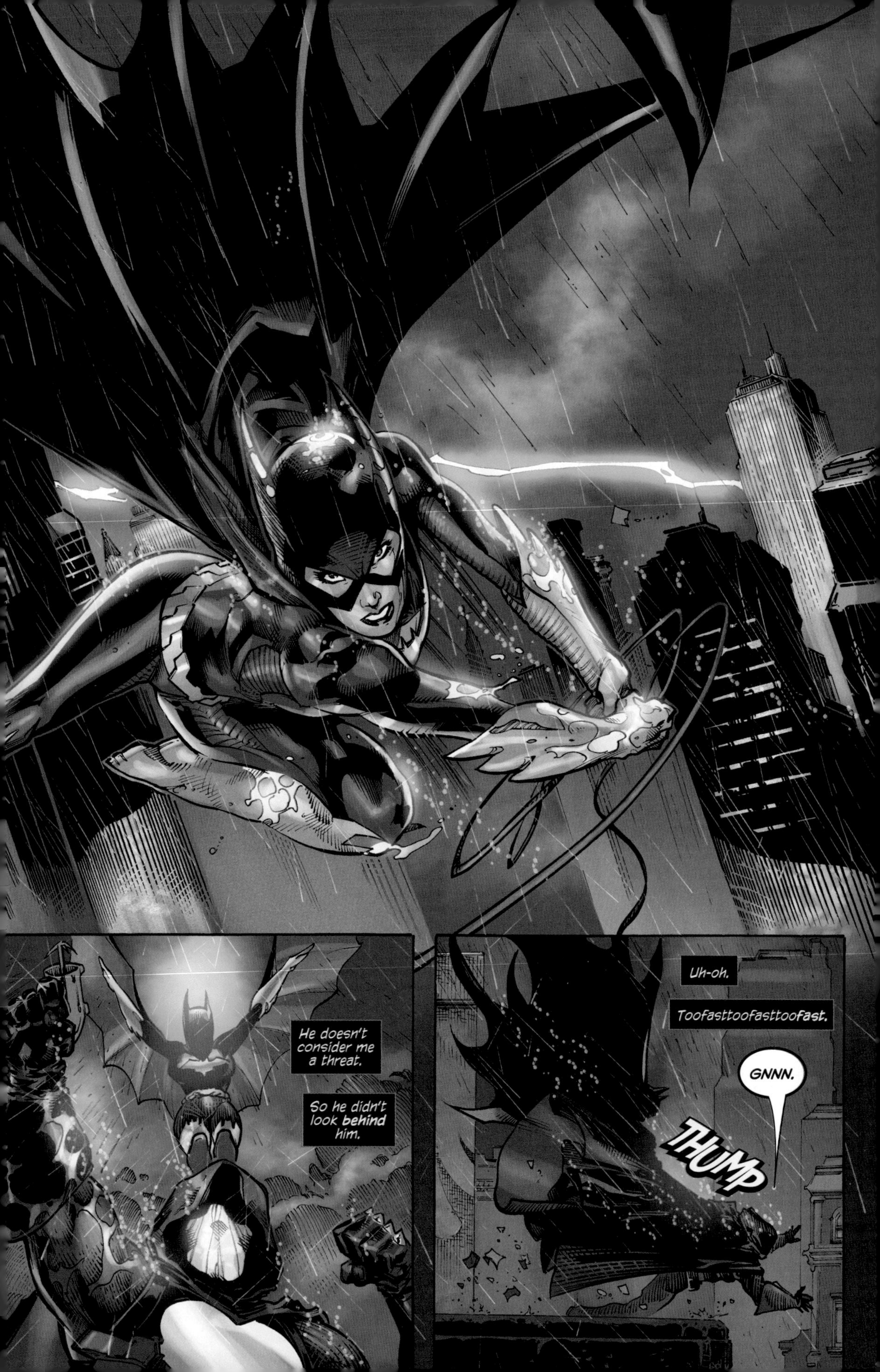
He doesn't consider me a threat.
So he didn't look **behind** him.
Uh-oh.
Toofasttoofasttoo**fast**.
GNNN.
THUMP

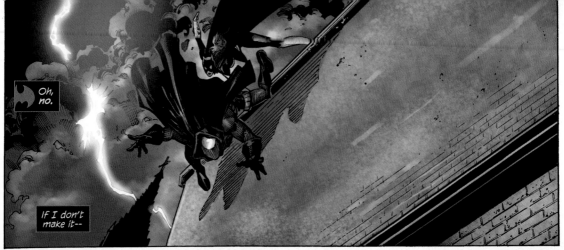

Oh, no.

If I don't make it--

--who's going to explain this to my dad?

"Commissioner Gordon... about your daughter--"

OW. OH, OW.

My legs.

He hit me way too hard. Too hard for a girl only recently out of a wheelchair.

I shouldn't be out here yet.

NO. NO.

I CAN'T DIE LIKE THIS!

ARE YOU KIDDING ME?

MAYBE YOU SHOULD HAVE THOUGHT OF THAT BEFORE YOU KILLED A COP, PAL.

ALL RIGHT. COME ON, TOUGH GUY. REACH.

YOU DON'T UNDERSTAND. I AM NOT SUPPOSED TO DIE THIS WAY...

...BUT YOU ARE, BATGIRL. YOU'RE ON THE LIST.

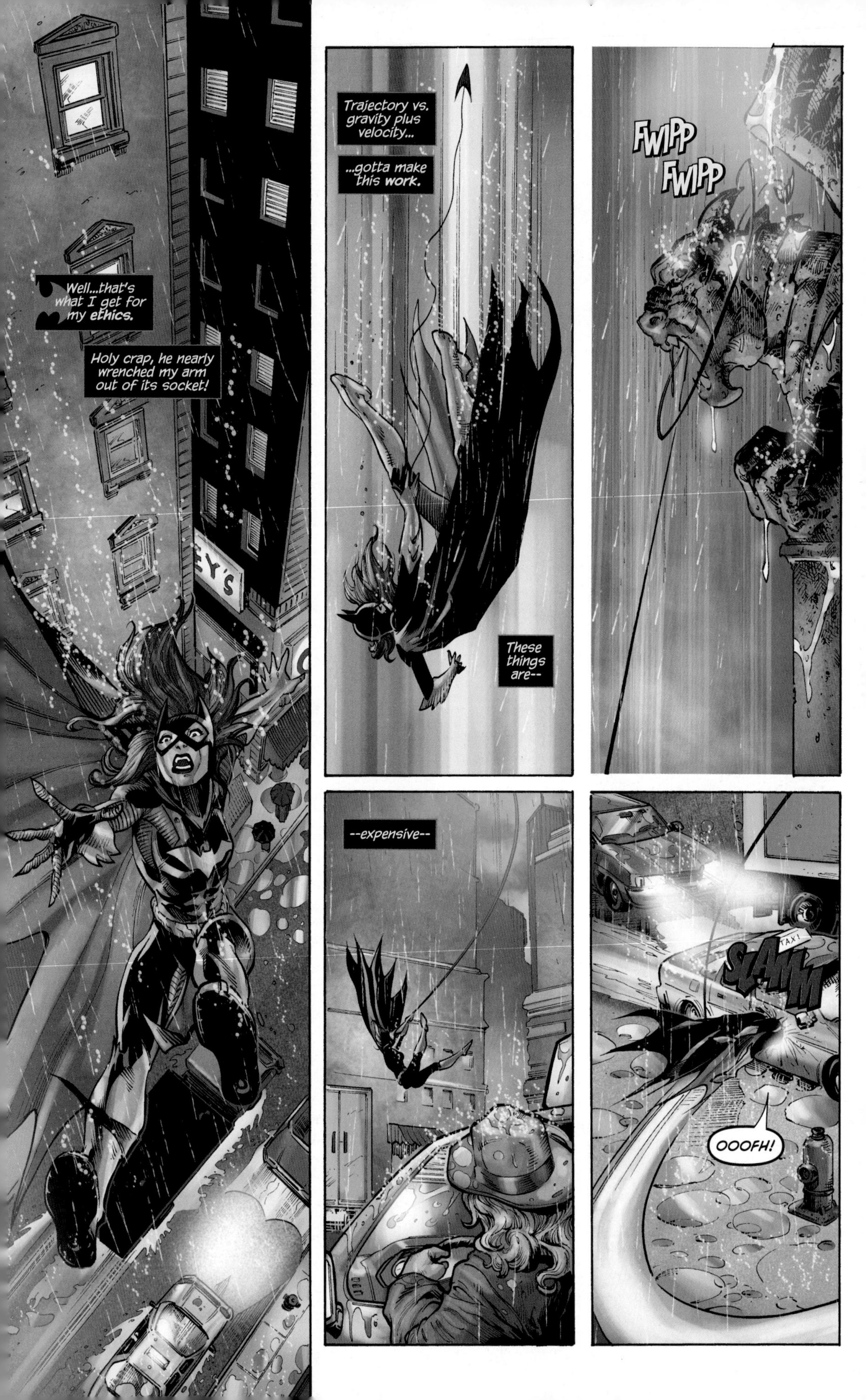

Well...that's what I get for my ethics.
Holy crap, he nearly wrenched my arm out of its socket!
EY'S
Trajectory vs. gravity plus velocity...
...gotta make this work.
These things are--
FWIPP
FWIPP
--expensive--
TAXI
SLAMM
OOOFH!

I'M GOING TO RECOMMEND A HEAD C.T. TO RULE OUT HEMORRHAGE.

WILL YOU GET THAT THING *AWAY* FROM ME?

MEL. TAKE IT *EASY*...

DETECTIVE *McKENNA*.

UH. COMMISSIONER *GORDON*. WE WERE JUST...

...DETECTIVE McKENNA WAS ABOUT TO--

SIT DOWN AND LET THE ATTENDING PHYSICIAN CHECK HER OVER, ISN'T THAT RIGHT, DETECTIVE?

SIR.

MY PARTNER. HE...

...HE...

...HE WAS *GOOD*. HE WAS A *GOOD MAN*.

YES. DOUGLAS PAULSON WAS A GOOD MAN.

AND BECAUSE I DON'T WANT THIS INCIDENT TO LOSE ME *TWO* GOOD COPS...

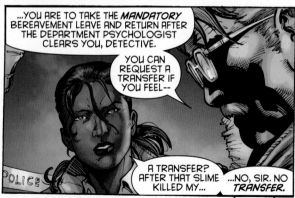

...YOU ARE TO TAKE THE *MANDATORY* BEREAVEMENT LEAVE AND RETURN AFTER THE DEPARTMENT PSYCHOLOGIST CLEARS YOU, DETECTIVE.

YOU CAN REQUEST A TRANSFER IF YOU FEEL--

A TRANSFER? AFTER THAT SLIME KILLED MY...

...NO, SIR. NO *TRANSFER*.

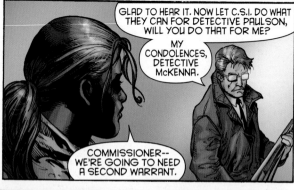

GLAD TO HEAR IT. NOW LET C.S.I. DO WHAT THEY CAN FOR DETECTIVE PAULSON, WILL YOU DO THAT FOR ME?

MY CONDOLENCES, DETECTIVE McKENNA.

COMMISSIONER-- WE'RE GOING TO NEED A SECOND WARRANT.

FOR *BATGIRL*.

SHE'S *BACK*.

Well.

I'm ninety-five *percent* sure, anyway.

UGHGNR.

I *may* have those numbers just a *wee bit* off.

WOOF. OKAY...I CAN'T OUTPUNCH YOU. WE BOTH KNOW THAT.

BUT I CAN OUT*THINK* YOU.

Oh, baby, let's hope I called his compulsion *correctly.*

AND I JUST BOOSTED THESE *PAPERS* YOU KEEP *OBSESSING* OVER.

YOU HAVE NO *RIGHT!*

YOU *DON'T* *GET* TO *SEE* *THAT!*

WRRRRRR

Then we both heard the *sirens.* Must have seen us on the surveillance cameras.

Like I said, this place holds a lot of *capitalists.*

And just like that, he was gone.

I couldn't follow. I could barely *move.*

YEAH. THAT'S RIGHT. RUN. YOU DON'T WANT...

...NONE OF *THIS.*

OH, MAN. OW.

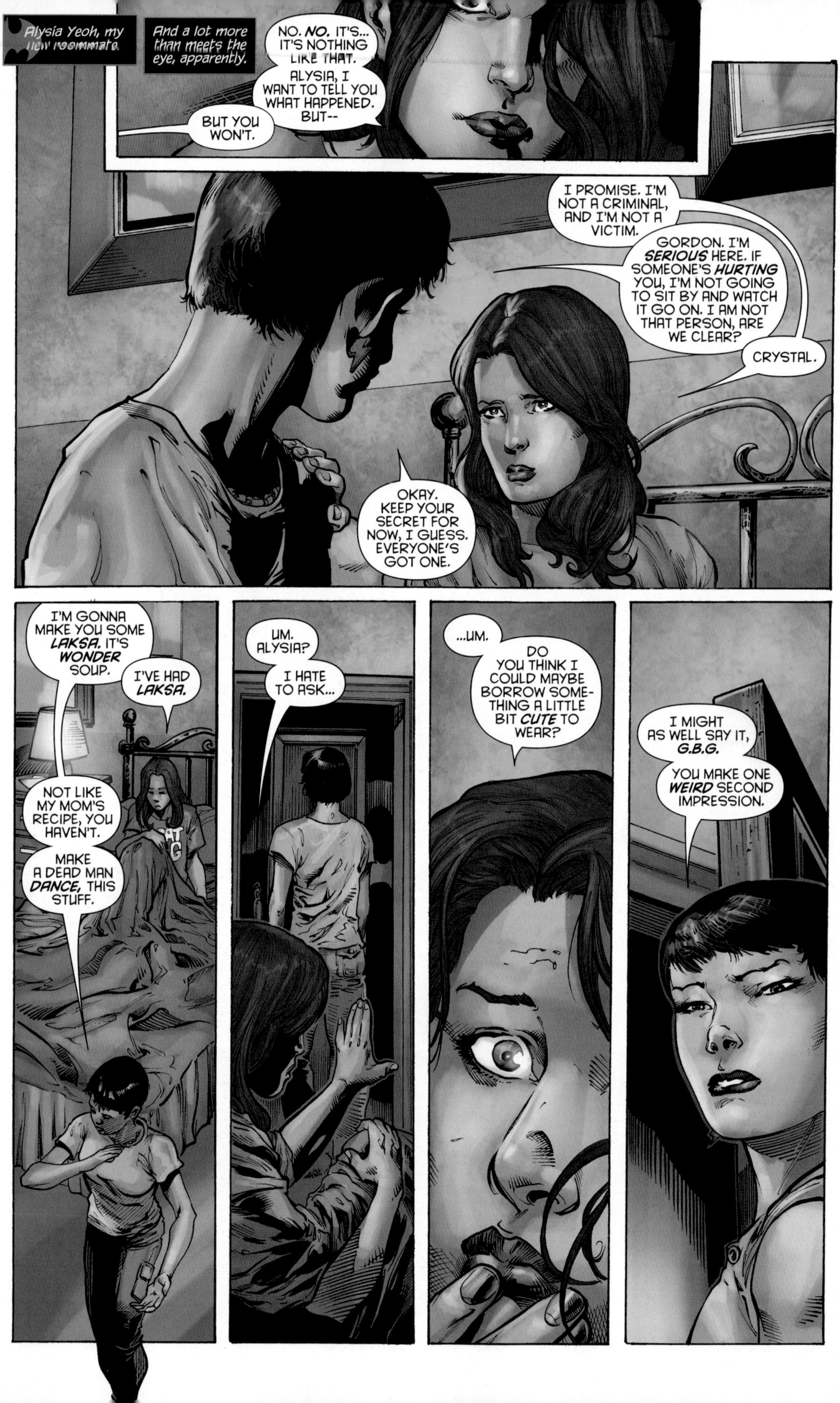
Alysia Yeoh, my new roommate.
And a lot more than meets the eye, apparently.
NO. NO. IT'S... IT'S NOTHING LIKE THAT.
ALYSIA, I WANT TO TELL YOU WHAT HAPPENED. BUT--
BUT YOU WON'T.
I PROMISE. I'M NOT A CRIMINAL, AND I'M NOT A VICTIM.
GORDON. I'M SERIOUS HERE. IF SOMEONE'S HURTING YOU, I'M NOT GOING TO SIT BY AND WATCH IT GO ON. I AM NOT THAT PERSON, ARE WE CLEAR?
CRYSTAL.
OKAY. KEEP YOUR SECRET FOR NOW, I GUESS. EVERYONE'S GOT ONE.
I'M GONNA MAKE YOU SOME LAKSA. IT'S WONDER SOUP.
I'VE HAD LAKSA.
NOT LIKE MY MOM'S RECIPE, YOU HAVEN'T.
MAKE A DEAD MAN DANCE, THIS STUFF.
UM. ALYSIA?
I HATE TO ASK...
...UM.
DO YOU THINK I COULD MAYBE BORROW SOMETHING A LITTLE BIT CUTE TO WEAR?
I MIGHT AS WELL SAY IT, G.B.G.
YOU MAKE ONE WEIRD SECOND IMPRESSION.

And what do you know?

The wonder soup *worked.*

WELL, YEAH, BUT THE QUESTION IS DO *YOU* LIKE IT?

WELL, I'M MALE AND STRAIGHT, BARBARA. OF *COURSE* I LIKE IT.

IT'S JUST THAT I'VE NEVER *WEAR* ANYTHING LIKE IT.

OH, YEAH, THIS OLD THING?

I WEAR STUFF LIKE THIS ALL THE TIME, HONEST.

And as if I weren't embarrassed enough, I had to go and get *carded* at lunch.

I offered to split the tab, but he insisted on paying. Because he's a *gentleman.*

What is it about *good guys* that gets me every *time?*

THAT'S THE PROBLEM WITH SEEING YOUR *PHYSICAL THERAPIST* SOCIALLY.

THEY ALREADY KNOW ALL YOUR SECRETS.

YOU'D *THINK* SO, WOULDN'T YOU?

IT'S NOT REALLY ETHICAL, BARBARA. MY BOSS WOULD--

YOU DON'T HAVE A BOSS, GREGOR. TECHNICALLY, *I'M* YOUR BOSS.

AND I PROMISE, IF WE GET MARRIED AND HAVE EIGHT KIDS?

I'LL GET A *NEW* THERAPIST.

WELL, YOU ASKED *ME* ON THIS DATE. WHERE TO?

I'M GOING TO IGNORE THAT UN-CHIVALROUS DECLARATION OF FACT AND SUGGEST THE PARK.

"YOU'LL *FIND* THE ANSWER. I *KNOW* IT."

HELLO, MORNING IN GOTHAM.

YOU LOOK *BEAUTIFUL*, TODAY.

And so I got in a workout and then spent a few hours at the *library*, doing *research*.

Mirror wasn't at that cemetery by accident. It was *sacred* to him. He was *visiting* someone.

He had mentioned a fire, like that was *important*.

I got stuck there for a bit, looking for people who were *buried* in the Hallows and had died in a building fire.

BUT THAT'S *NOT QUITE* RIGHT, IS IT, MIRROR?

I'd forgotten how *beautiful* morning is here, after a hard rain.

Anyway, then it hit me...not all fires happen in *buildings*.

I looked at the most recent graves and worked backwards, cross-referencing people with access to *money* and *commando* experience.

PROFESSOR STEIN SALIVE

FEDERAL AGENT AND WAR HERO SOLE SURVIVOR OF HOLIDAY CRASH

Authorities have released the full names of the victims in a horrific crash that occurred just south of the Gotham Bay Bridge this past weekend. It's known that the crash took the lives of a young wife and mother, Shanda Mills, a vast fortune in food commodities, and her two-year daughter, Jonathan Mills, escaped without serious injury. The father, Jonathan Mills, When pressed by reporters as to whether this tragedy had been engineered by Gotham crime bosses currently under investigation by both local and federal authorities, Police Commissioner Gordon had no comment.

FREAKIN' *BINGO*.

The skills he displayed. *And* his wife had the money for a plot in the *Hallows*. And his *family* had burned.

HUH. TRIP WIRES ON THE WINDOW.

They were just the standard alarm stuff, nothing *too* serious.

I'm sure there's a more *delicate* way to do this.

KABRAKK

ANYONE HOME?

This place might not be *homey...*

WOW.

...but you can't say it's not fully *loaded*.

There's gotta be hundreds of thousands of dollars' worth of surveillance stuff here. All *completely* state of the art.

But he left the *window* alarm off? *Why?*

BATGIRL.

MIRROR.

YES.

YOU SAW THE LIST.

I DID. I'M *ON* IT, REMEMBER.

In *both* my identities. And so is my *father*. And the Ortega family I saved from the *Brisby Killers*.

All people who *should* have died recently, but somehow survived.

YOU HAVE MADE YOURSELF A PART OF THIS. YOU WILL BE A WITNESS.

I KNOW WHO YOU *ARE*, MR. MILLS... I KNOW ABOUT YOUR *FAMILY*.

DO *YOU*?

DO YOU KNOW ABOUT MY *FAMILY*?

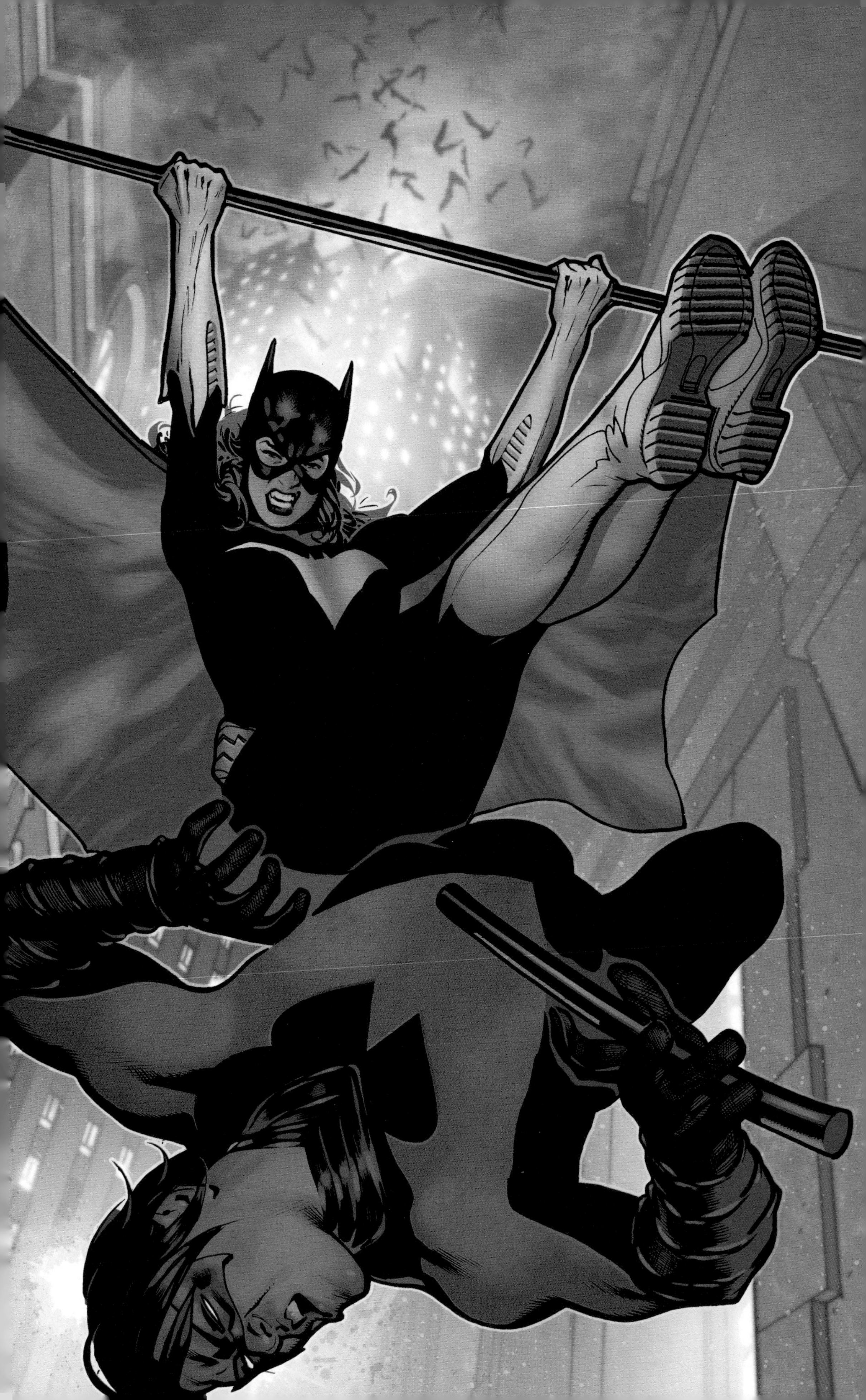

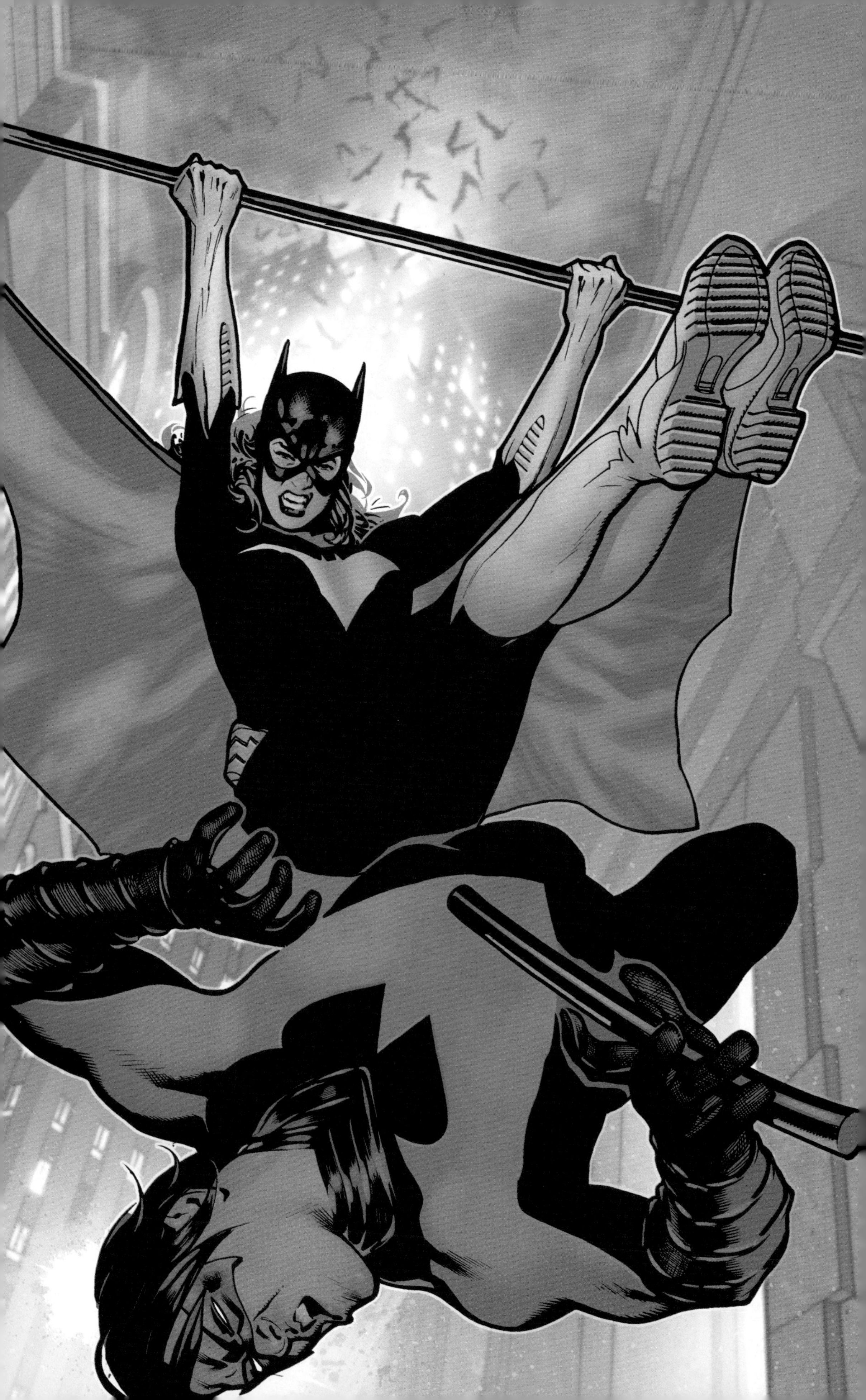

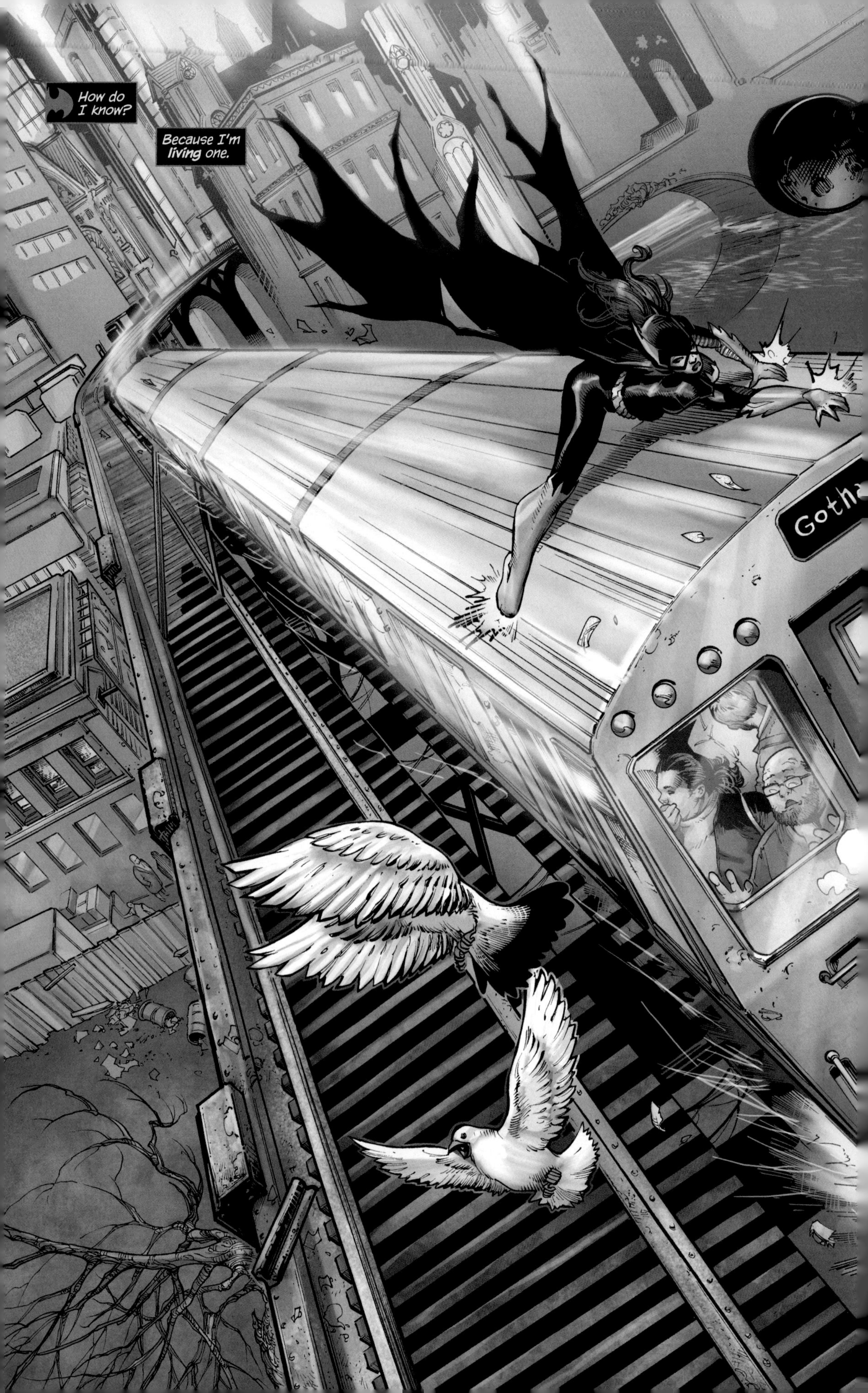
How do I know?
Because I'm *living* one.
Gotha

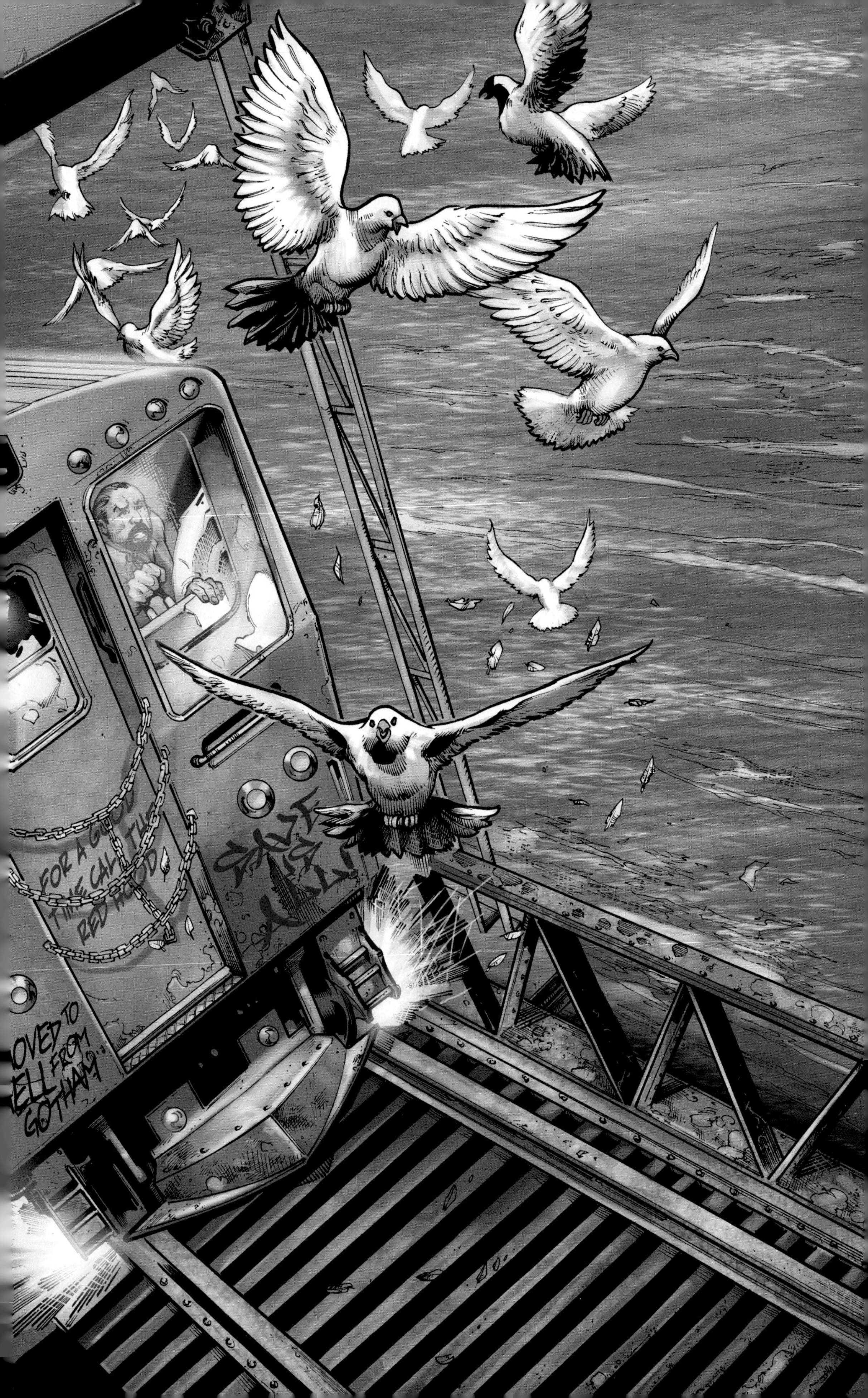
FOR A GOOD TIME CALL THE RED HOOD
OVED TO
ELL FROM
GOTHAM

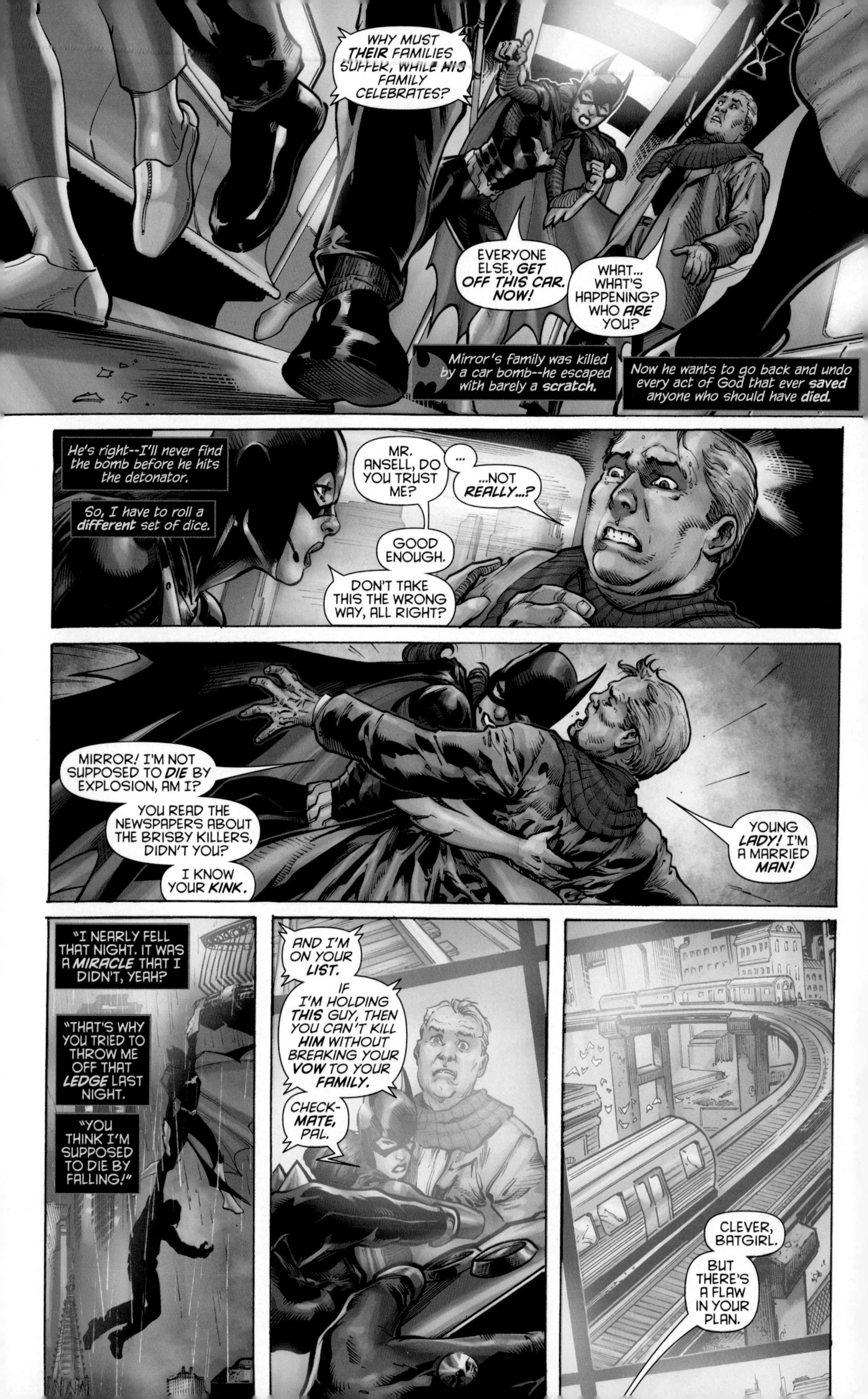
WHY MUST THEIR FAMILIES SUFFER, WHILE HIS FAMILY CELEBRATES?
EVERYONE ELSE, GET OFF THIS CAR. NOW!
WHAT... WHAT'S HAPPENING? WHO ARE YOU?
Mirror's family was killed by a car bomb--he escaped with barely a scratch.
Now he wants to go back and undo every act of God that ever saved anyone who should have died.
He's right--I'll never find the bomb before he hits the detonator.
So, I have to roll a different set of dice.
MR. ANSELL, DO YOU TRUST ME?
...
...NOT REALLY...?
GOOD ENOUGH.
DON'T TAKE THIS THE WRONG WAY, ALL RIGHT?
MIRROR! I'M NOT SUPPOSED TO DIE BY EXPLOSION, AM I?
YOU READ THE NEWSPAPERS ABOUT THE BRISBY KILLERS, DIDN'T YOU?
I KNOW YOUR KINK.
YOUNG LADY! I'M A MARRIED MAN!
"I NEARLY FELL THAT NIGHT. IT WAS A MIRACLE THAT I DIDN'T, YEAH?
"THAT'S WHY YOU TRIED TO THROW ME OFF THAT LEDGE LAST NIGHT.
"YOU THINK I'M SUPPOSED TO DIE BY FALLING!"
AND I'M ON YOUR LIST.
IF I'M HOLDING THIS GUY, THEN YOU CAN'T KILL HIM WITHOUT BREAKING YOUR VOW TO YOUR FAMILY.
CHECK-MATE, PAL.
CLEVER, BATGIRL.
BUT THERE'S A FLAW IN YOUR PLAN.

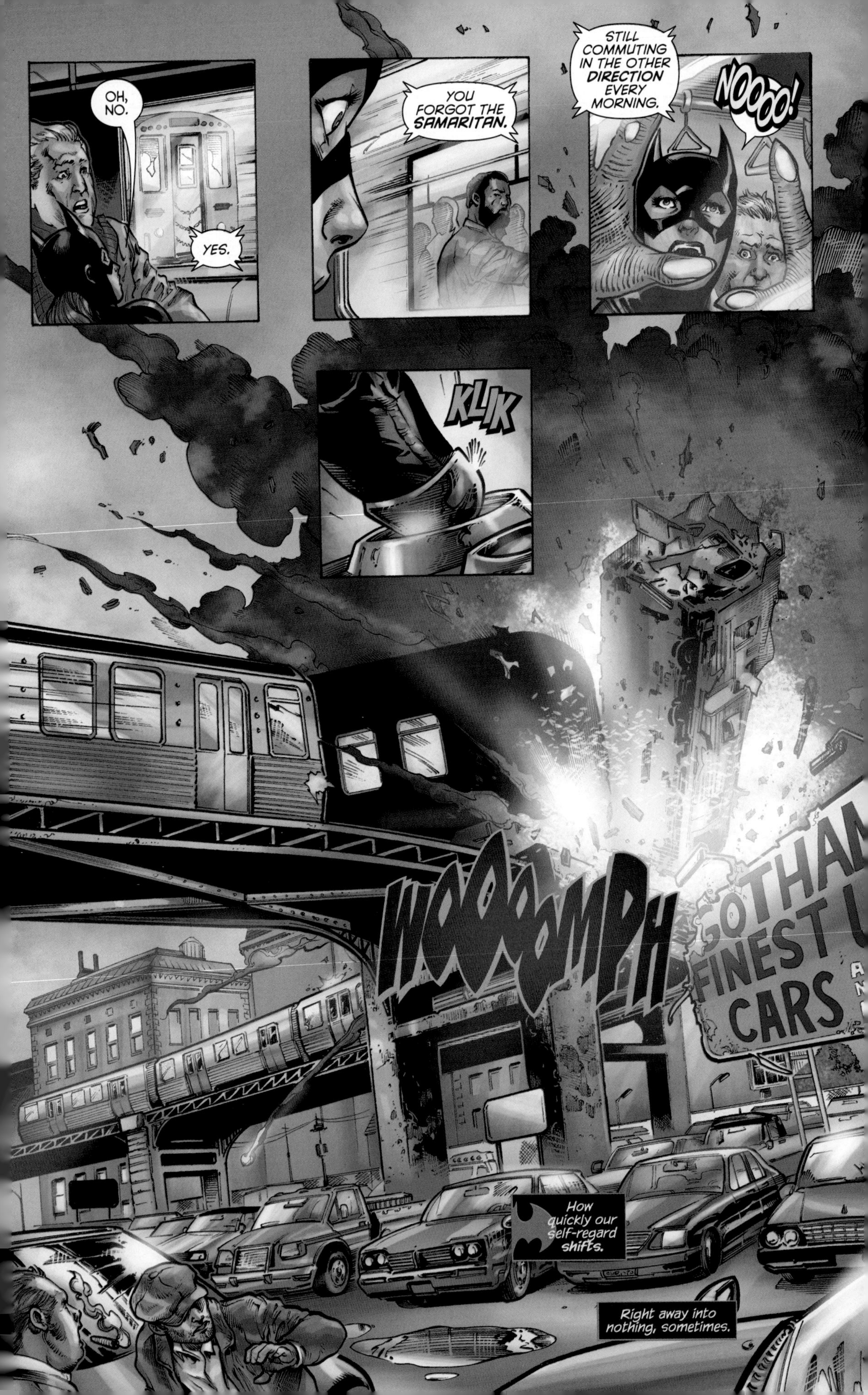
OH, NO.
YES.
YOU FORGOT THE SAMARITAN.
STILL COMMUTING IN THE OTHER DIRECTION EVERY MORNING.
NOOOO!
KLIK
WOOOOMPH
How quickly our self-regard shifts.
Right away into nothing, sometimes.

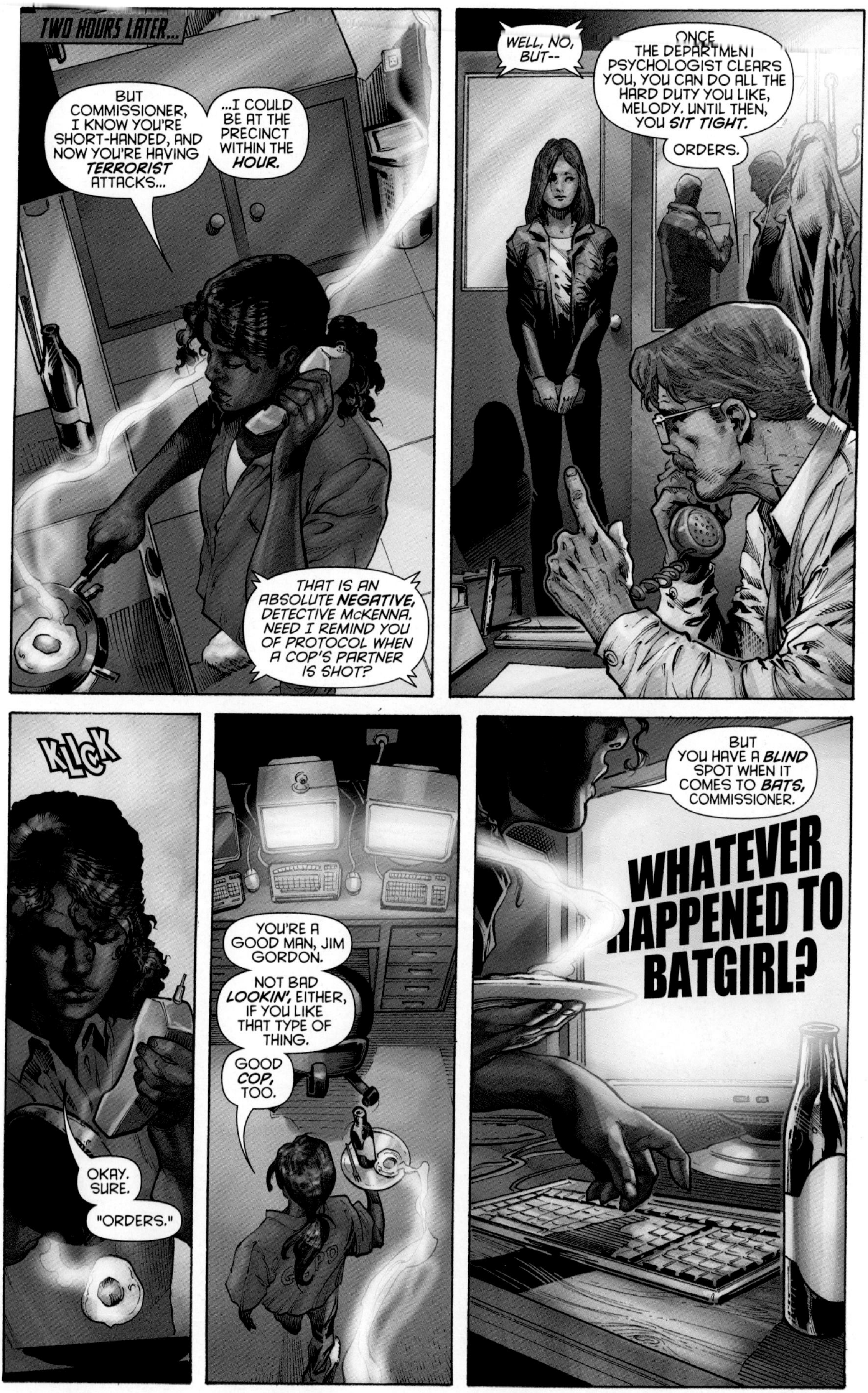
TWO HOURS LATER...
BUT COMMISSIONER, I KNOW YOU'RE SHORT-HANDED, AND NOW YOU'RE HAVING TERRORIST ATTACKS...
...I COULD BE AT THE PRECINCT WITHIN THE HOUR.
THAT IS AN ABSOLUTE NEGATIVE, DETECTIVE McKENNA. NEED I REMIND YOU OF PROTOCOL WHEN A COP'S PARTNER IS SHOT?
WELL, NO, BUT--
ONCE THE DEPARTMENT PSYCHOLOGIST CLEARS YOU, YOU CAN DO ALL THE HARD DUTY YOU LIKE, MELODY. UNTIL THEN, YOU SIT TIGHT.
ORDERS.
KLICK
OKAY. SURE.
"ORDERS."
YOU'RE A GOOD MAN, JIM GORDON.
NOT BAD LOOKIN', EITHER, IF YOU LIKE THAT TYPE OF THING.
GOOD COP, TOO.
BUT YOU HAVE A BLIND SPOT WHEN IT COMES TO BATS, COMMISSIONER.
WHATEVER HAPPENED TO BATGIRL?

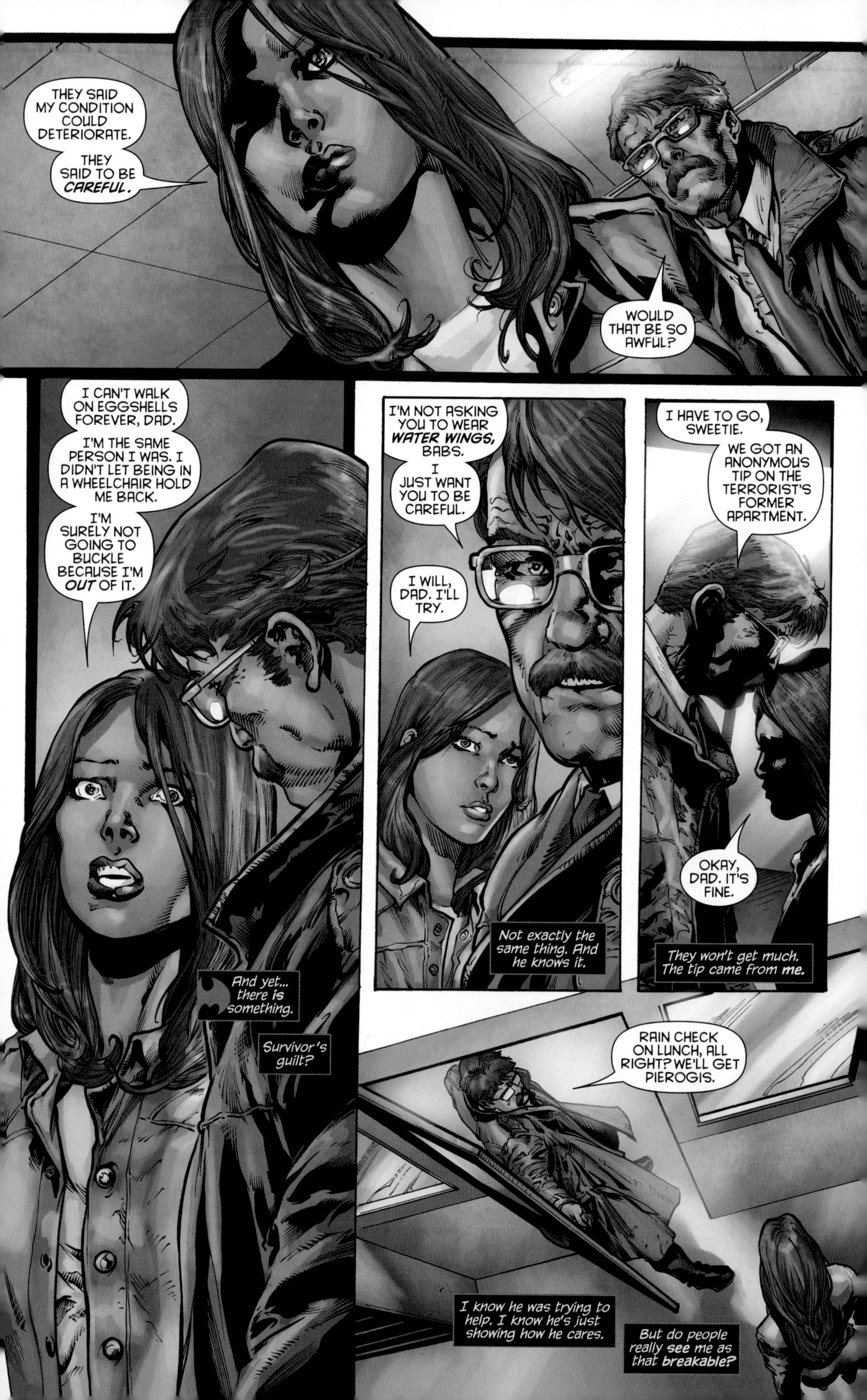
THEY SAID MY CONDITION COULD DETERIORATE.
THEY SAID TO BE *CAREFUL*.
WOULD THAT BE SO AWFUL?
I CAN'T WALK ON EGGSHELLS FOREVER, DAD.
I'M THE SAME PERSON I WAS. I DIDN'T LET BEING IN A WHEELCHAIR HOLD ME BACK.
I'M SURELY NOT GOING TO BUCKLE BECAUSE I'M *OUT* OF IT.
And yet... there is something.
Survivor's guilt?
I'M NOT ASKING YOU TO WEAR **WATER WINGS,** BABS.
I JUST WANT YOU TO BE CAREFUL.
I WILL, DAD. I'LL TRY.
Not exactly the same thing. And he knows it.
I HAVE TO GO, SWEETIE.
WE GOT AN ANONYMOUS TIP ON THE TERRORIST'S FORMER APARTMENT.
OKAY, DAD. IT'S FINE.
They won't get much. The tip came from ***me.***
RAIN CHECK ON LUNCH, ALL RIGHT? WE'LL GET PIEROGIS.
I know he was trying to help. I know he's just showing how he cares.
But do people really ***see*** *me as that* ***breakable?***

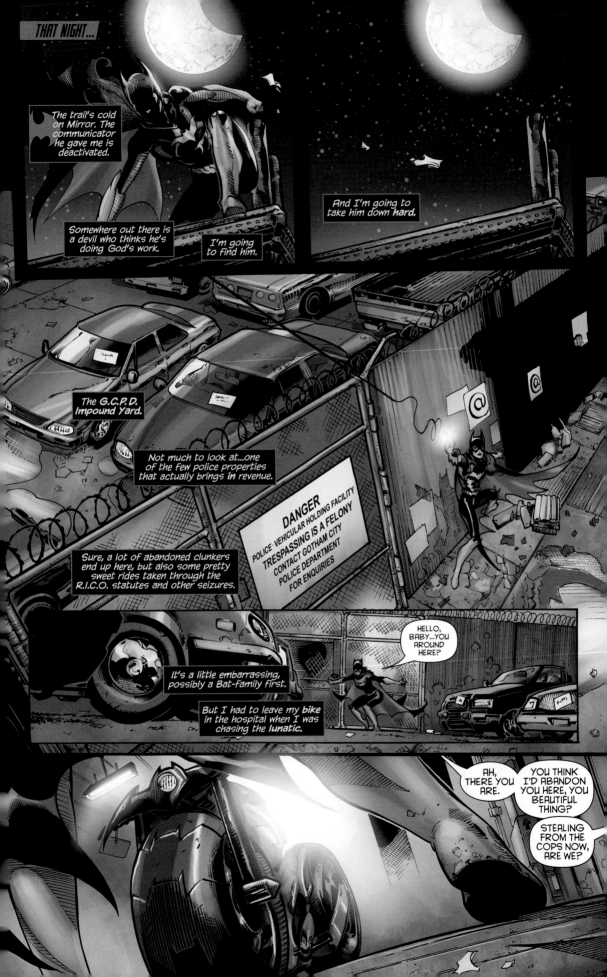

THAT NIGHT...

The trail's cold on Mirror. The communicator he gave me is deactivated.

Somewhere out there is a devil who thinks he's doing God's work.

I'm going to find him.

And I'm going to take him down *hard*.

The G.C.P.D. Impound Yard.

Not much to look at...one of the few police properties that actually brings *in* revenue.

Sure, a lot of abandoned clunkers end up here, but also some pretty sweet rides taken through the R.I.C.O. statutes and other seizures.

DANGER
POLICE - VEHICULAR HOLDING FACILITY
TRESPASSING IS A FELONY
CONTACT GOTHAM CITY
POLICE DEPARTMENT
FOR ENQUIRIES

It's a little embarrassing, possibly a Bat-family first.

But I had to leave my *bike* in the hospital when I was chasing the *lunatic*.

HELLO, BABY...YOU AROUND HERE?

AH, THERE YOU ARE.

YOU THINK I'D ABANDON YOU HERE, YOU BEAUTIFUL THING?

STEALING FROM THE COPS NOW, ARE WE?

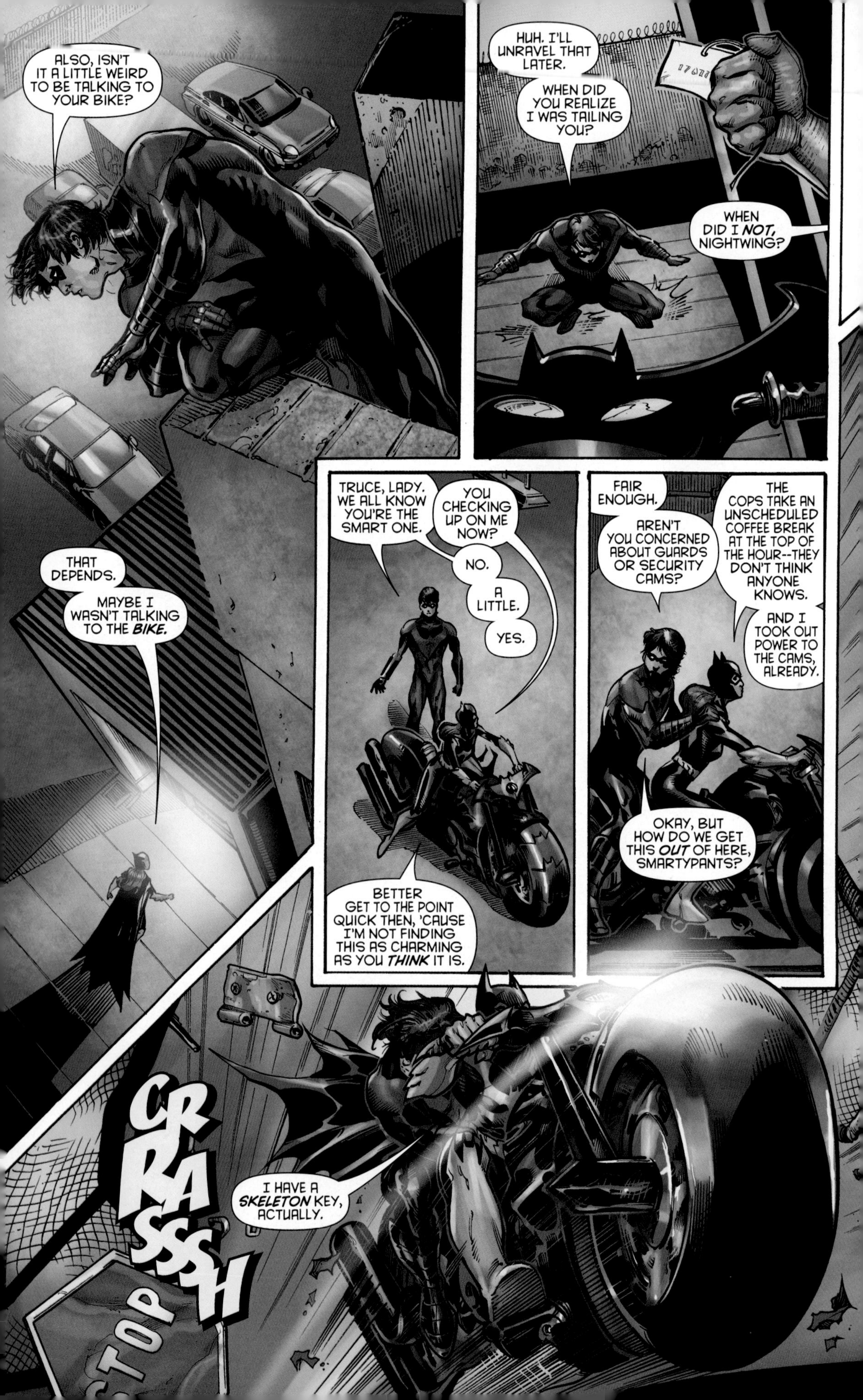
ALSO, ISN'T IT A LITTLE WEIRD TO BE TALKING TO YOUR BIKE?
THAT DEPENDS.
MAYBE I WASN'T TALKING TO THE *BIKE.*
HUH. I'LL UNRAVEL THAT LATER.
WHEN DID YOU REALIZE I WAS TAILING YOU?
WHEN DID I *NOT,* NIGHTWING?
TRUCE, LADY. WE ALL KNOW YOU'RE THE SMART ONE.
YOU CHECKING UP ON ME NOW?
NO.
A LITTLE.
YES.
BETTER GET TO THE POINT QUICK THEN, 'CAUSE I'M NOT FINDING THIS AS CHARMING AS YOU *THINK* IT IS.
FAIR ENOUGH.
AREN'T YOU CONCERNED ABOUT GUARDS OR SECURITY CAMS?
THE COPS TAKE AN UNSCHEDULED COFFEE BREAK AT THE TOP OF THE HOUR--THEY DON'T THINK ANYONE KNOWS.
AND I TOOK OUT POWER TO THE CAMS, ALREADY.
OKAY, BUT HOW DO WE GET THIS *OUT* OF HERE, SMARTYPANTS?
CRRASSSH
I HAVE A *SKELETON* KEY, ACTUALLY.
STOP

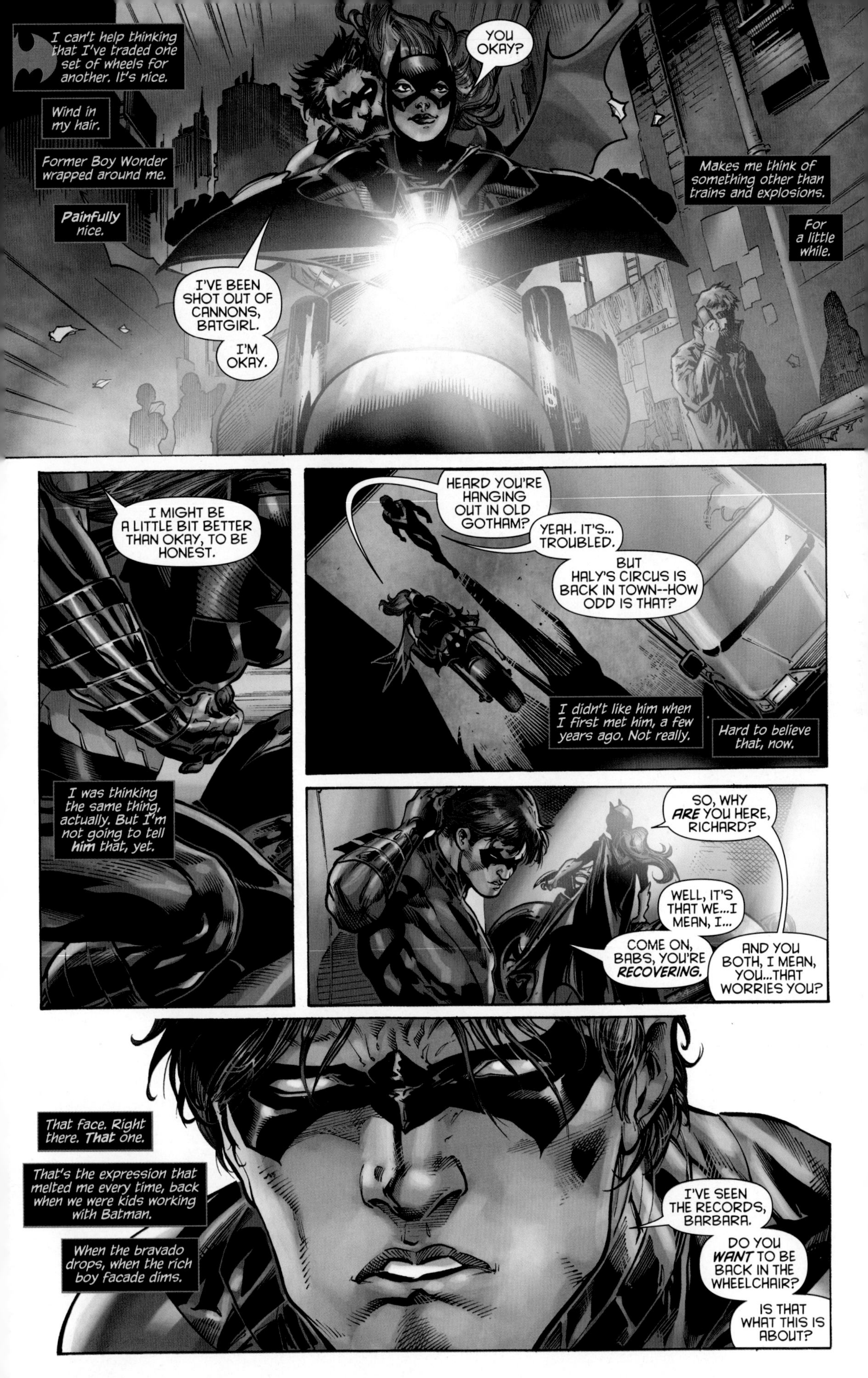

I can't help thinking that I've traded one set of wheels for another. It's nice.
Wind in my hair.
Former Boy Wonder wrapped around me.
Painfully nice.
YOU OKAY?
I'VE BEEN SHOT OUT OF CANNONS, BATGIRL.
I'M OKAY.
Makes me think of something other than trains and explosions.
For a little while.
I MIGHT BE A LITTLE BIT BETTER THAN OKAY, TO BE HONEST.
I was thinking the same thing, actually. But I'm not going to tell *him* that, yet.
HEARD YOU'RE HANGING OUT IN OLD GOTHAM?
YEAH. IT'S... TROUBLED.
BUT HALY'S CIRCUS IS BACK IN TOWN--HOW ODD IS THAT?
I didn't like him when I first met him, a few years ago. Not really.
Hard to believe that, now.
SO, WHY *ARE* YOU HERE, RICHARD?
WELL, IT'S THAT WE...I MEAN, I...
AND YOU BOTH, I MEAN, YOU...THAT WORRIES YOU?
COME ON, BABS, YOU'RE *RECOVERING.*
That face. Right there. *That* one.
That's the expression that melted me every time, back when we were kids working with Batman.
When the bravado drops, when the rich boy facade dims.
I'VE SEEN THE RECORDS, BARBARA.
DO YOU *WANT* TO BE BACK IN THE WHEELCHAIR?
IS THAT WHAT THIS IS ABOUT?

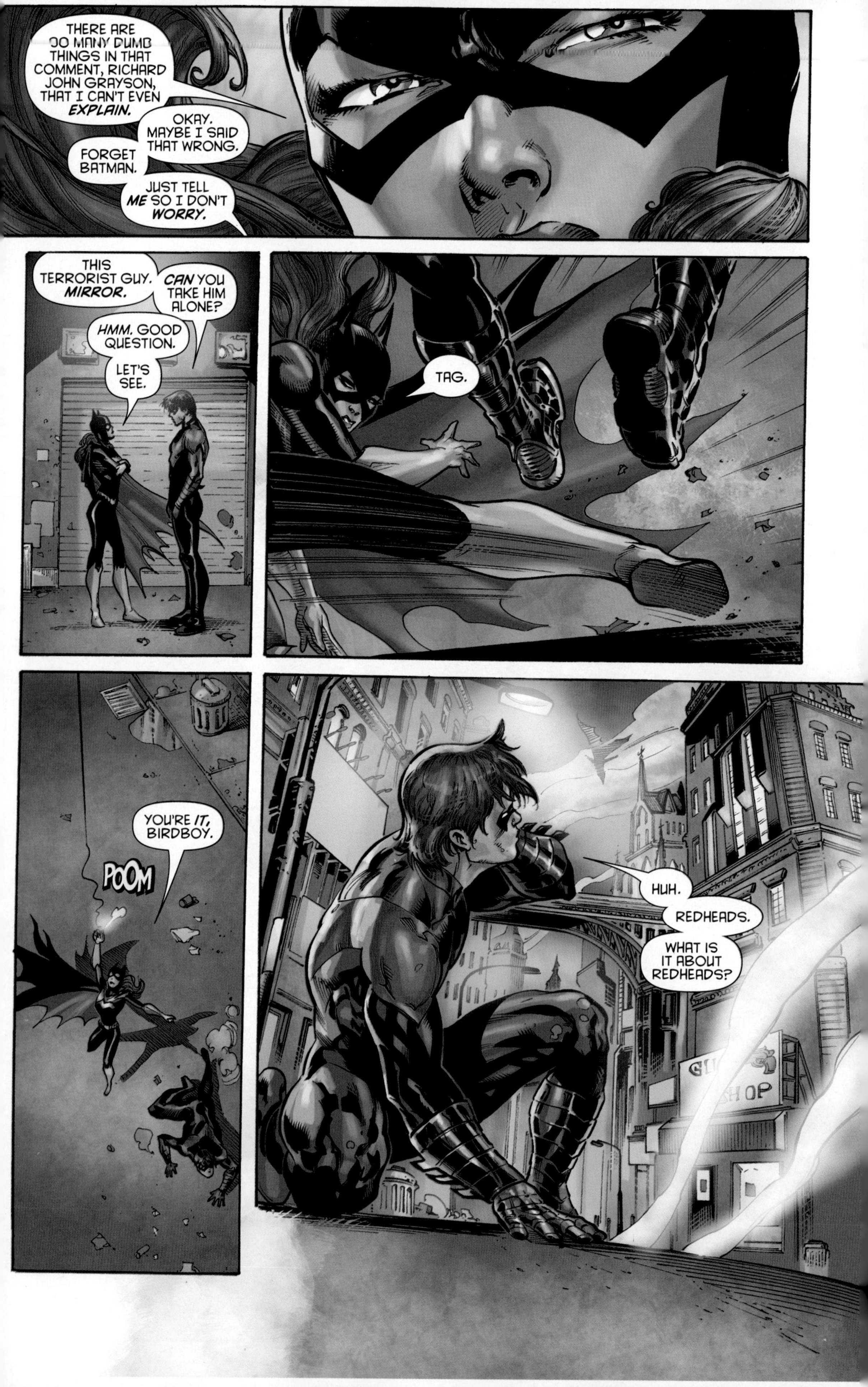
THERE ARE SO MANY DUMB THINGS IN THAT COMMENT, RICHARD JOHN GRAYSON, THAT I CAN'T EVEN EXPLAIN.
OKAY. MAYBE I SAID THAT WRONG.
FORGET BATMAN.
JUST TELL ME SO I DON'T WORRY.
THIS TERRORIST GUY. MIRROR.
CAN YOU TAKE HIM ALONE?
HMM. GOOD QUESTION.
LET'S SEE.
TAG.
YOU'RE IT, BIRDBOY.
POOM
HUH.
REDHEADS.
WHAT IS IT ABOUT REDHEADS?
GU
SHOP

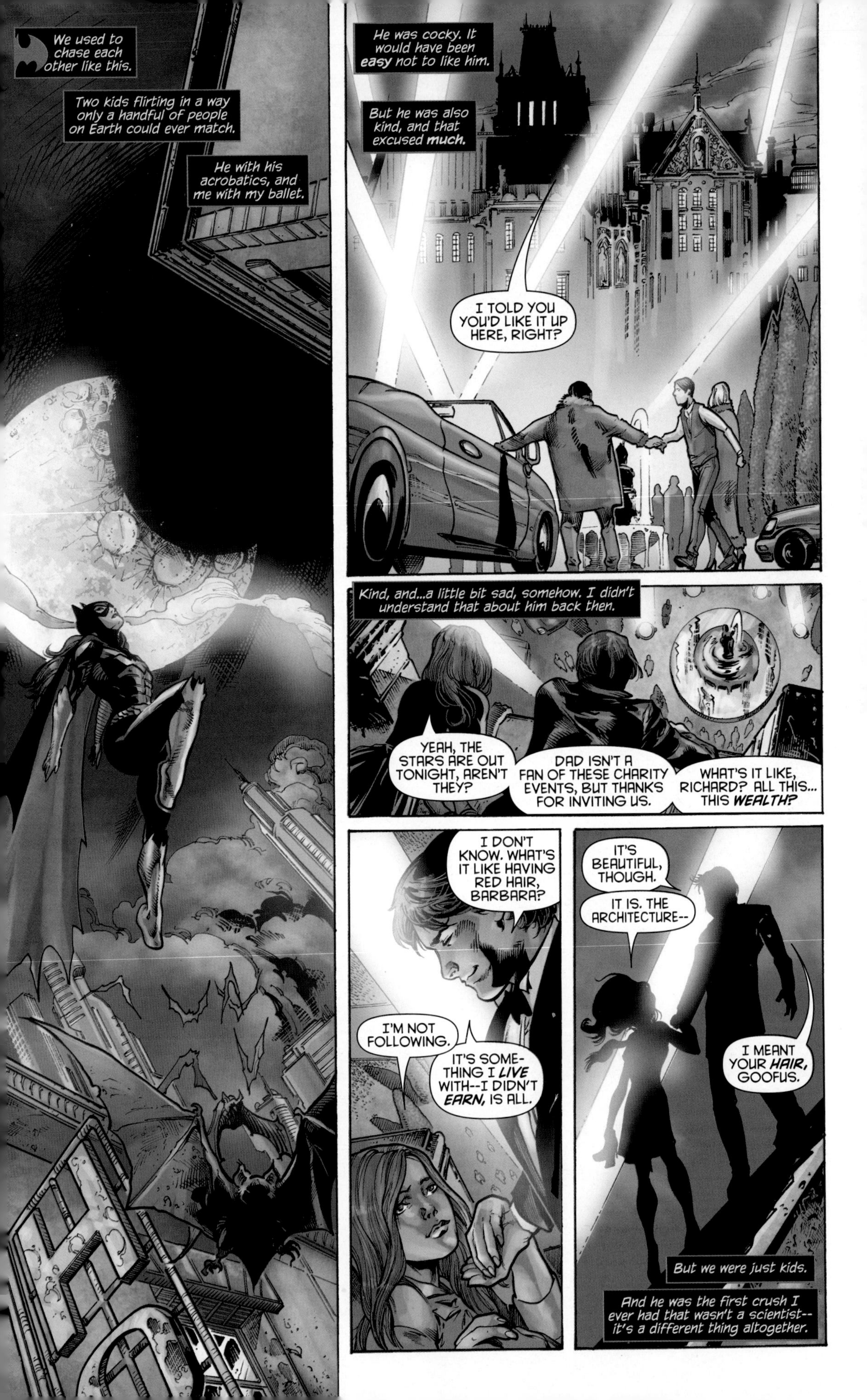
We used to chase each other like this.
Two kids flirting in a way only a handful of people on Earth could ever match.
He with his acrobatics, and me with my ballet.
He was cocky. It would have been easy not to like him.
But he was also kind, and that excused much.
I TOLD YOU YOU'D LIKE IT UP HERE, RIGHT?
Kind, and...a little bit sad, somehow. I didn't understand that about him back then.
YEAH, THE STARS ARE OUT TONIGHT, AREN'T THEY?
DAD ISN'T A FAN OF THESE CHARITY EVENTS, BUT THANKS FOR INVITING US.
WHAT'S IT LIKE, RICHARD? ALL THIS... THIS WEALTH?
I DON'T KNOW. WHAT'S IT LIKE HAVING RED HAIR, BARBARA?
I'M NOT FOLLOWING.
IT'S SOME-THING I LIVE WITH--I DIDN'T EARN, IS ALL.
IT'S BEAUTIFUL, THOUGH.
IT IS. THE ARCHITECTURE--
I MEANT YOUR HAIR, GOOFUS.
But we were just kids.
And he was the first crush I ever had that wasn't a scientist--it's a different thing altogether.

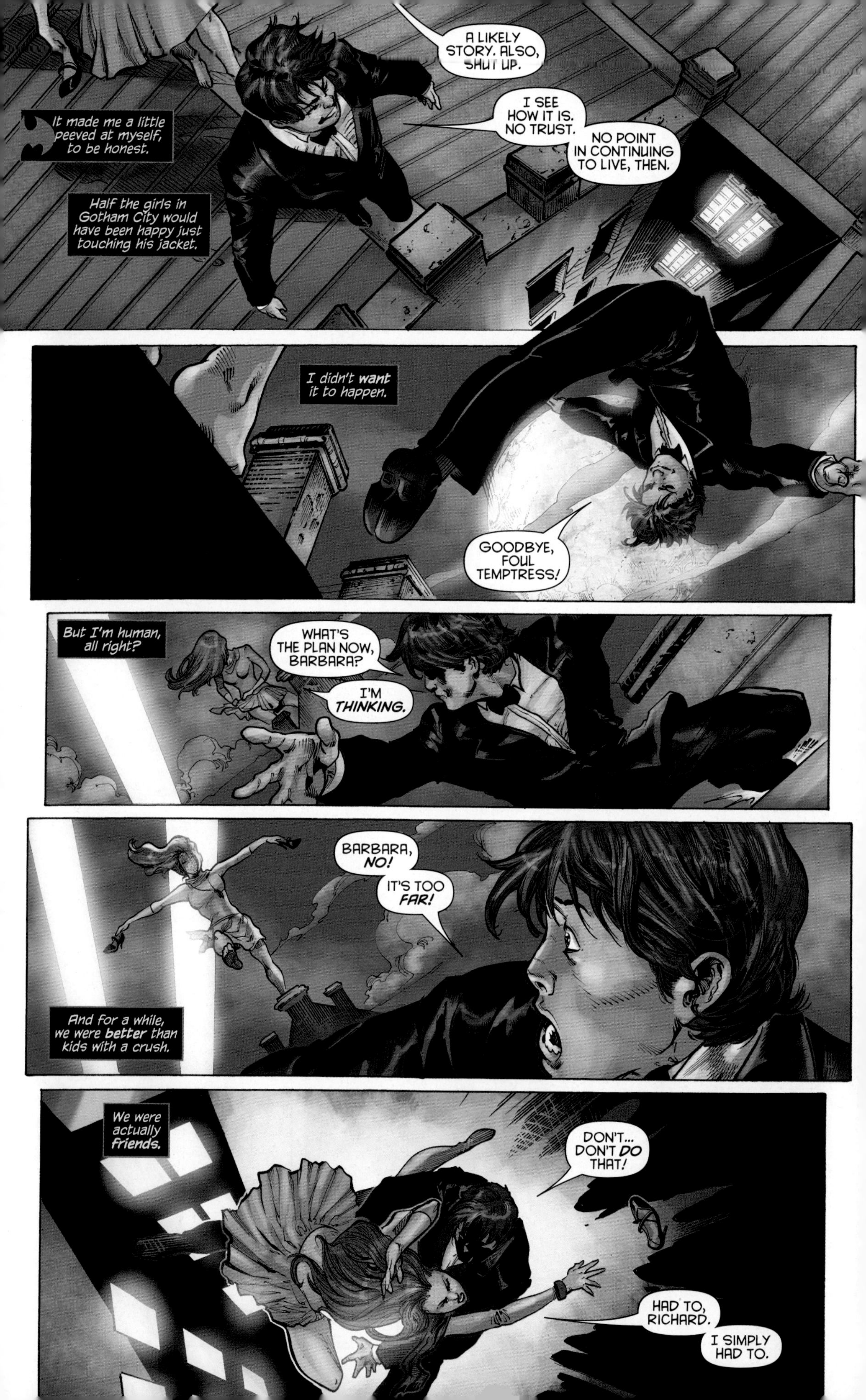

A LIKELY STORY. ALSO, SHUT UP.
It made me a little peeved at myself, to be honest.
I SEE HOW IT IS. NO TRUST.
NO POINT IN CONTINUING TO LIVE, THEN.
Half the girls in Gotham City would have been happy just touching his jacket.
I didn't **want** it to happen.
GOODBYE, FOUL TEMPTRESS!
But I'm human, all right?
WHAT'S THE PLAN NOW, BARBARA?
I'M ***THINKING.***
BARBARA, ***NO!***
IT'S TOO ***FAR!***
And for a while, we were **better** than kids with a crush.
We were actually **friends.**
DON'T... DON'T ***DO*** THAT!
HAD TO, RICHARD.
I SIMPLY HAD TO.

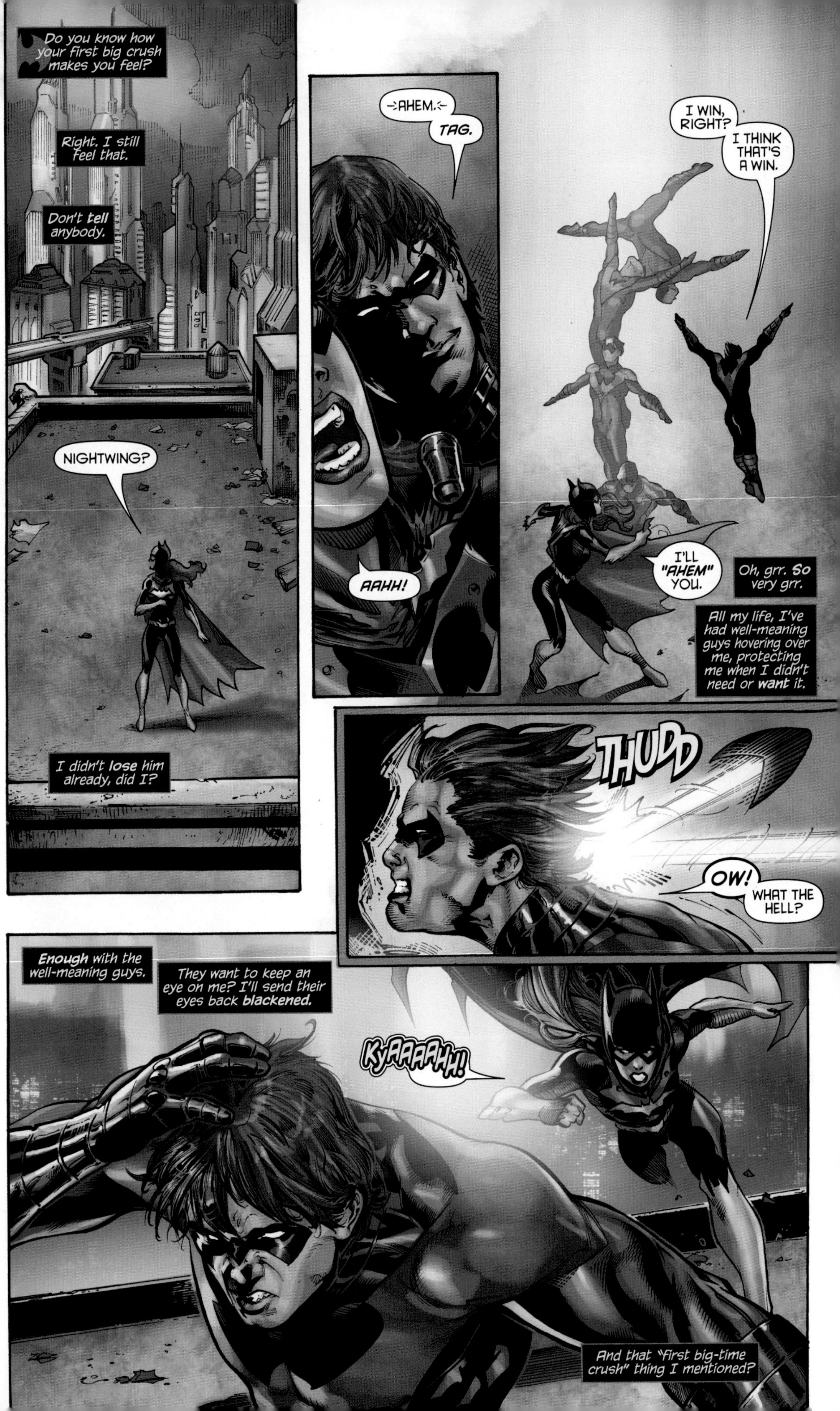

Do you know how your first big crush makes you feel?
Right. I still feel that.
Don't tell anybody.
NIGHTWING?
I didn't lose him already, did I?
AHEM.
TAG.
AAHH!
I WIN, RIGHT?
I THINK THAT'S A WIN.
I'LL "AHEM" YOU.
Oh, grr. So very grr.
All my life, I've had well-meaning guys hovering over me, protecting me when I didn't need or want it.
THUDD
OW!
WHAT THE HELL?
Enough with the well-meaning guys.
They want to keep an eye on me? I'll send their eyes back blackened.
KYAAAAAHH!
And that "first big-time crush" thing I mentioned?

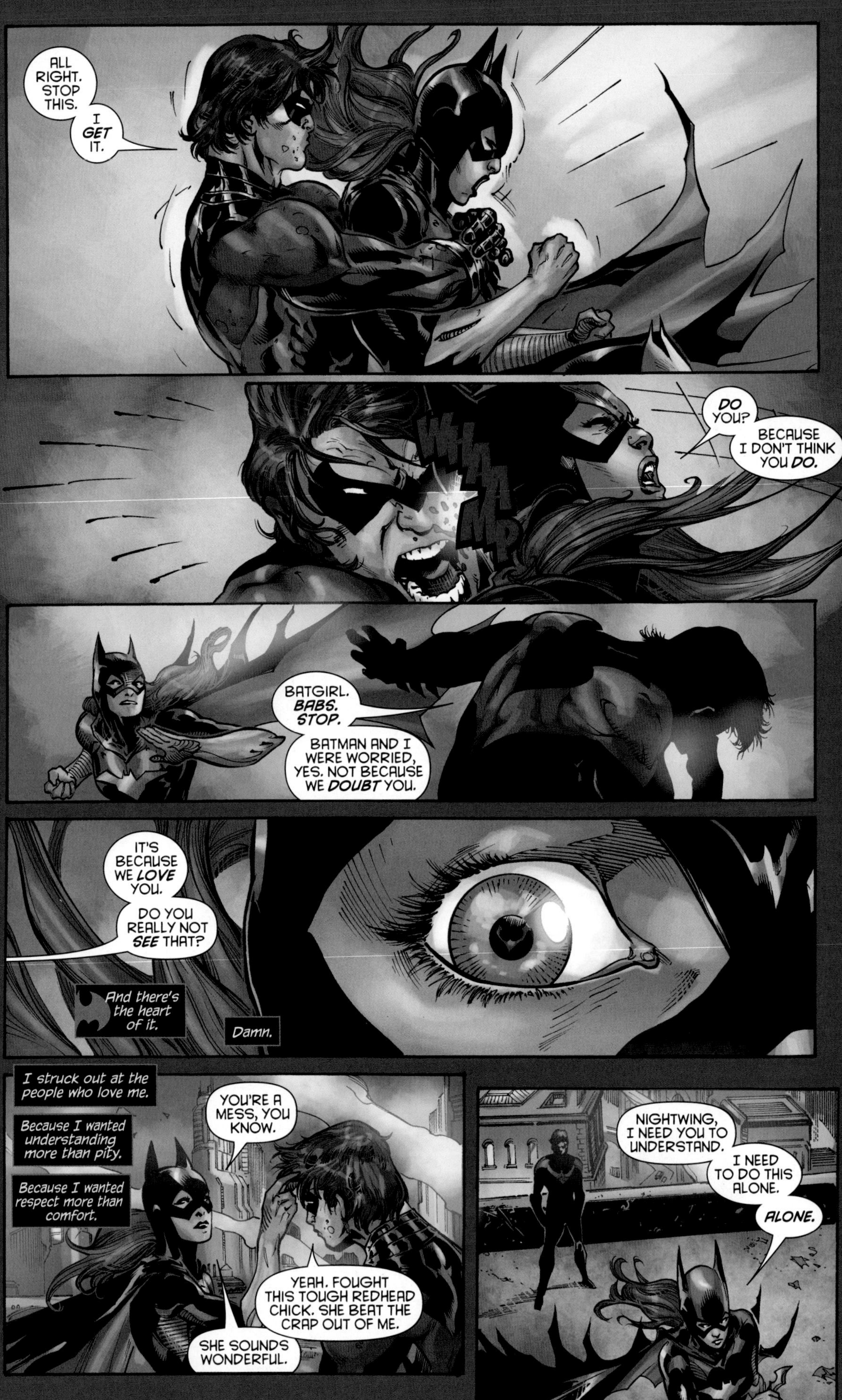

ALL RIGHT. STOP THIS. I GET IT.
DO YOU? BECAUSE I DON'T THINK YOU DO.
WHAAMP
BATGIRL. BABS. STOP.
BATMAN AND I WERE WORRIED, YES. NOT BECAUSE WE DOUBT YOU.
IT'S BECAUSE WE LOVE YOU.
DO YOU REALLY NOT SEE THAT?
And there's the heart of it.
Damn.
I struck out at the people who love me.
Because I wanted understanding more than pity.
Because I wanted respect more than comfort.
YOU'RE A MESS, YOU KNOW.
YEAH. FOUGHT THIS TOUGH REDHEAD CHICK. SHE BEAT THE CRAP OUT OF ME.
SHE SOUNDS WONDERFUL.
NIGHTWING, I NEED YOU TO UNDERSTAND.
I NEED TO DO THIS ALONE.
ALONE.

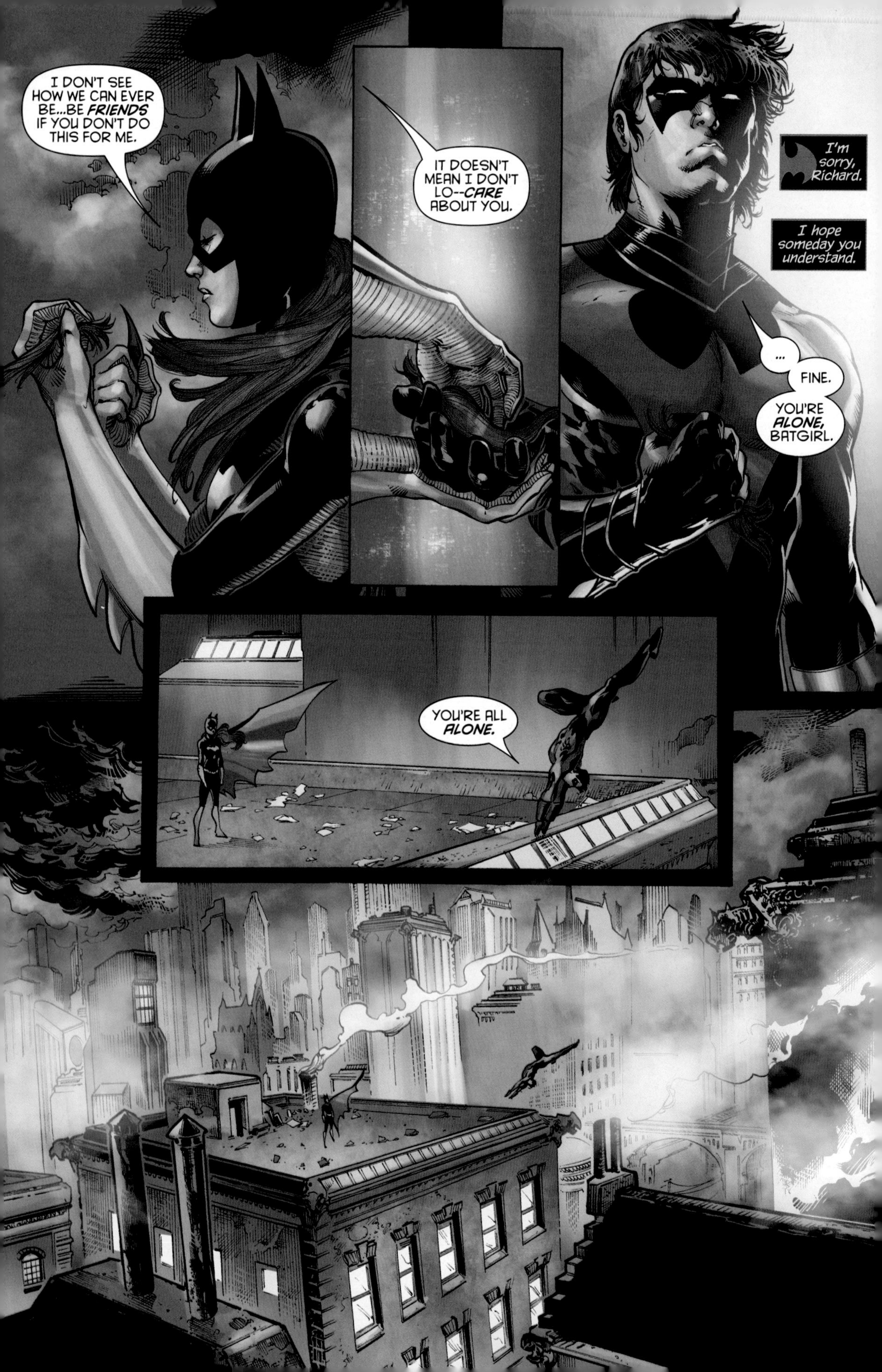
I DON'T SEE HOW WE CAN EVER BE...BE FRIENDS IF YOU DON'T DO THIS FOR ME.
IT DOESN'T MEAN I DON'T LO--CARE ABOUT YOU.
I'm sorry, Richard.
I hope someday you understand.
...
FINE.
YOU'RE ALONE, BATGIRL.
YOU'RE ALL ALONE.

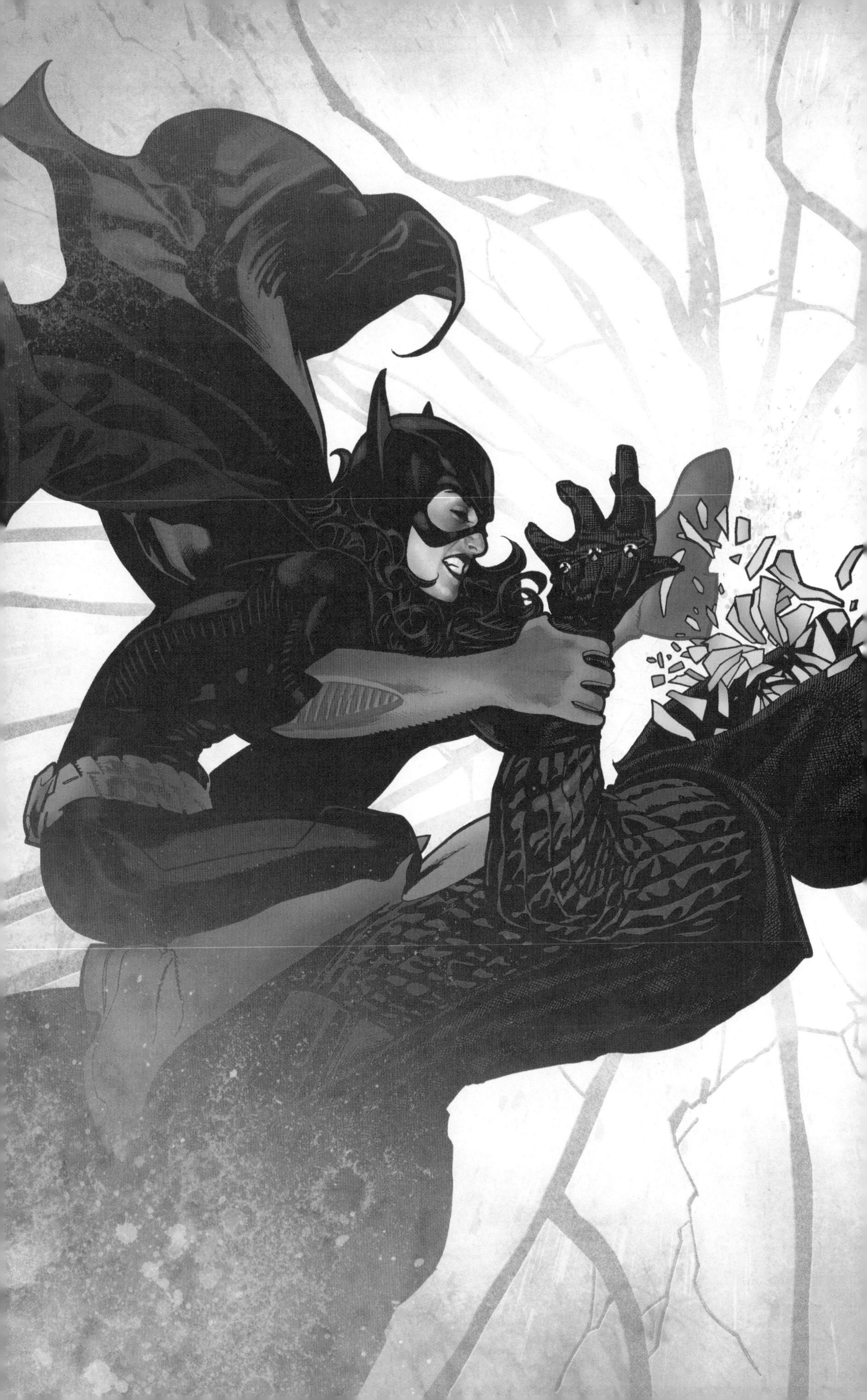

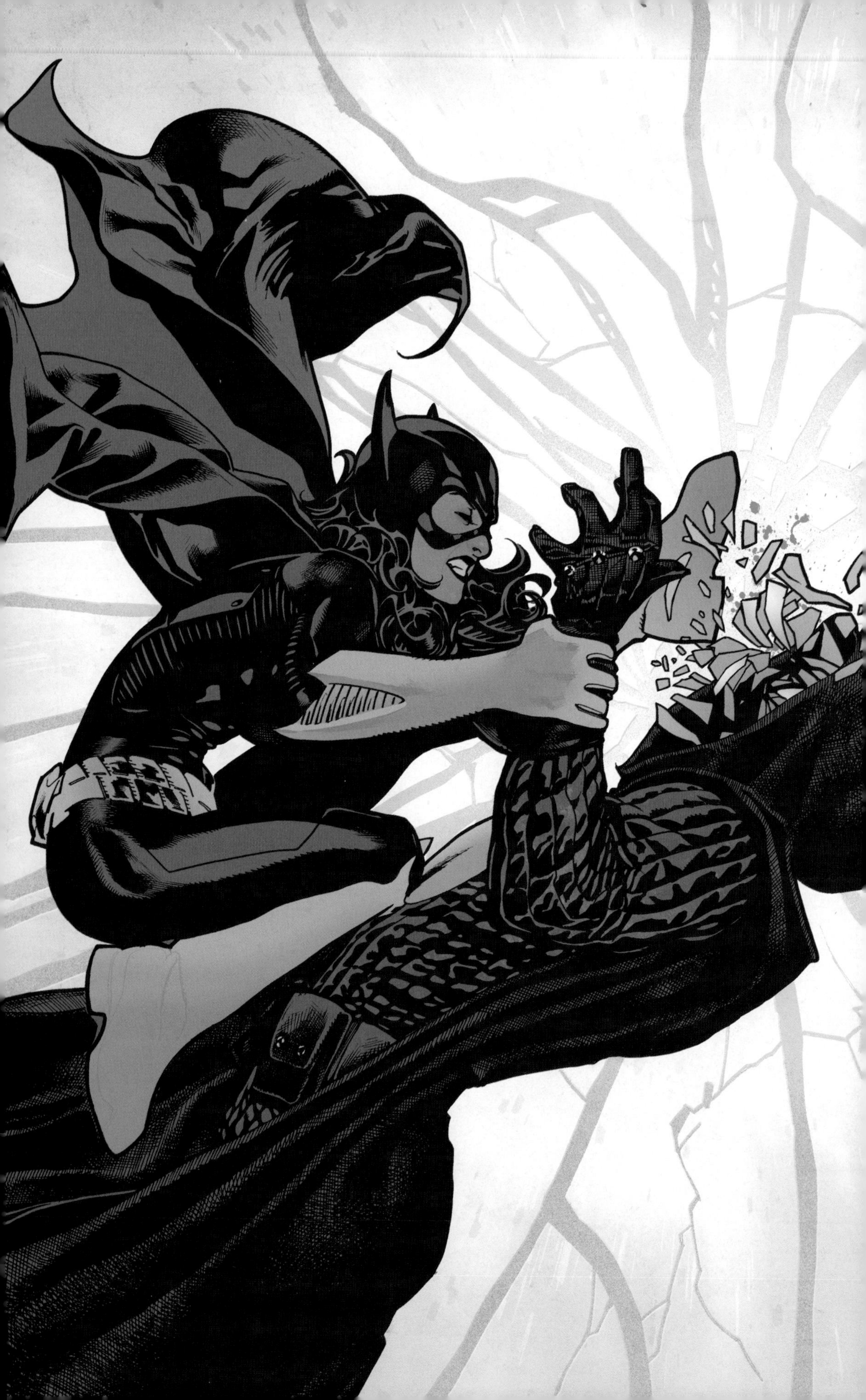

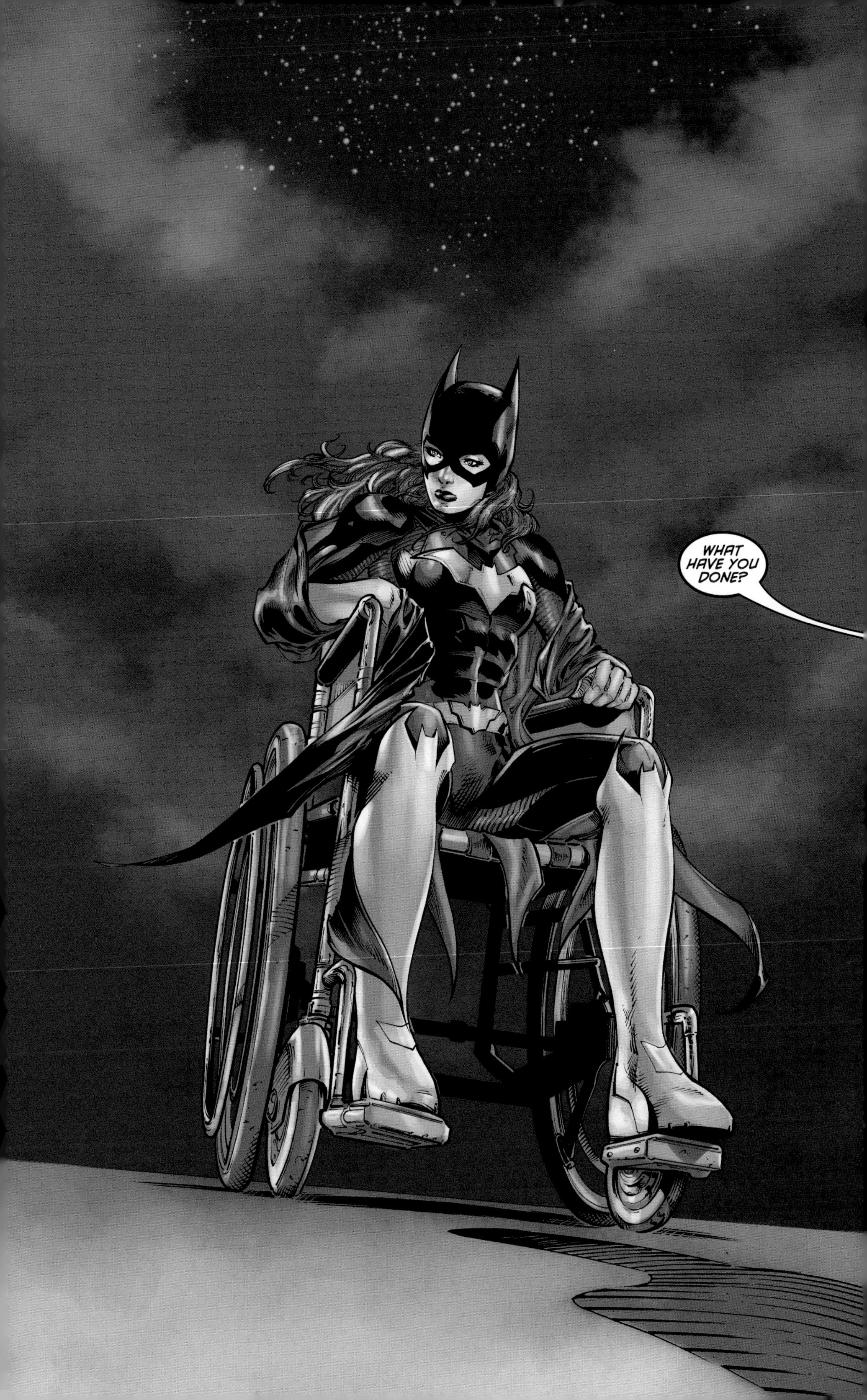
WHAT HAVE YOU DONE?

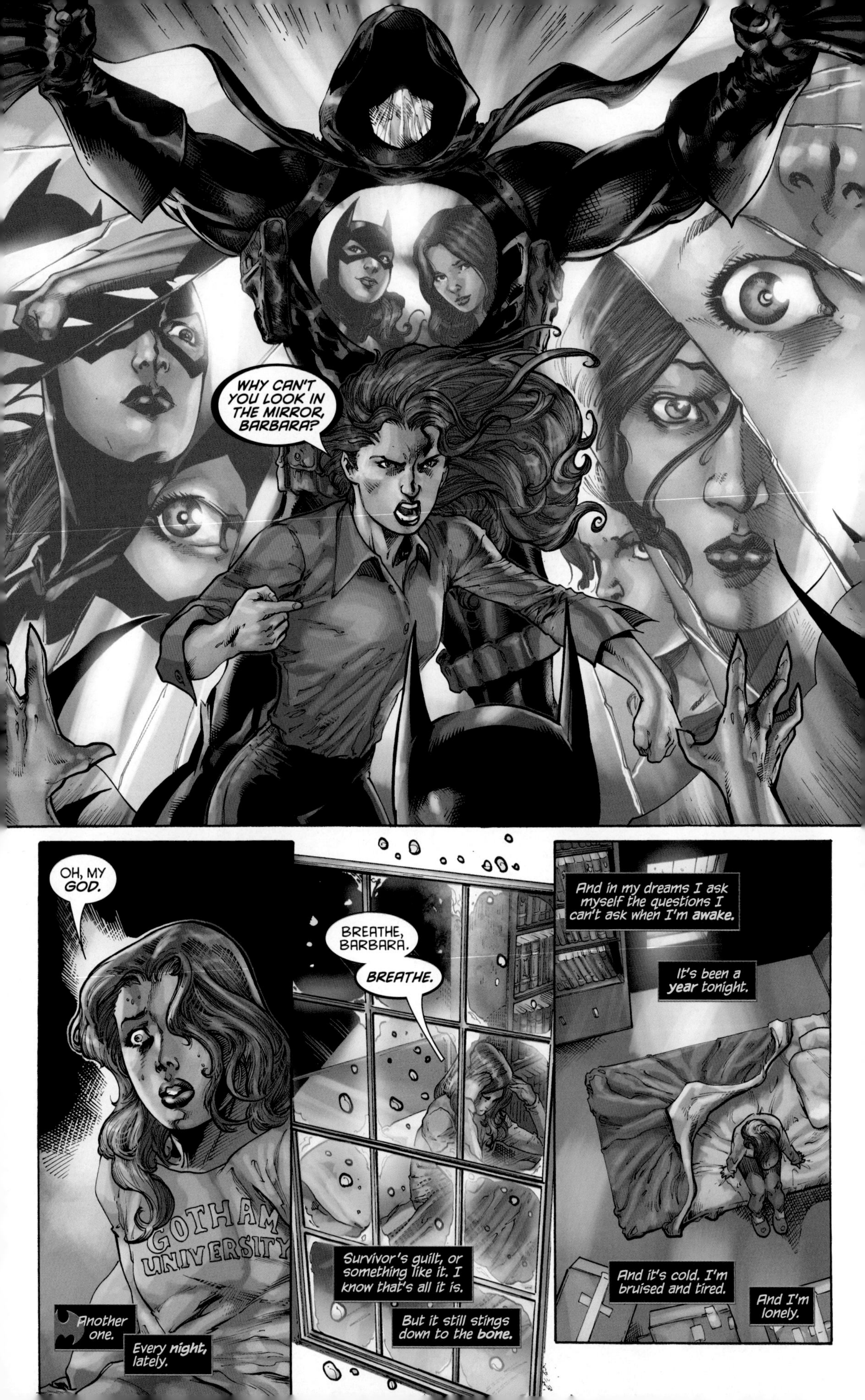
WHY CAN'T YOU LOOK IN THE MIRROR, BARBARA?
OH, MY GOD.
Another one.
Every night, lately.
BREATHE, BARBARA.
BREATHE.
Survivor's guilt, or something like it. I know that's all it is.
But it still stings down to the bone.
And in my dreams I ask myself the questions I can't ask when I'm awake.
It's been a year tonight.
And it's cold. I'm bruised and tired.
And I'm lonely.
GOTHAM UNIVERSITY

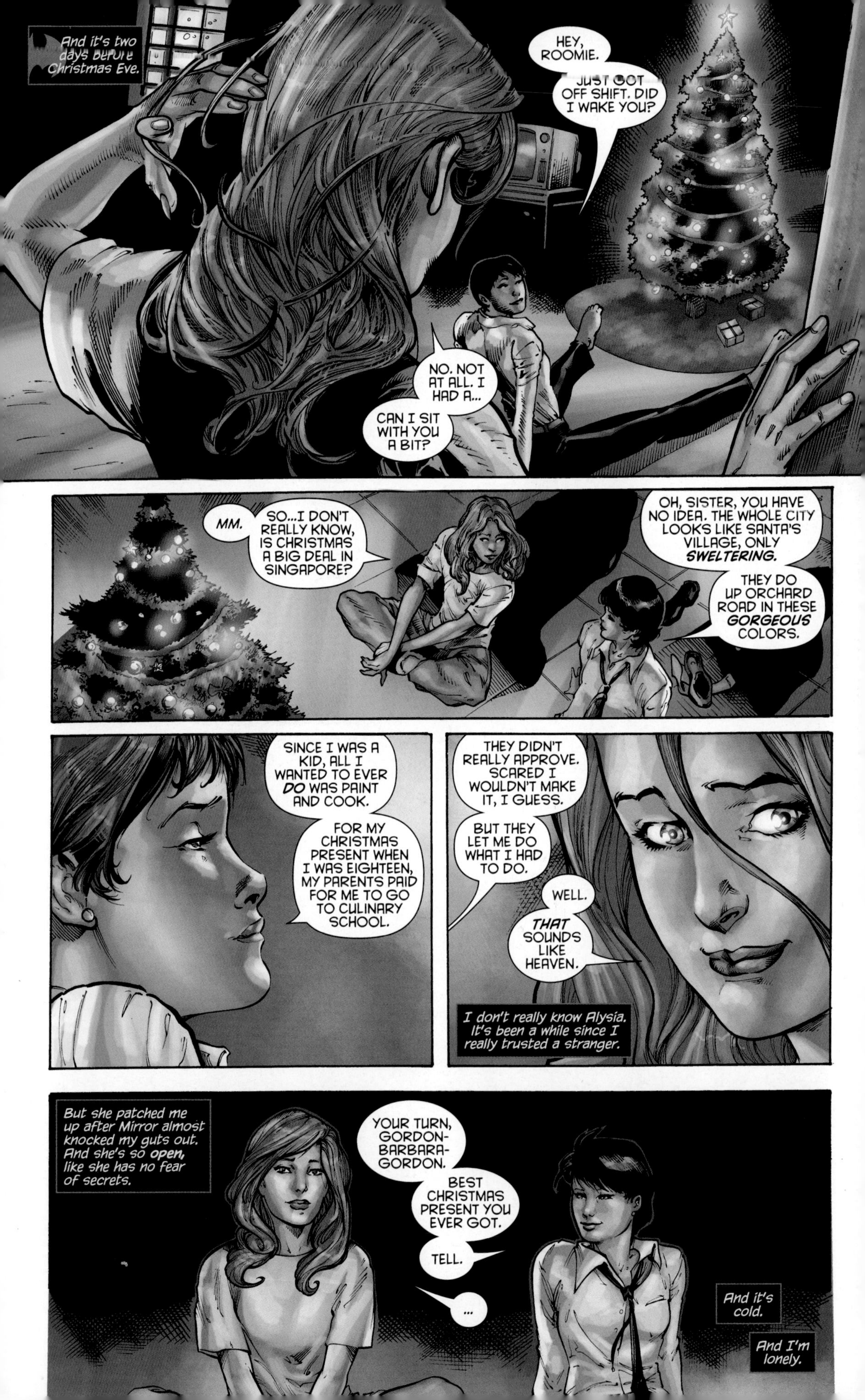
And it's two days before Christmas Eve.
HEY, ROOMIE.
JUST GOT OFF SHIFT. DID I WAKE YOU?
NO. NOT AT ALL. I HAD A...
CAN I SIT WITH YOU A BIT?
MM.
SO...I DON'T REALLY KNOW, IS CHRISTMAS A BIG DEAL IN SINGAPORE?
OH, SISTER, YOU HAVE NO IDEA. THE WHOLE CITY LOOKS LIKE SANTA'S VILLAGE, ONLY SWELTERING.
THEY DO UP ORCHARD ROAD IN THESE GORGEOUS COLORS.
SINCE I WAS A KID, ALL I WANTED TO EVER DO WAS PAINT AND COOK.
FOR MY CHRISTMAS PRESENT WHEN I WAS EIGHTEEN, MY PARENTS PAID FOR ME TO GO TO CULINARY SCHOOL.
THEY DIDN'T REALLY APPROVE. SCARED I WOULDN'T MAKE IT, I GUESS.
BUT THEY LET ME DO WHAT I HAD TO DO.
WELL.
THAT SOUNDS LIKE HEAVEN.
I don't really know Alysia. It's been a while since I really trusted a stranger.
But she patched me up after Mirror almost knocked my guts out. And she's so open, like she has no fear of secrets.
YOUR TURN, GORDON-BARBARA-GORDON.
BEST CHRISTMAS PRESENT YOU EVER GOT.
TELL.
...
And it's cold.
And I'm lonely.

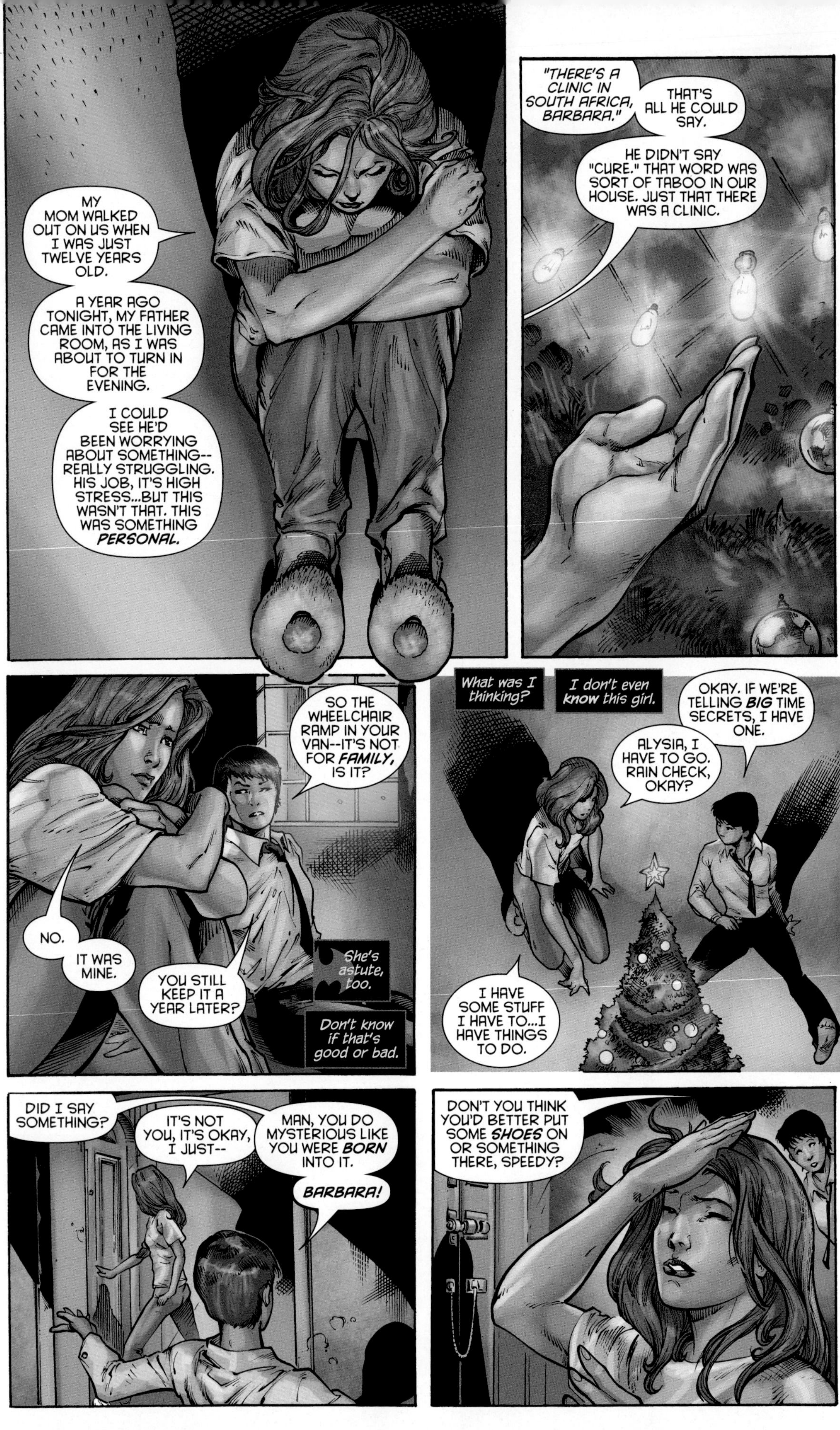
MY MOM WALKED OUT ON US WHEN I WAS JUST TWELVE YEARS OLD.
A YEAR AGO TONIGHT, MY FATHER CAME INTO THE LIVING ROOM, AS I WAS ABOUT TO TURN IN FOR THE EVENING.
I COULD SEE HE'D BEEN WORRYING ABOUT SOMETHING-- REALLY STRUGGLING. HIS JOB, IT'S HIGH STRESS...BUT THIS WASN'T THAT. THIS WAS SOMETHING *PERSONAL.*
"THERE'S A CLINIC IN SOUTH AFRICA, BARBARA."
THAT'S ALL HE COULD SAY.
HE DIDN'T SAY "CURE." THAT WORD WAS SORT OF TABOO IN OUR HOUSE. JUST THAT THERE WAS A CLINIC.
SO THE WHEELCHAIR RAMP IN YOUR VAN--IT'S NOT FOR *FAMILY,* IS IT?
NO.
IT WAS MINE.
YOU STILL KEEP IT A YEAR LATER?
She's astute, too.
Don't know if that's good or bad.
What was I thinking?
I don't even *know* this girl.
OKAY. IF WE'RE TELLING *BIG* TIME SECRETS, I HAVE ONE.
ALYSIA, I HAVE TO GO. RAIN CHECK, OKAY?
I HAVE SOME STUFF I HAVE TO...I HAVE THINGS TO DO.
DID I SAY SOMETHING?
IT'S NOT YOU, IT'S OKAY, I JUST--
MAN, YOU DO MYSTERIOUS LIKE YOU WERE *BORN* INTO IT.
BARBARA!
DON'T YOU THINK YOU'D BETTER PUT SOME *SHOES* ON OR SOMETHING THERE, SPEEDY?

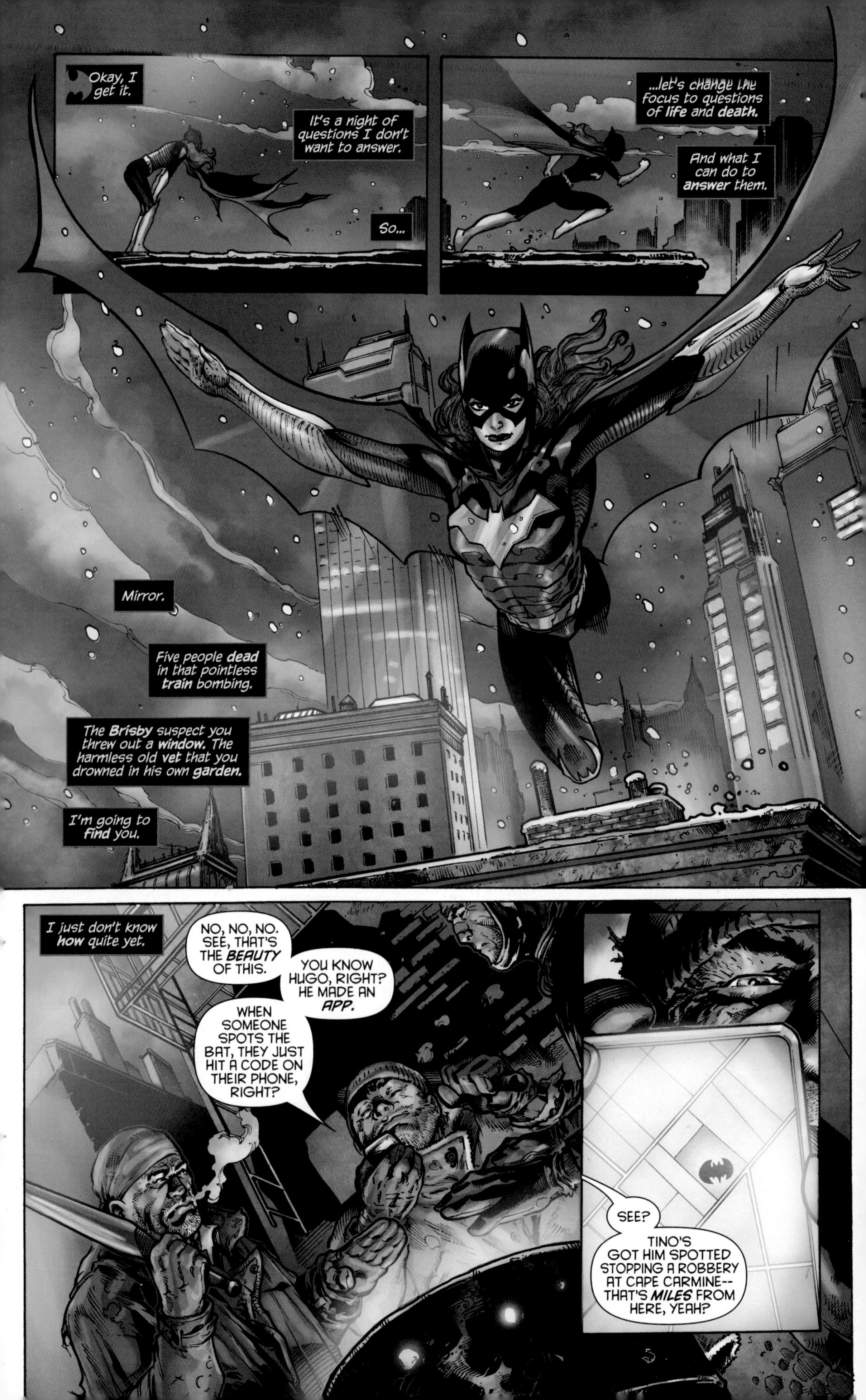
Okay, I get it.
It's a night of questions I don't want to answer.
So...
...let's change the focus to questions of life and death.
And what I can do to answer them.
Mirror.
Five people dead in that pointless train bombing.
The Brisby suspect you threw out a window. The harmless old vet that you drowned in his own garden.
I'm going to find you.
I just don't know how quite yet.
NO, NO, NO. SEE, THAT'S THE BEAUTY OF THIS.
YOU KNOW HUGO, RIGHT? HE MADE AN APP.
WHEN SOMEONE SPOTS THE BAT, THEY JUST HIT A CODE ON THEIR PHONE, RIGHT?
SEE?
TINO'S GOT HIM SPOTTED STOPPING A ROBBERY AT CAPE CARMINE-- THAT'S MILES FROM HERE, YEAH?

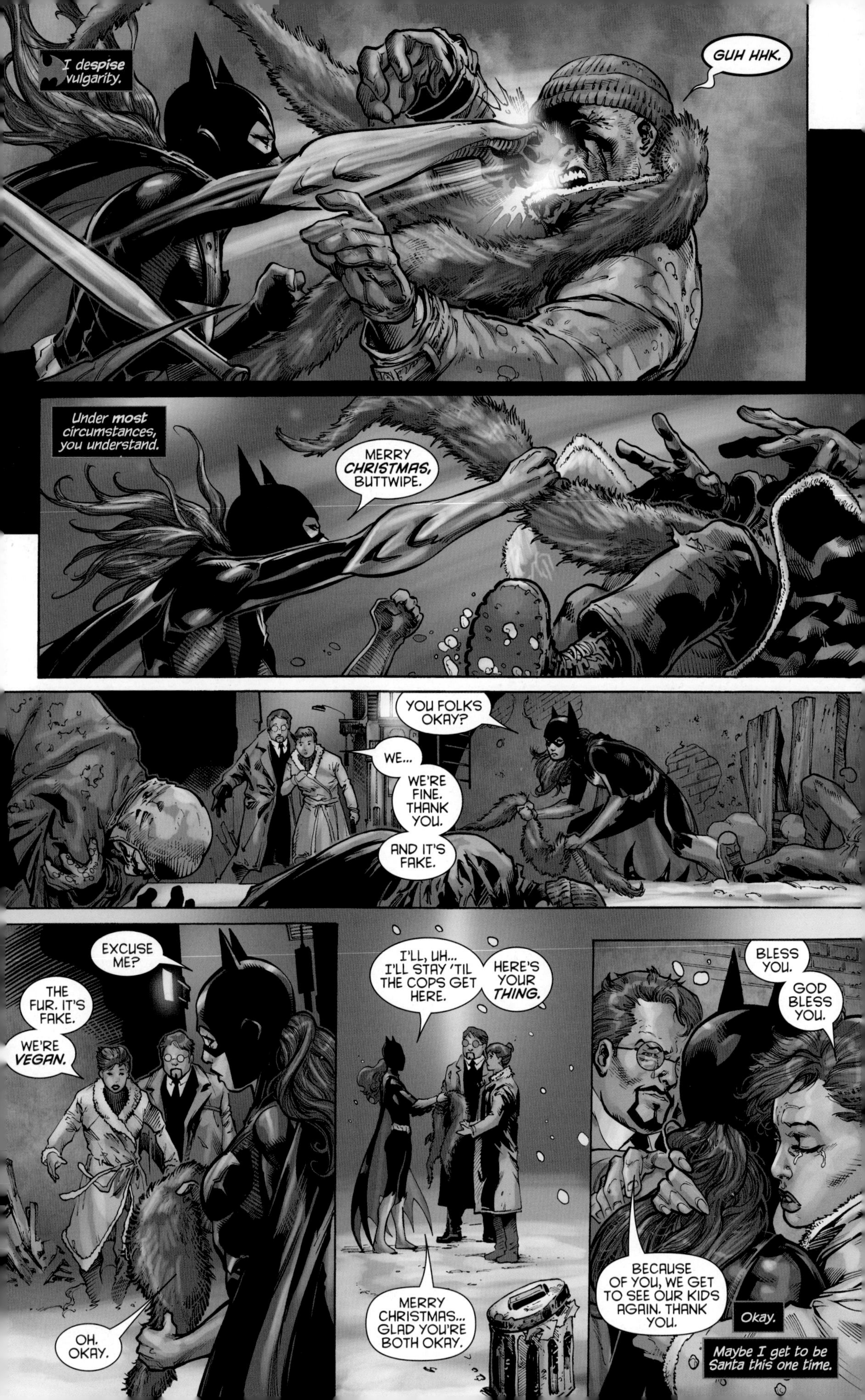
I despise vulgarity.
GUH HHK.
Under most circumstances, you understand.
MERRY CHRISTMAS, BUTTWIPE.
YOU FOLKS OKAY?
WE...
WE'RE FINE. THANK YOU.
AND IT'S FAKE.
EXCUSE ME?
THE FUR. IT'S FAKE.
WE'RE VEGAN.
OH. OKAY.
I'LL, UH... I'LL STAY 'TIL THE COPS GET HERE.
HERE'S YOUR THING.
MERRY CHRISTMAS... GLAD YOU'RE BOTH OKAY.
BLESS YOU.
GOD BLESS YOU.
BECAUSE OF YOU, WE GET TO SEE OUR KIDS AGAIN. THANK YOU.
Okay.
Maybe I get to be Santa this one time.

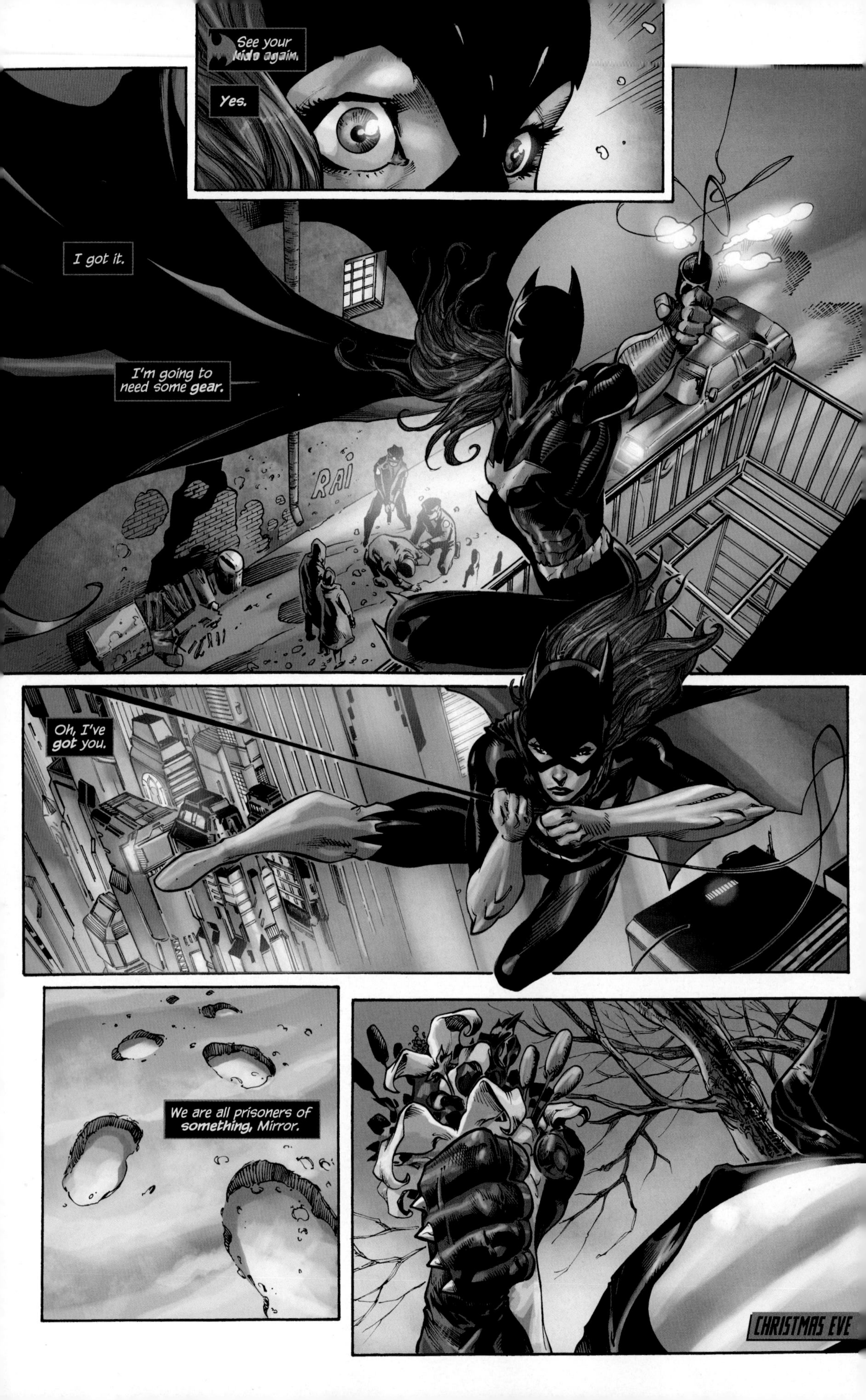
See your kids again.
Yes.
I got it.
I'm going to need some gear.
RAI
Oh, I've got you.
We are all prisoners of something, Mirror.
CHRISTMAS EVE

Mirror wasn't always a killer of innocents.

He was D.E.A. once, the best agent they *had*.

Until a cartel out for revenge planted a car bomb.

He miraculously survived.

SHANDRA MILLS
BELOVED WIFE
AND MOTHER

TABITHA MILLS

JENNIFER MILLS

His wife and twin daughters did not.

It didn't break his mind.

It broke his universe.

And now he believes that miracles, people surviving against impossible odds--

--are a *curse*, not a blessing.

He's been keeping a list of such Gotham citizens.

So that he could *correct* God's *"mistakes."*

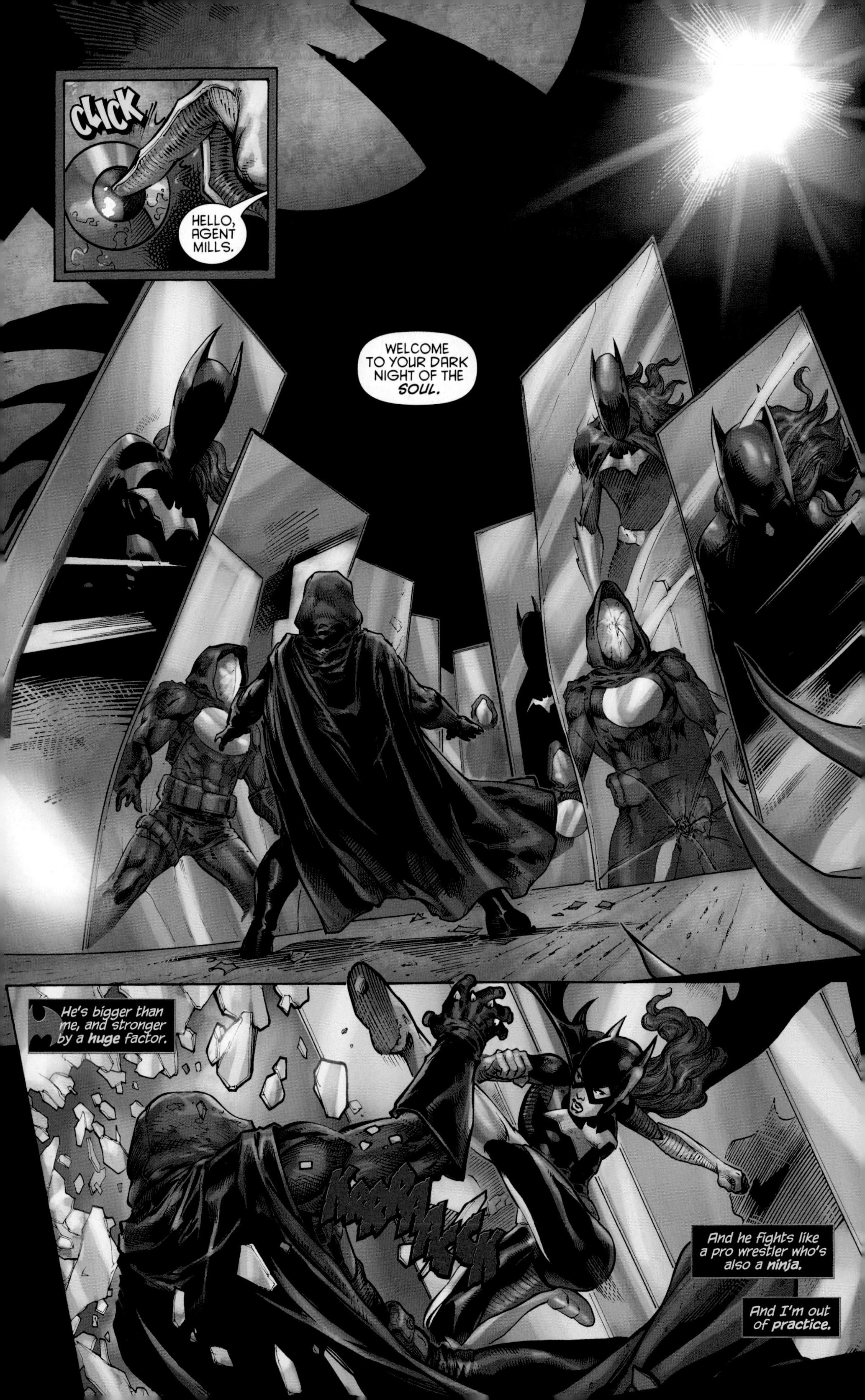
CLICK
HELLO, AGENT MILLS.
WELCOME TO YOUR DARK NIGHT OF THE *SOUL.*
He's bigger than me, and stronger by a **huge** factor.
And he fights like a pro wrestler who's also a **ninja.**
And I'm out of **practice.**

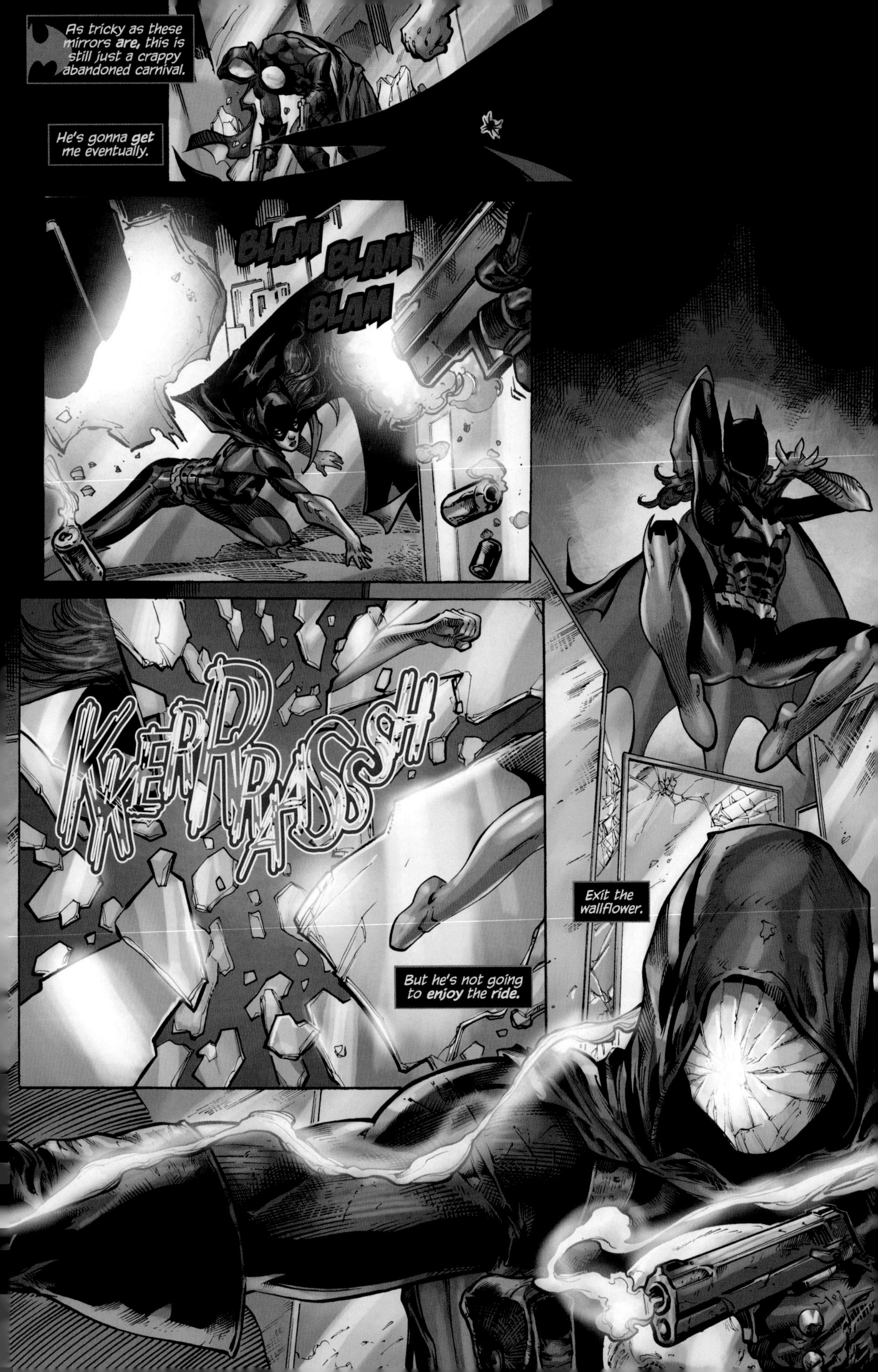
As tricky as these mirrors are, this is still just a crappy abandoned carnival.
He's gonna get me eventually.
BLAM
BLAM
BLAM
KKERRRASSH
But he's not going to enjoy the ride.
Exit the wallflower.

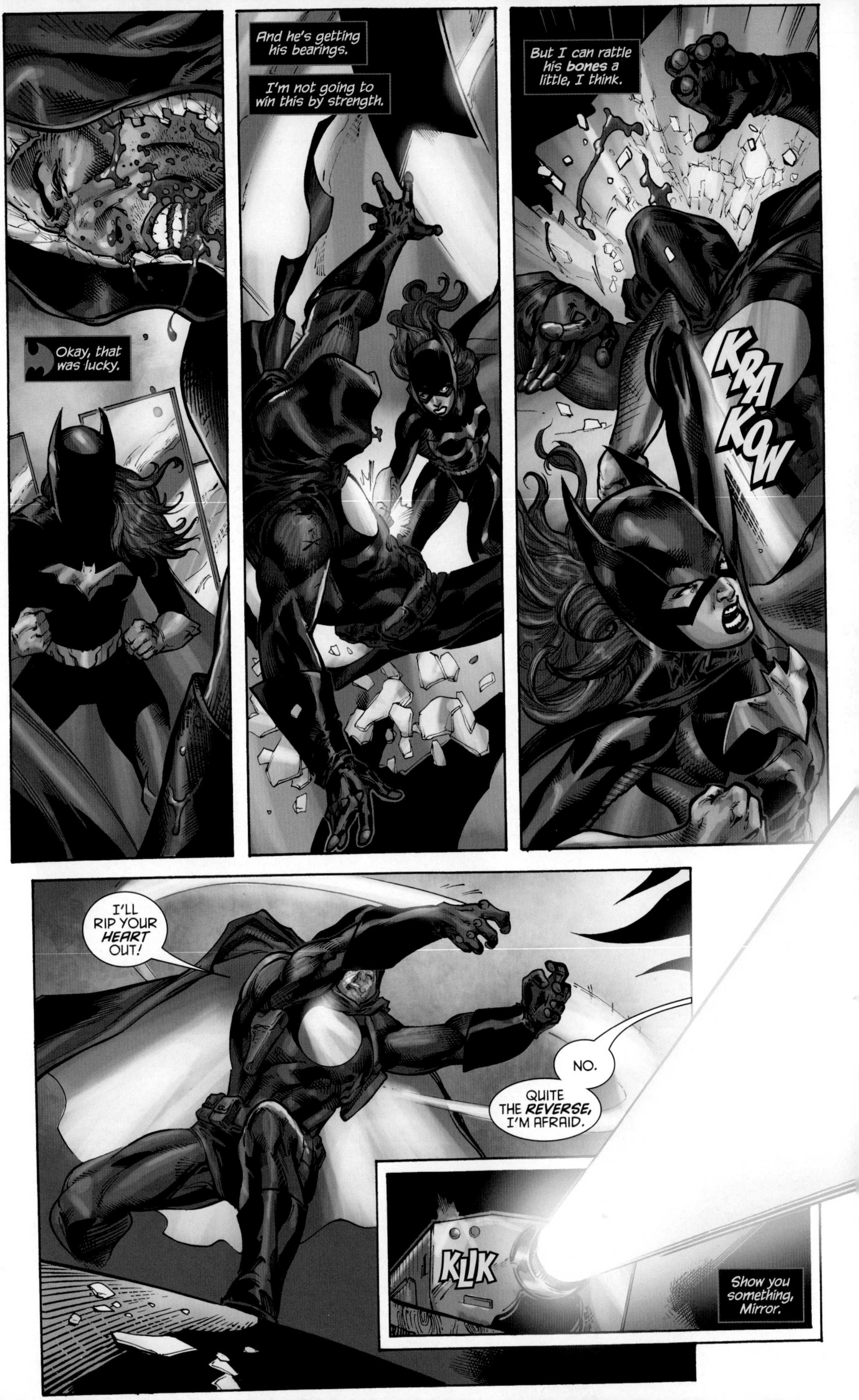
Okay, that was lucky.
And he's getting his bearings.
I'm not going to win this by strength.
But I can rattle his bones a little, I think.
KRAKOW
I'LL RIP YOUR HEART OUT!
NO.
QUITE THE REVERSE, I'M AFRAID.
KLIK
Show you something, Mirror.

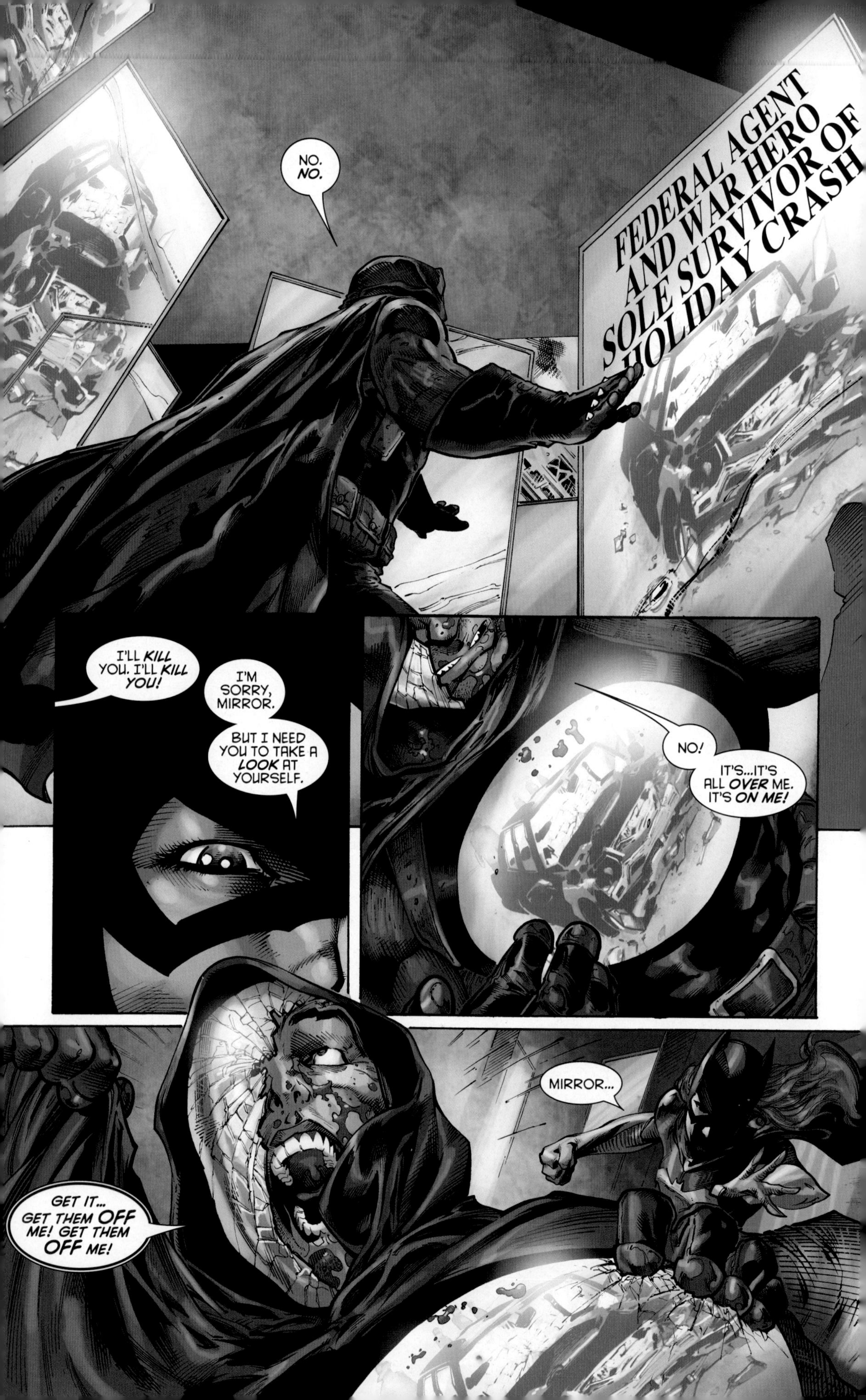
FEDERAL AGENT AND WAR HERO SOLE SURVIVOR OF HOLIDAY CRASH
NO. NO.
I'LL KILL YOU. I'LL KILL YOU!
I'M SORRY, MIRROR.
BUT I NEED YOU TO TAKE A LOOK AT YOURSELF.
NO!
IT'S...IT'S ALL OVER ME. IT'S ON ME!
MIRROR...
GET IT... GET THEM OFF ME! GET THEM OFF ME!

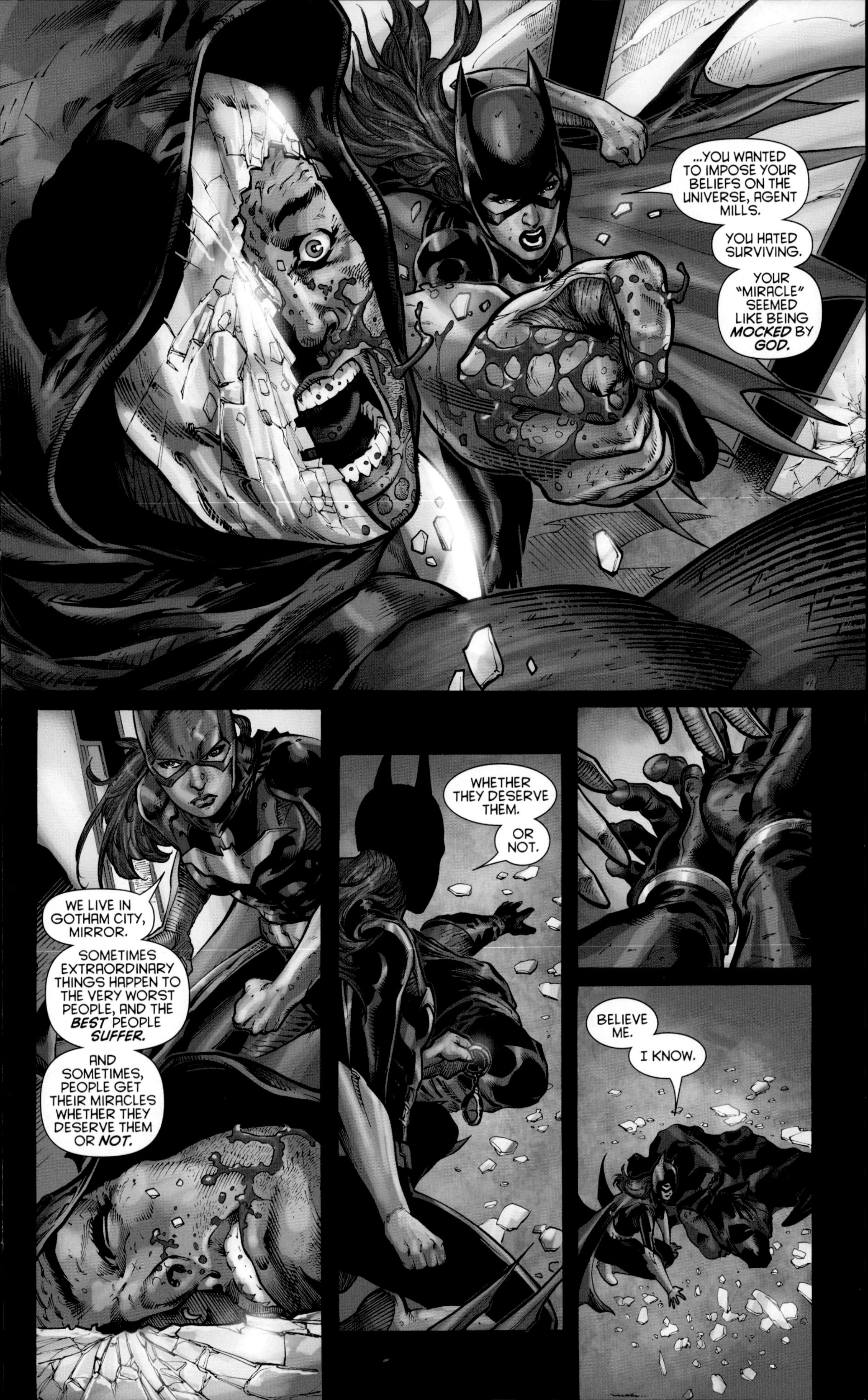
...YOU WANTED TO IMPOSE YOUR BELIEFS ON THE UNIVERSE, AGENT MILLS.
YOU HATED SURVIVING.
YOUR "MIRACLE" SEEMED LIKE BEING ***MOCKED*** BY ***GOD.***
WE LIVE IN GOTHAM CITY, MIRROR.
SOMETIMES EXTRAORDINARY THINGS HAPPEN TO THE VERY WORST PEOPLE, AND THE ***BEST*** PEOPLE ***SUFFER.***
AND SOMETIMES, PEOPLE GET THEIR MIRACLES WHETHER THEY DESERVE THEM OR ***NOT.***
WHETHER THEY DESERVE THEM.
OR NOT.
BELIEVE ME.
I KNOW.

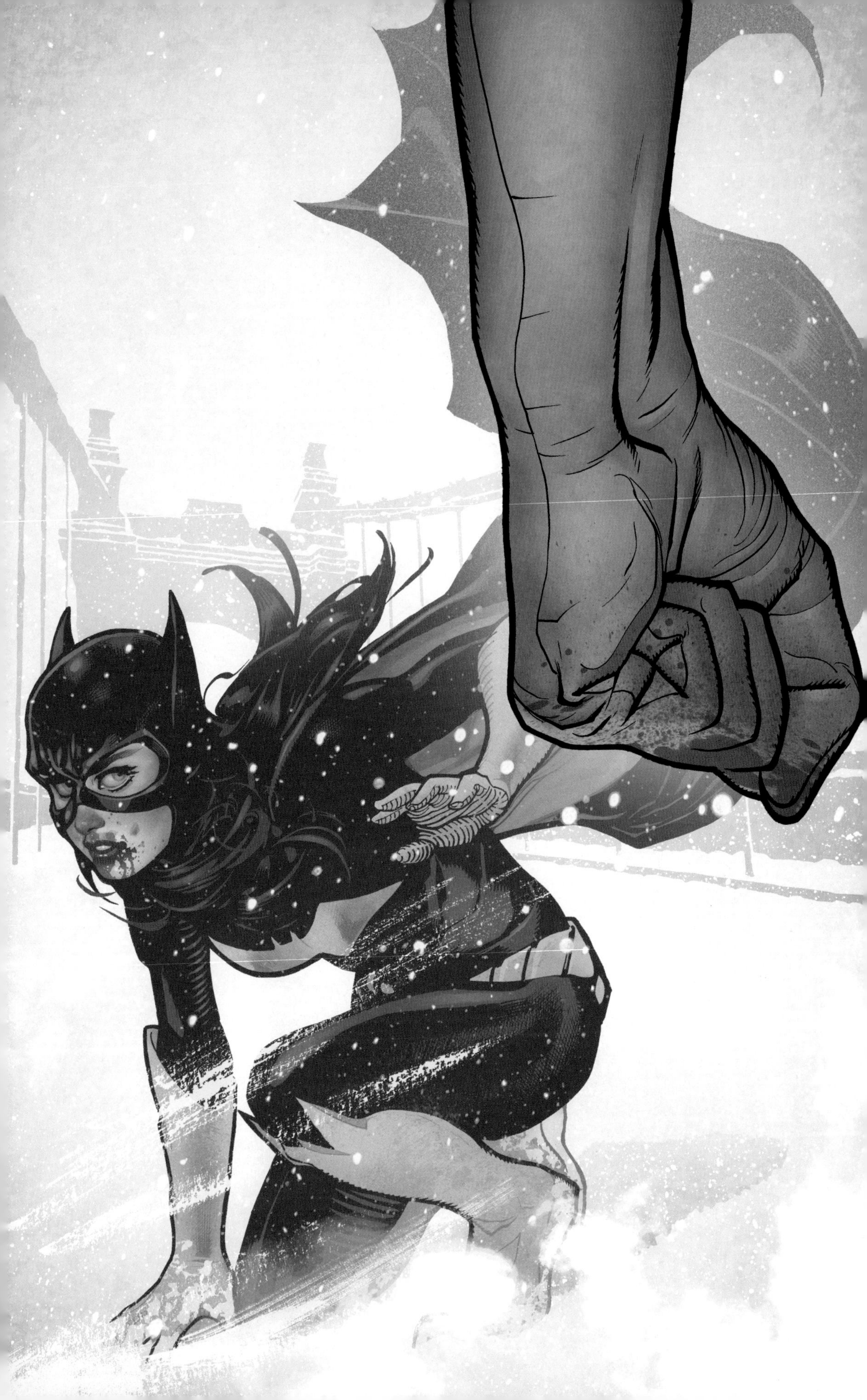

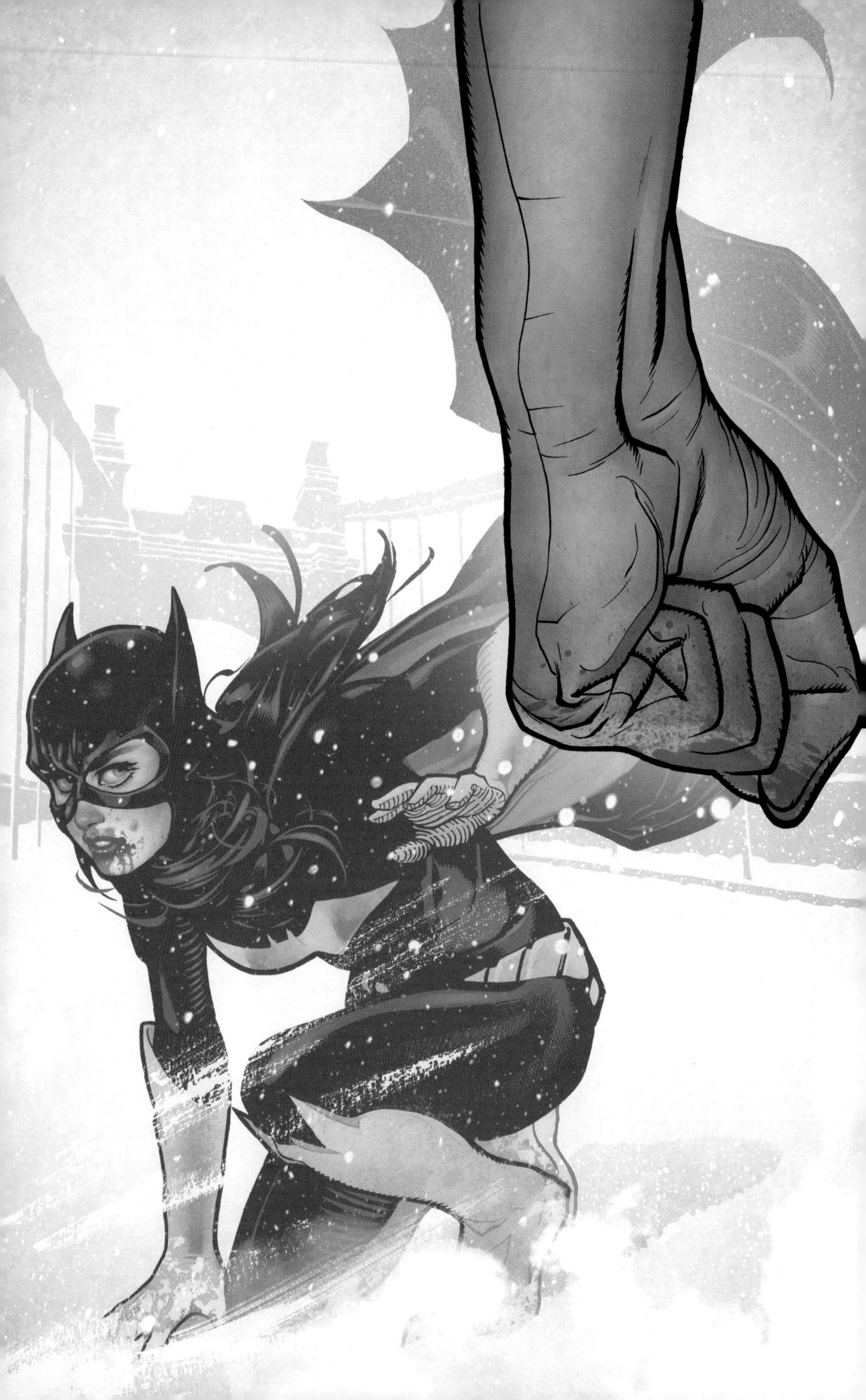

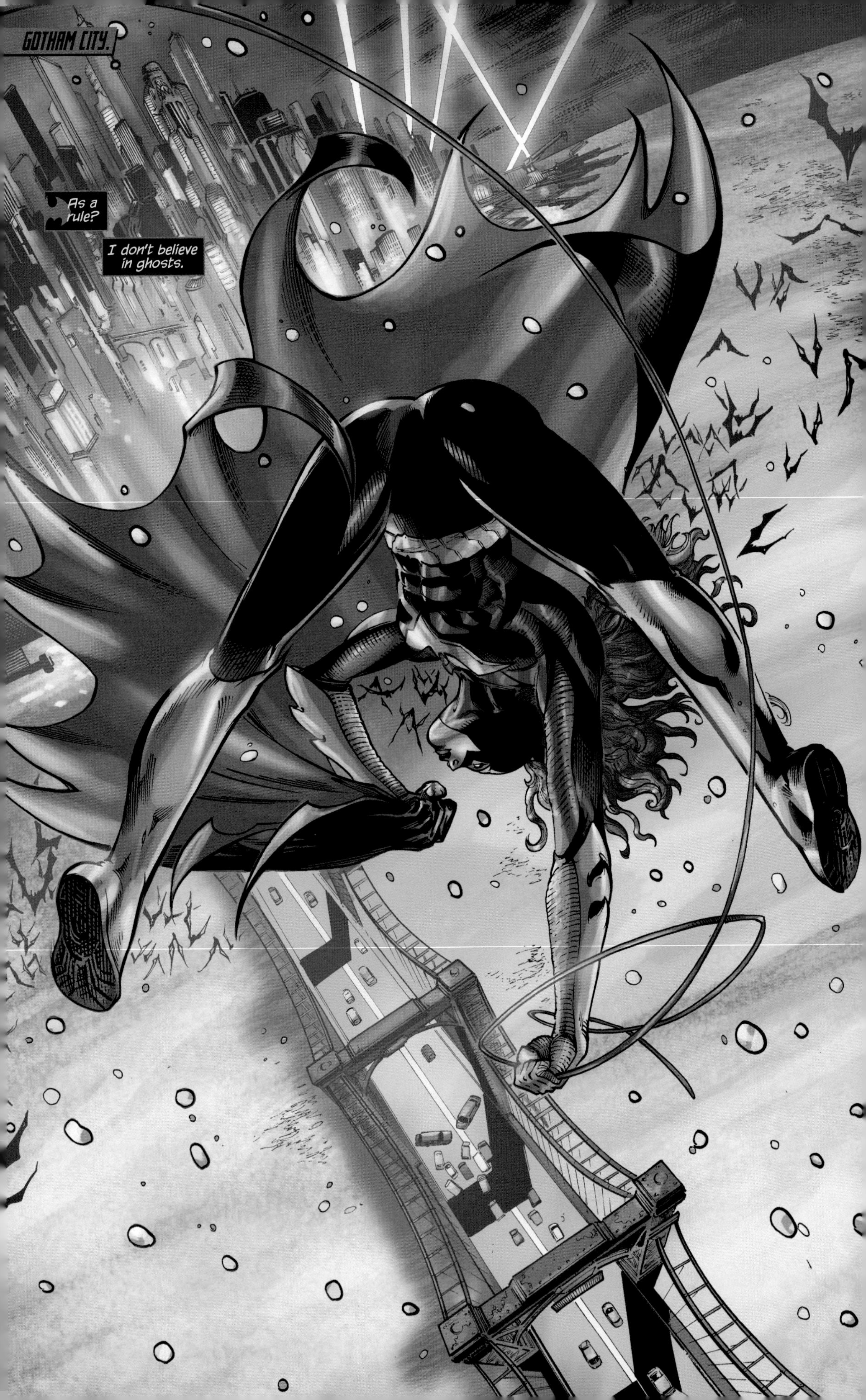
GOTHAM CITY.
As a rule?
I don't believe in ghosts.

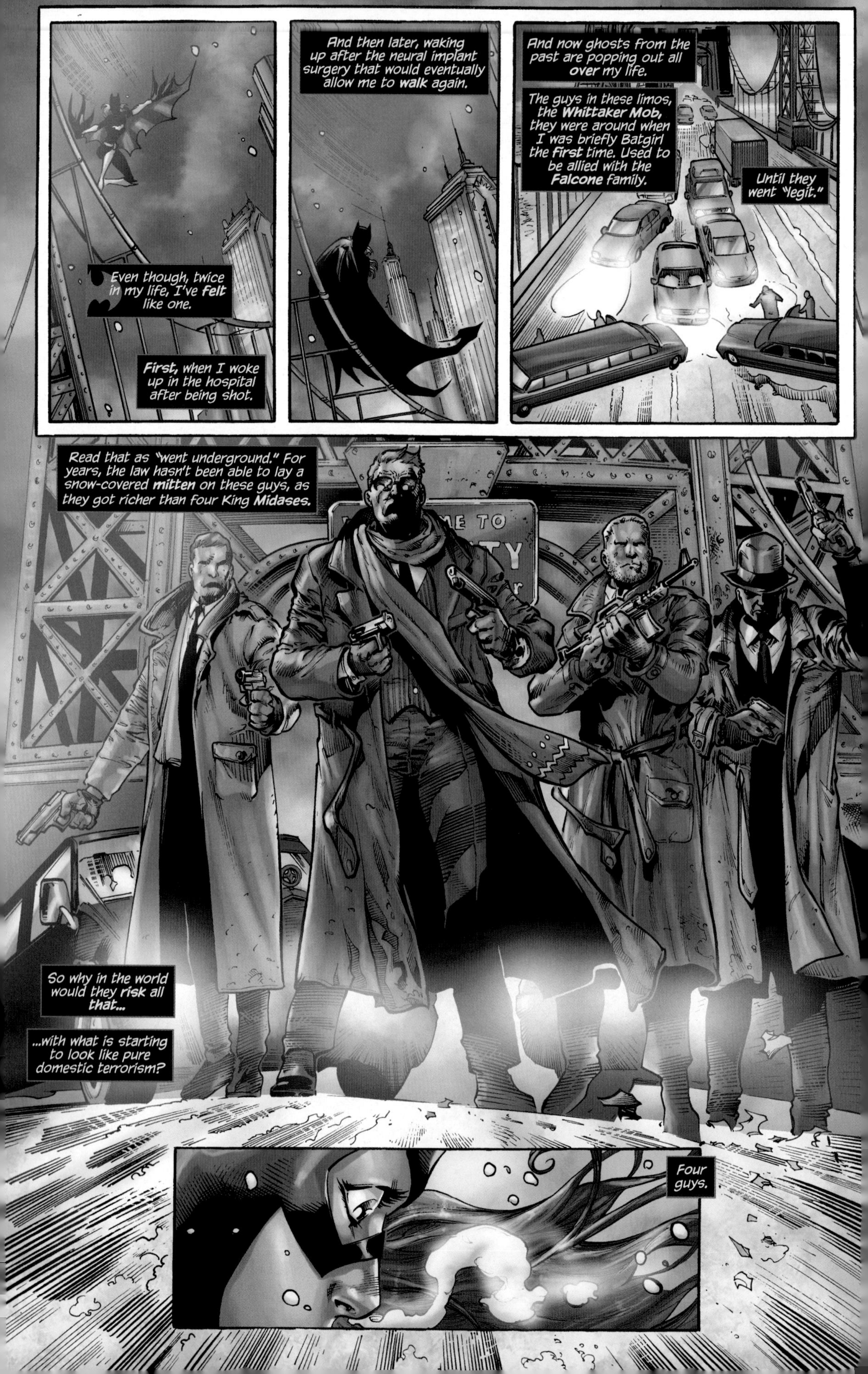
Even though, twice in my life, I've felt like one.
First, when I woke up in the hospital after being shot.
And then later, waking up after the neural implant surgery that would eventually allow me to walk again.
And now ghosts from the past are popping out all over my life.
The guys in these limos, the Whittaker Mob, they were around when I was briefly Batgirl the first time. Used to be allied with the Falcone family.
Until they went "legit."
Read that as "went underground." For years, the law hasn't been able to lay a snow-covered mitten on these guys, as they got richer than four King Midases.
So why in the world would they risk all that...
...with what is starting to look like pure domestic terrorism?
Four guys.

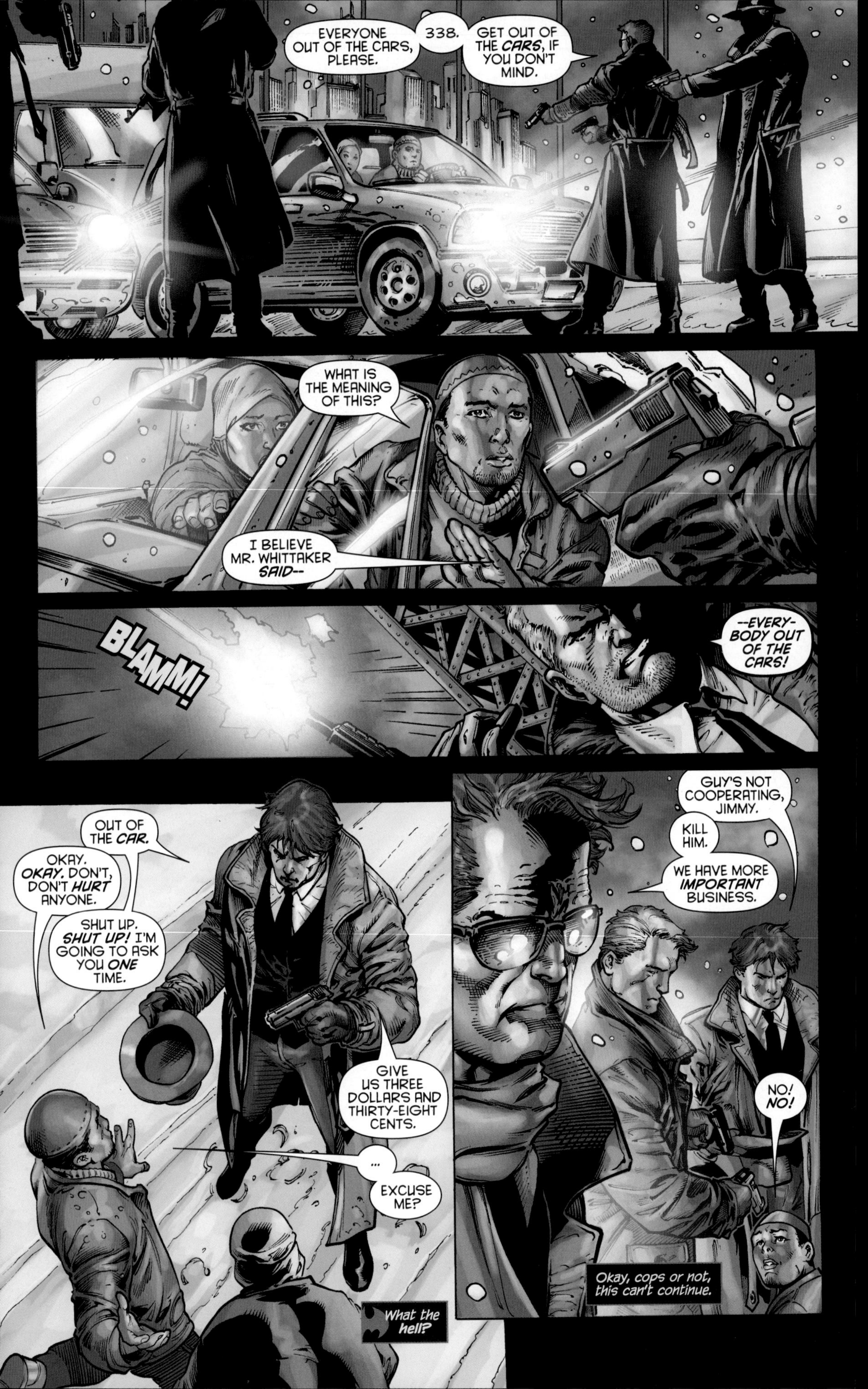
EVERYONE OUT OF THE CARS, PLEASE.
338.
GET OUT OF THE *CARS*, IF YOU DON'T MIND.
WHAT IS THE MEANING OF THIS?
I BELIEVE MR. WHITTAKER *SAID--*
BLAMM!
--EVERYBODY OUT OF THE CARS!
OUT OF THE *CAR.*
OKAY. *OKAY.* DON'T, DON'T *HURT* ANYONE.
SHUT UP. *SHUT UP!* I'M GOING TO ASK YOU *ONE* TIME.
GIVE US THREE DOLLARS AND THIRTY-EIGHT CENTS.
...
EXCUSE ME?
What the hell?
GUY'S NOT COOPERATING, JIMMY.
KILL HIM.
WE HAVE MORE *IMPORTANT* BUSINESS.
NO! *NO!*
Okay, cops or not, this can't continue.

His family.
His sons.

These were his sons.

I FEEL ALL DIRTY.

I COULD USE A COLD BATH.

Okay. It's *Gotham.*

Crazy lives here on a long-term *lease.*

That's Gotham.

But this... I don't know *what* this is.

I think I'm gonna be *sick.*

NO. WAIT.

MR. *WHITTAKER.*

STOP!

FORGOT MY SHOWER CAP.

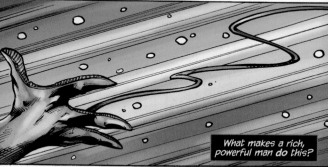

What makes a rich, powerful man *do* this?

FWIP FWIP

Oh, man.

I *lucked* out with that throw. I so *lucked* out.

Guy might have a sprain...but he'll *live.*

Maybe.

If my *arms* hold out.

BURNS, DOESN'T IT?

FEEL LIKE YOUR JOINTS'LL POP, MUSCLES'LL TEAR RIGHT OUT OF YOUR SKIN?

Oh, God, what *now?*

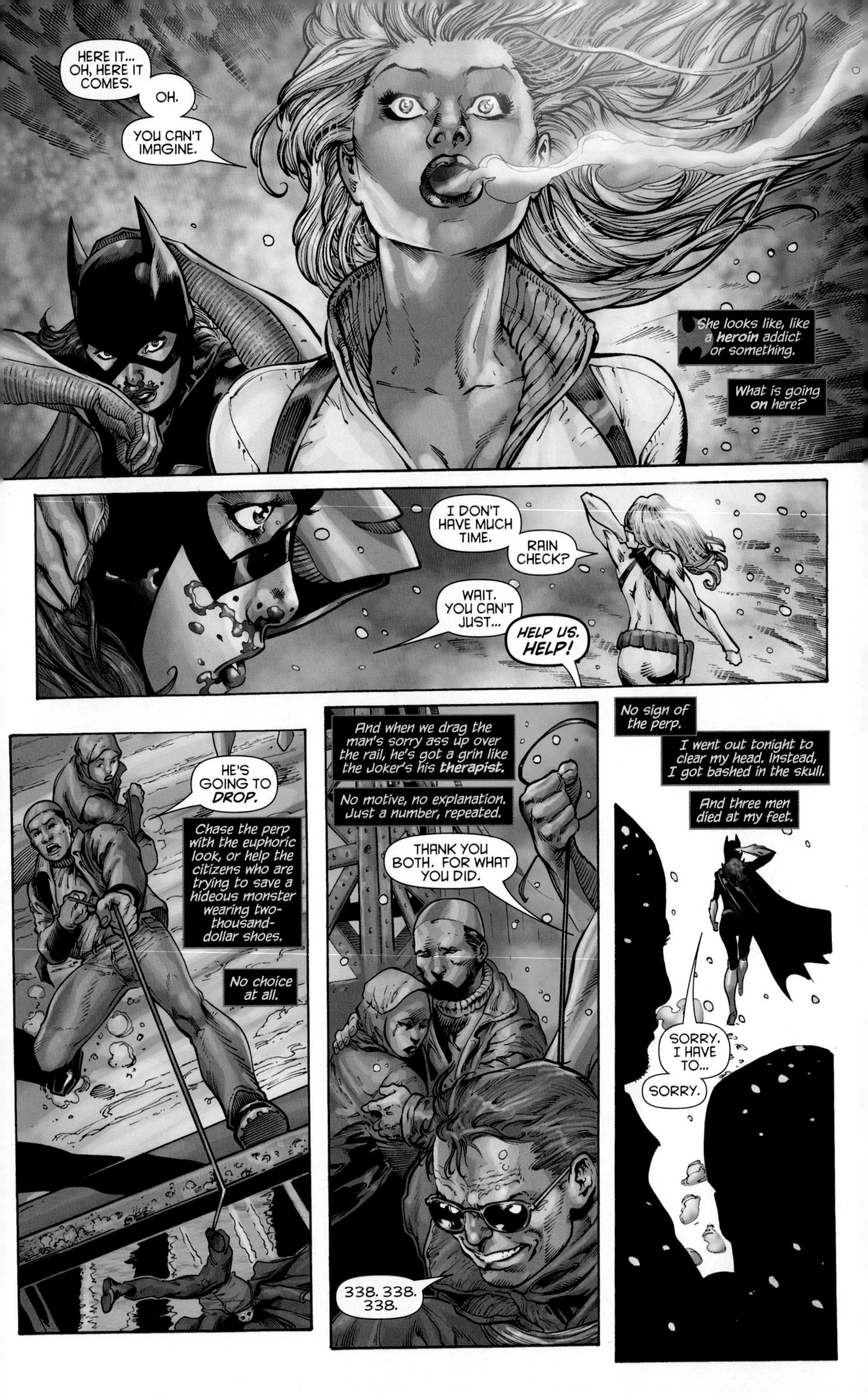

HERE IT... OH, HERE IT COMES.
OH.
YOU CAN'T IMAGINE.
She looks like, like a heroin addict or something.
What is going on here?
I DON'T HAVE MUCH TIME.
RAIN CHECK?
WAIT. YOU CAN'T JUST...
HELP US. HELP!
HE'S GOING TO DROP.
Chase the perp with the euphoric look, or help the citizens who are trying to save a hideous monster wearing two-thousand-dollar shoes.
No choice at all.
And when we drag the man's sorry ass up over the rail, he's got a grin like the Joker's his therapist.
No motive, no explanation. Just a number, repeated.
THANK YOU BOTH. FOR WHAT YOU DID.
338. 338. 338.
No sign of the perp.
I went out tonight to clear my head. Instead, I got bashed in the skull.
And three men died at my feet.
SORRY. I HAVE TO...
SORRY.

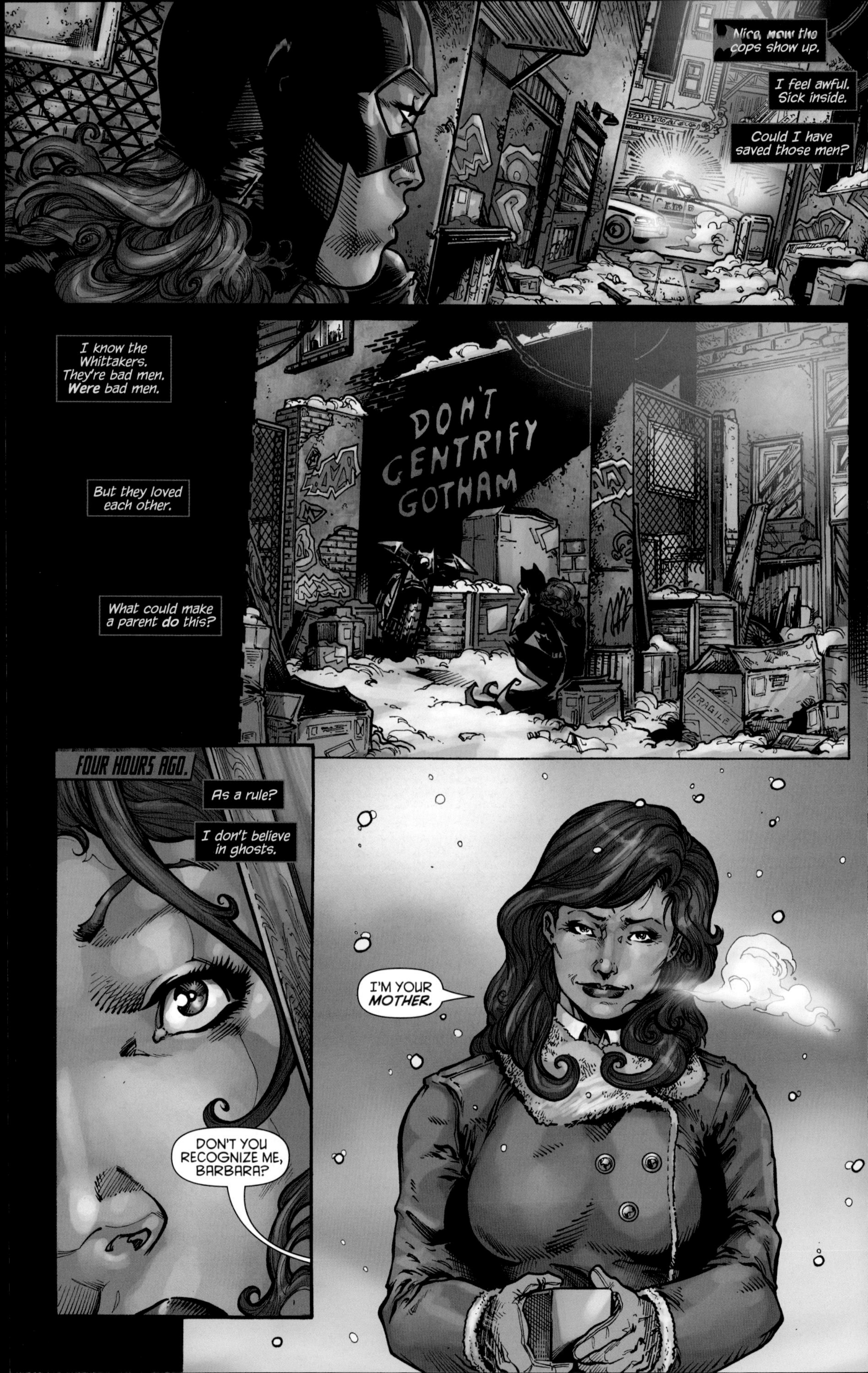

Nice, now the cops show up.
I feel awful. Sick inside.
Could I have saved those men?
I know the Whittakers. They're bad men. **Were** bad men.
DON'T GENTRIFY GOTHAM
But they loved each other.
What could make a parent **do** this?
FRAGILE
FOUR HOURS AGO.
As a rule?
I don't believe in ghosts.
DON'T YOU RECOGNIZE ME, BARBARA?
I'M YOUR *MOTHER.*

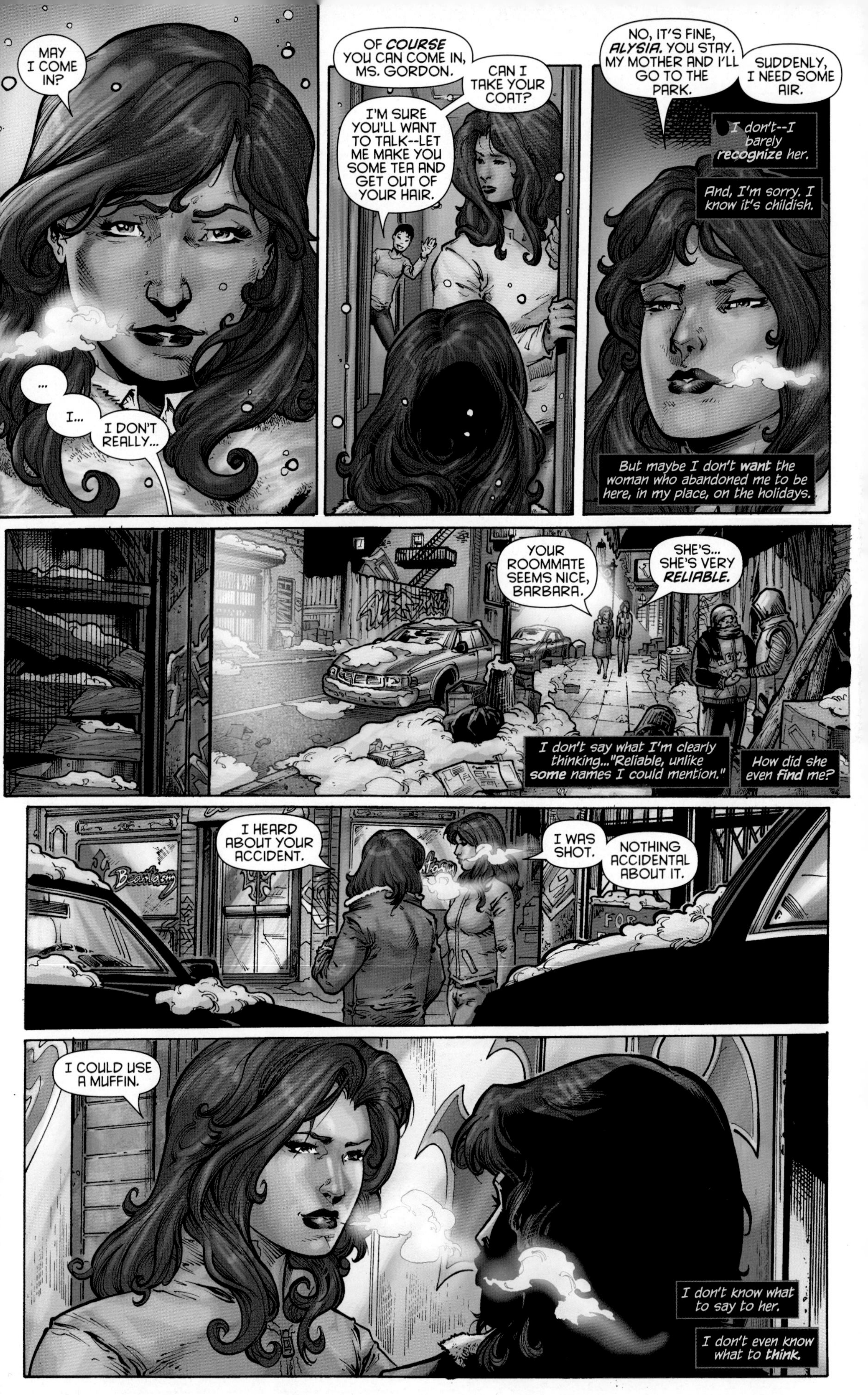

MAY I COME IN?
...
I...
I DON'T REALLY...
OF COURSE YOU CAN COME IN, MS. GORDON.
CAN I TAKE YOUR COAT?
I'M SURE YOU'LL WANT TO TALK--LET ME MAKE YOU SOME TEA AND GET OUT OF YOUR HAIR.
NO, IT'S FINE, ALYSIA. YOU STAY. MY MOTHER AND I'LL GO TO THE PARK.
SUDDENLY, I NEED SOME AIR.
I don't--I barely recognize her.
And, I'm sorry. I know it's childish.
But maybe I don't want the woman who abandoned me to be here, in my place, on the holidays.
YOUR ROOMMATE SEEMS NICE, BARBARA.
SHE'S... SHE'S VERY RELIABLE.
I don't say what I'm clearly thinking..."Reliable, unlike some names I could mention."
How did she even find me?
I HEARD ABOUT YOUR ACCIDENT.
I WAS SHOT.
NOTHING ACCIDENTAL ABOUT IT.
I COULD USE A MUFFIN.
I don't know what to say to her.
I don't even know what to think.

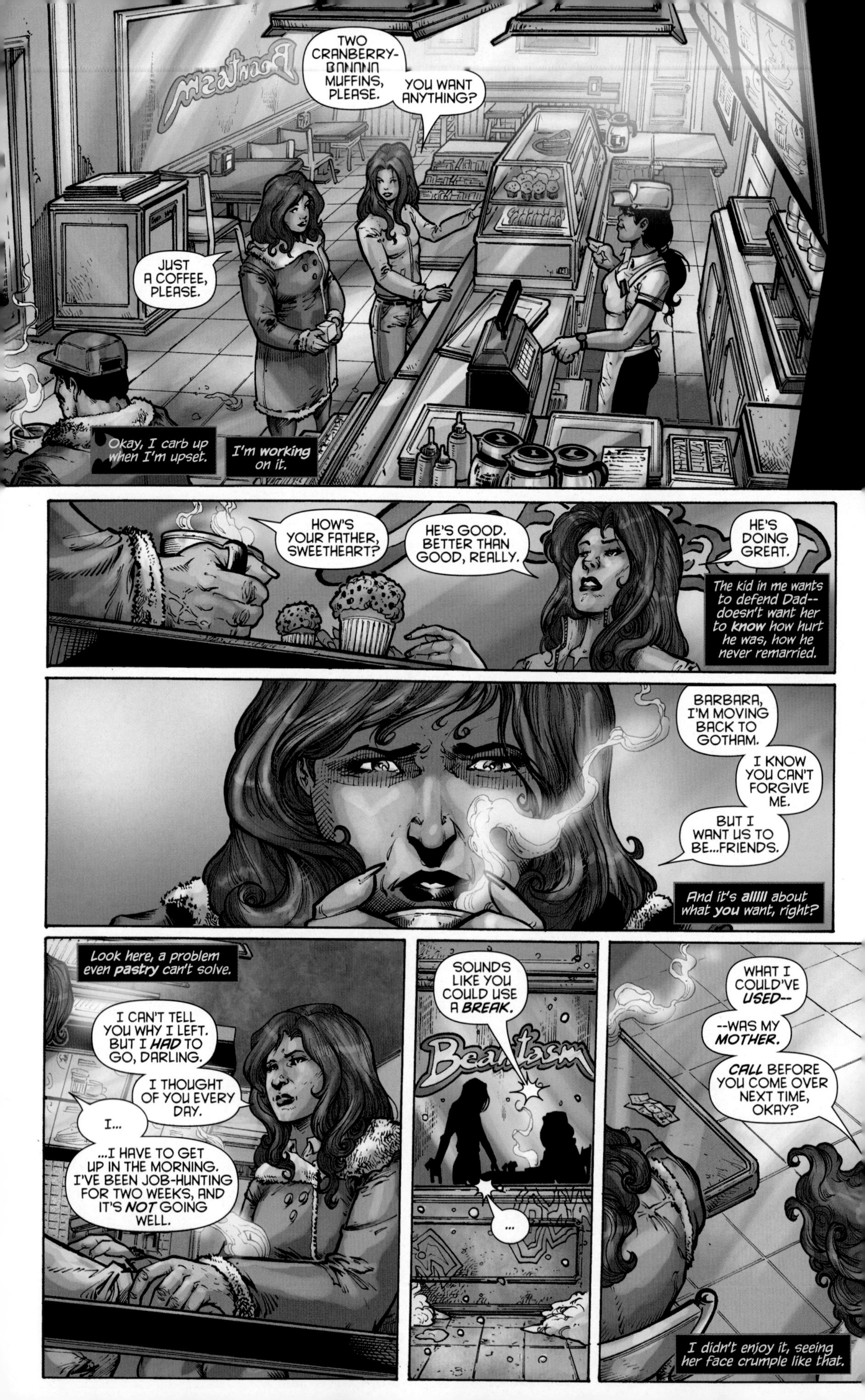
TWO CRANBERRY-BANANA MUFFINS, PLEASE.
YOU WANT ANYTHING?
JUST A COFFEE, PLEASE.
Okay, I carb up when I'm upset.
I'm working on it.
HOW'S YOUR FATHER, SWEETHEART?
HE'S GOOD. BETTER THAN GOOD, REALLY.
HE'S DOING GREAT.
The kid in me wants to defend Dad--doesn't want her to know how hurt he was, how he never remarried.
BARBARA, I'M MOVING BACK TO GOTHAM.
I KNOW YOU CAN'T FORGIVE ME.
BUT I WANT US TO BE...FRIENDS.
And it's allll about what you want, right?
Look here, a problem even pastry can't solve.
I CAN'T TELL YOU WHY I LEFT. BUT I HAD TO GO, DARLING.
I THOUGHT OF YOU EVERY DAY.
I...
...I HAVE TO GET UP IN THE MORNING. I'VE BEEN JOB-HUNTING FOR TWO WEEKS, AND IT'S NOT GOING WELL.
SOUNDS LIKE YOU COULD USE A BREAK.
...
WHAT I COULD'VE USED--
--WAS MY MOTHER.
CALL BEFORE YOU COME OVER NEXT TIME, OKAY?
I didn't enjoy it, seeing her face crumple like that.

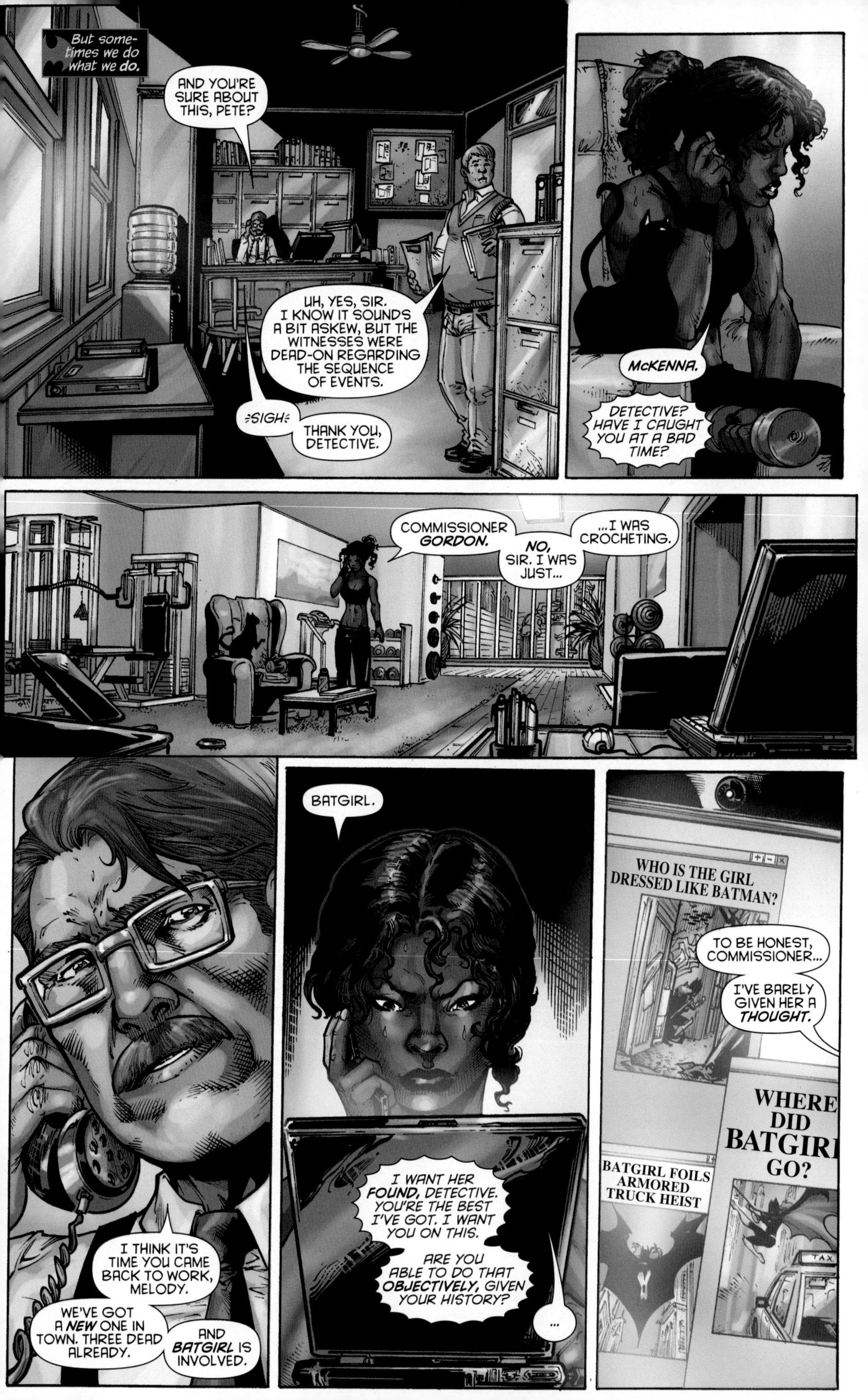

But sometimes we do what we do.
AND YOU'RE SURE ABOUT THIS, PETE?
UH, YES, SIR. I KNOW IT SOUNDS A BIT ASKEW, BUT THE WITNESSES WERE DEAD-ON REGARDING THE SEQUENCE OF EVENTS.
SIGH
THANK YOU, DETECTIVE.
McKENNA.
DETECTIVE? HAVE I CAUGHT YOU AT A BAD TIME?
COMMISSIONER GORDON.
NO, SIR. I WAS JUST...
...I WAS CROCHETING.
I THINK IT'S TIME YOU CAME BACK TO WORK, MELODY.
WE'VE GOT A NEW ONE IN TOWN. THREE DEAD ALREADY.
AND BATGIRL IS INVOLVED.
BATGIRL.
I WANT HER FOUND, DETECTIVE. YOU'RE THE BEST I'VE GOT. I WANT YOU ON THIS.
ARE YOU ABLE TO DO THAT OBJECTIVELY, GIVEN YOUR HISTORY?
...
WHO IS THE GIRL DRESSED LIKE BATMAN?
TO BE HONEST, COMMISSIONER...
I'VE BARELY GIVEN HER A THOUGHT.
WHERE DID BATGIRL GO?
BATGIRL FOILS ARMORED TRUCK HEIST

338. So weird. Such a specific trigger.

Room 38 on the third floor?

A date of some kind... March 1938?

HEY, GORDON. YOU OKAY?

I'M FINE, ALYSIA. THANKS, THOUGH.

WANT TO TALK ABOUT IT?

TALK ABOUT WHAT?

OH, WHATEVER, YOU KNOW--TAXES, THE WEATHER.

YOUR MOM, GOOFUS.

MIND IF I TURN THE TV ON, FOR A SEC?

IT'S FINE, I'M FINE. JUST DOING A BIT OF--

SOME FRIENDS OF MINE ARE PROTESTING THAT RIDICULOUS URBAN RENEWAL PROJECT WAYNE'S GOT GOING DOWNTOWN.

ONE-HUNDRED-FIFTY-YEAR-OLD BUILDINGS COMING DOWN, FOR WHAT? A NEW SKYSCRAPER?

FDT NEWS

OCCUPY GOTHAM!

OCCUPY

OCCUPY

NO WAYNE, NO HOW!

Sounds like Bruce has a bit of a PR problem.

...SYMBOLIC GESTURE ON BRUCE WAYNE'S PART, TO HOLD A PRESS CONFERENCE ON THE FRONT STEPS OF THIS CONDEMNED BUILDING, IN ONE OF GOTHAM'S HIGHEST-CRIME AREAS.

OCCUPY GOTHAM!

NO WAYNE, NO HOW!

NO WAYNE, NO HOW!

AN ATTEMPT TO DRUM UP SUPPORT FOR HIS MASSIVE DOWNTOWN RENEWAL INITITIAVE, DESPITE THE PRESENCE OF THE OBLIGATORY PROTESTORS...

OH.

OH, MAN.

338 GREEN LAKE DRIVE

AND MISTER WAYNE HIMSELF WILL BE ADDRESSING THE PRESS AND PUBLIC ON THESE SAME STEPS SHORTLY, IN PERSON.

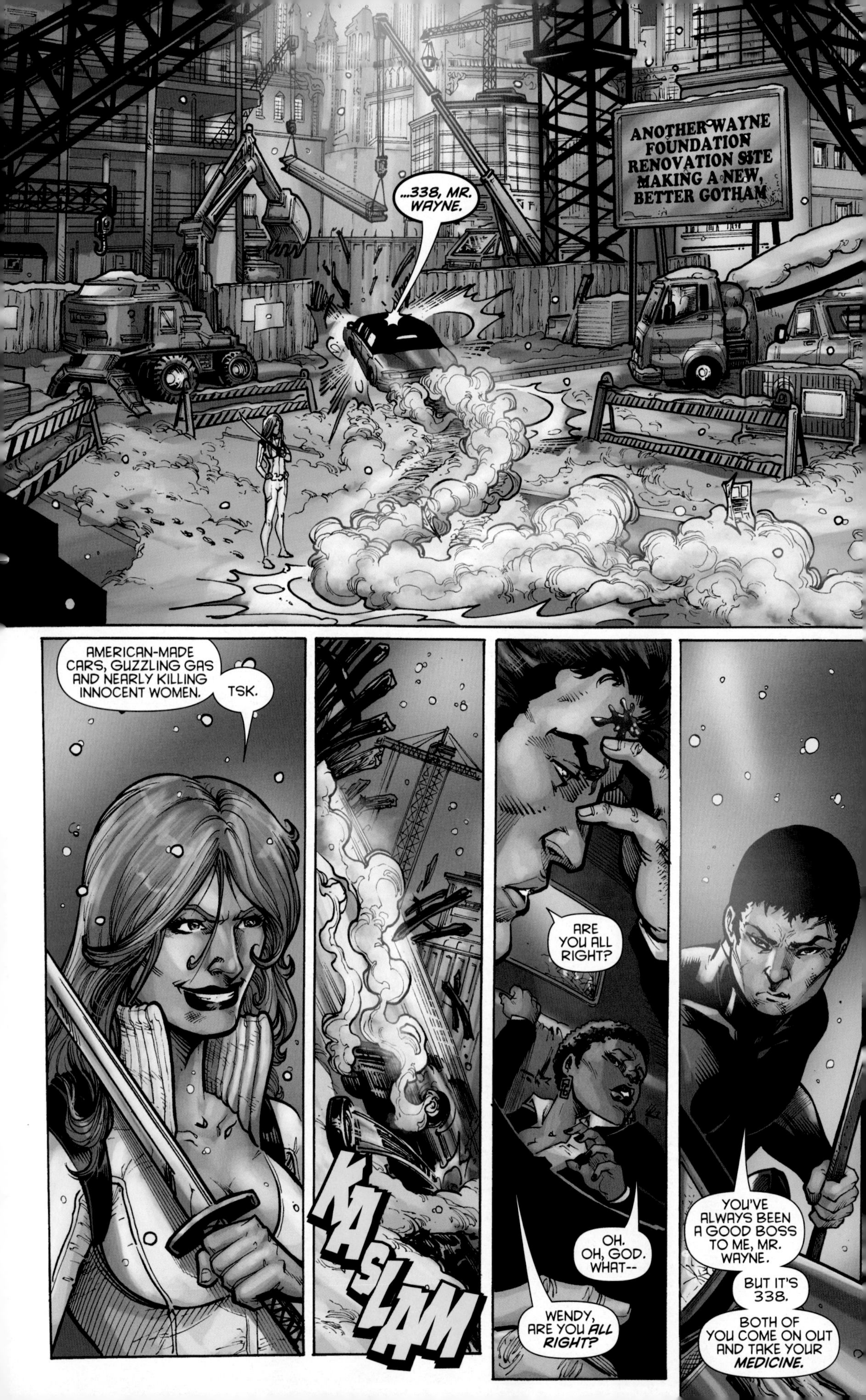
ANOTHER WAYNE FOUNDATION RENOVATION SITE MAKING A NEW, BETTER GOTHAM
...338, MR. WAYNE.
AMERICAN-MADE CARS, GUZZLING GAS AND NEARLY KILLING INNOCENT WOMEN.
TSK.
KASLAM
ARE YOU ALL RIGHT?
OH. OH, GOD. WHAT--
WENDY, ARE YOU *ALL RIGHT?*
YOU'VE ALWAYS BEEN A GOOD BOSS TO ME, MR. WAYNE.
BUT IT'S 338.
BOTH OF YOU COME ON OUT AND TAKE YOUR *MEDICINE.*

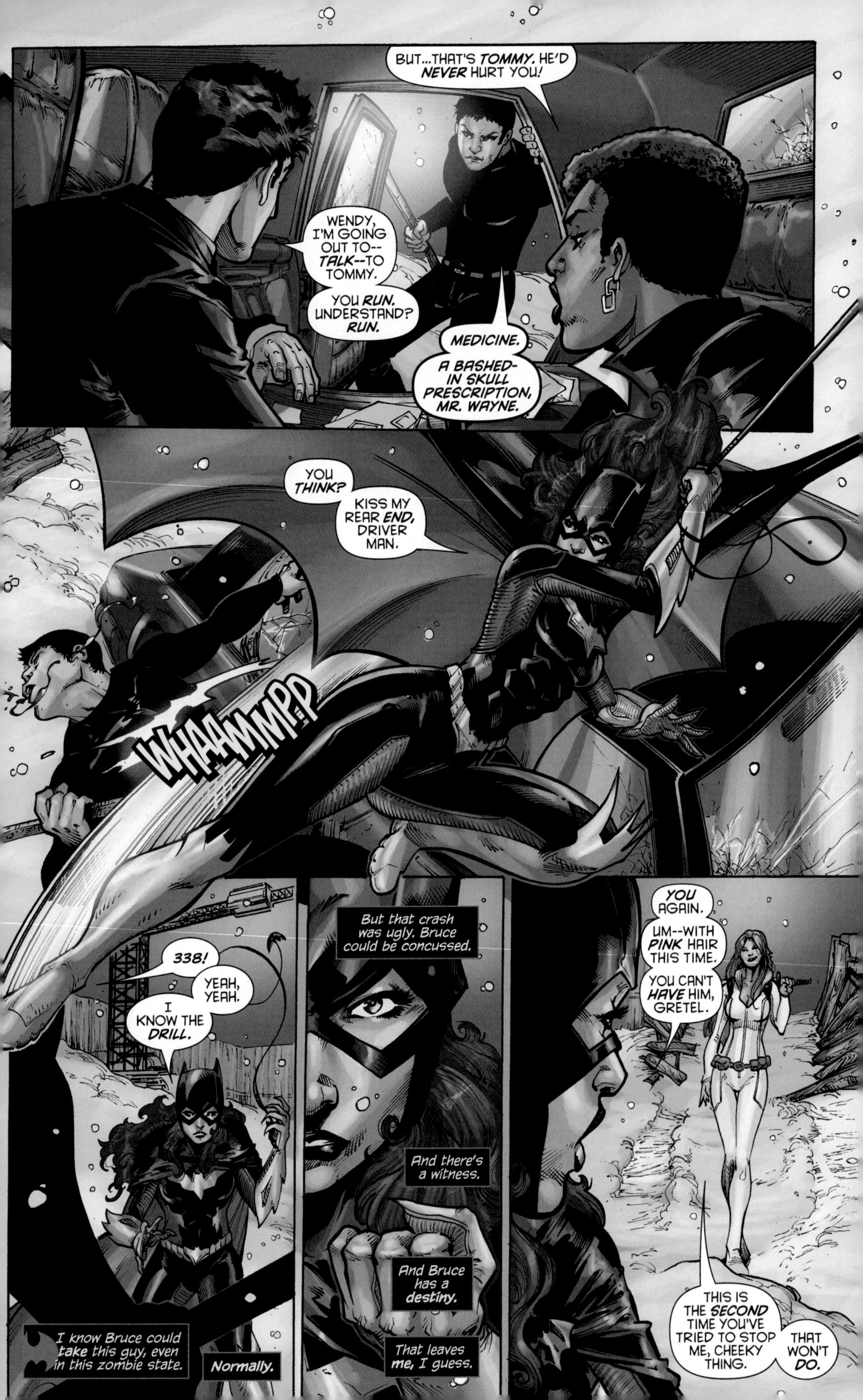

BUT...THAT'S TOMMY. HE'D NEVER HURT YOU!
WENDY, I'M GOING OUT TO--TALK--TO TOMMY.
YOU RUN. UNDERSTAND? RUN.
MEDICINE.
A BASHED-IN SKULL PRESCRIPTION, MR. WAYNE.
YOU THINK?
KISS MY REAR END, DRIVER MAN.
WHAAMMPP
338!
YEAH, YEAH.
I KNOW THE DRILL.
I know Bruce could take this guy, even in this zombie state.
Normally.
But that crash was ugly. Bruce could be concussed.
And there's a witness.
And Bruce has a destiny.
That leaves me, I guess.
YOU AGAIN.
UM--WITH PINK HAIR THIS TIME.
YOU CAN'T HAVE HIM, GRETEL.
THIS IS THE SECOND TIME YOU'VE TRIED TO STOP ME, CHEEKY THING.
THAT WON'T DO.

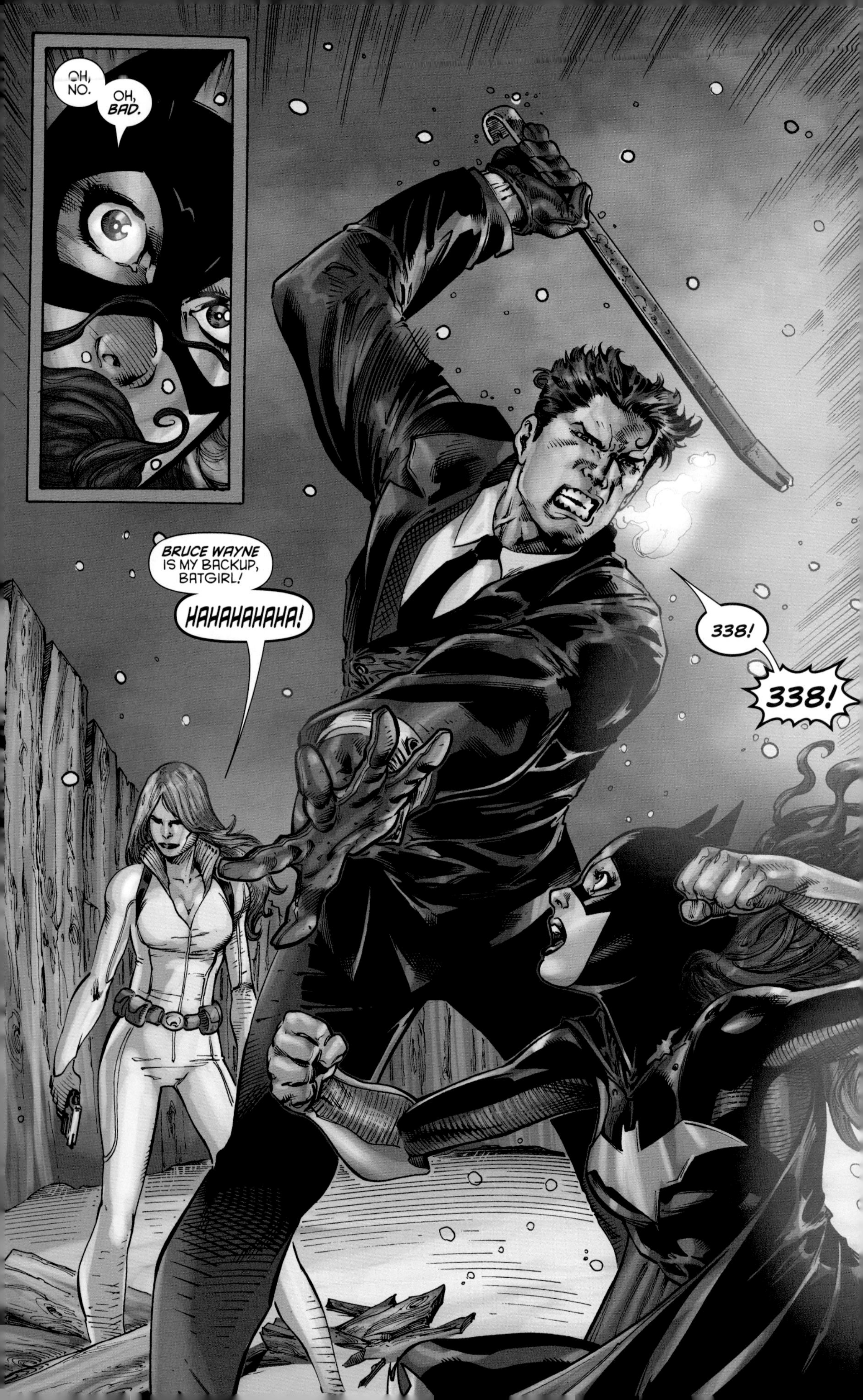
OH, NO.
OH, BAD.
BRUCE WAYNE IS MY BACKUP, BATGIRL!
HAHAHAHAHA!
338!
338!

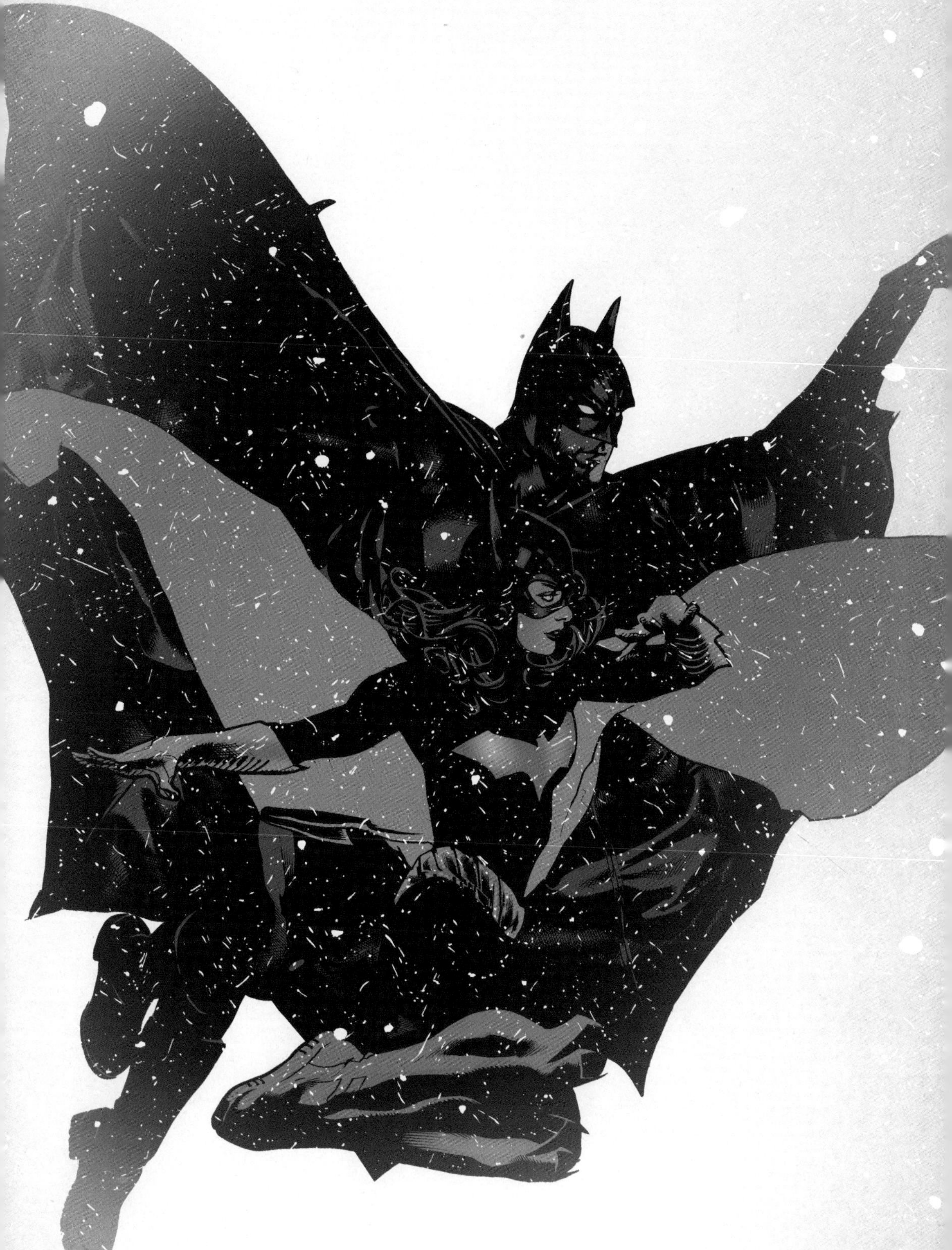

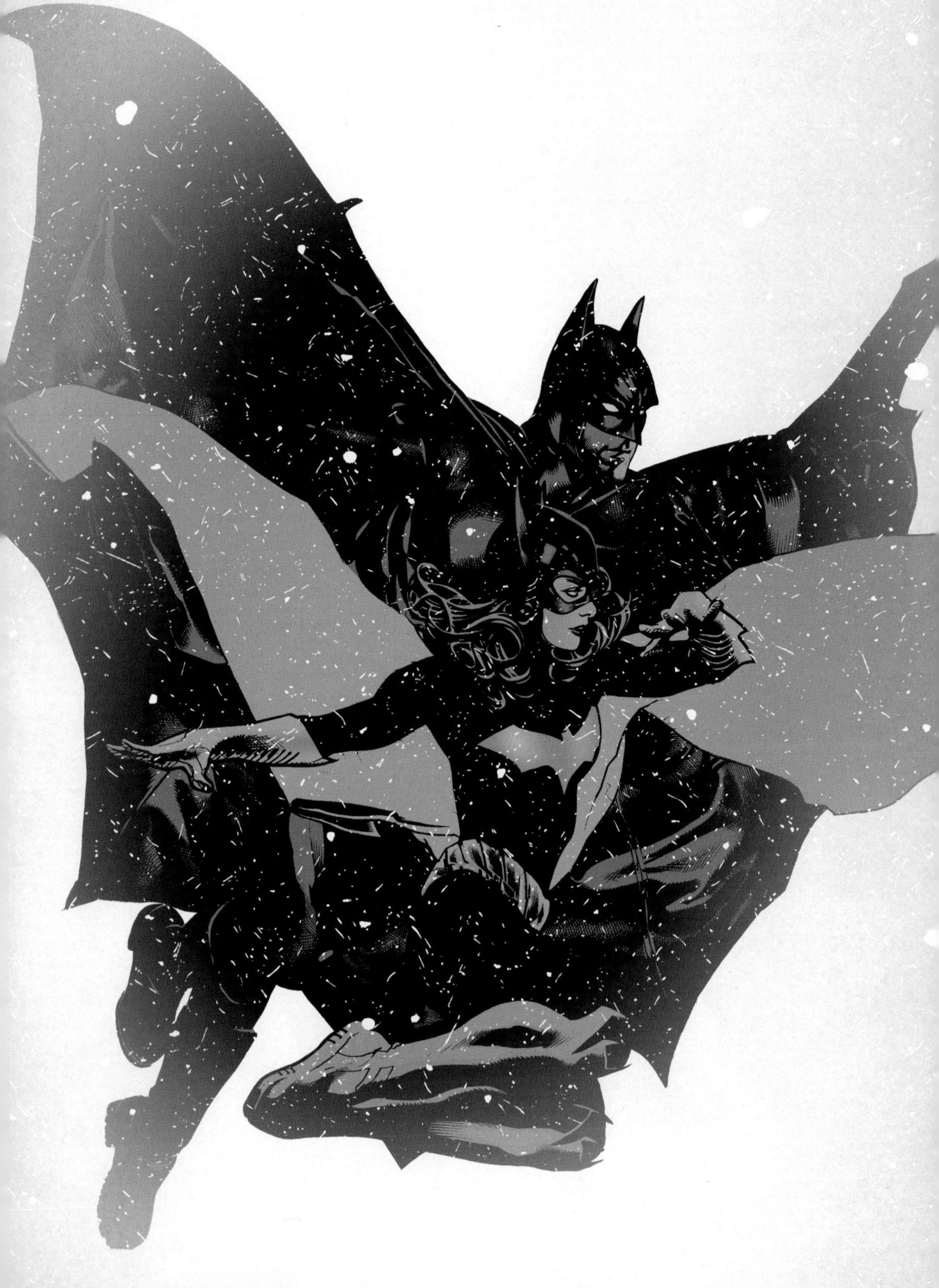

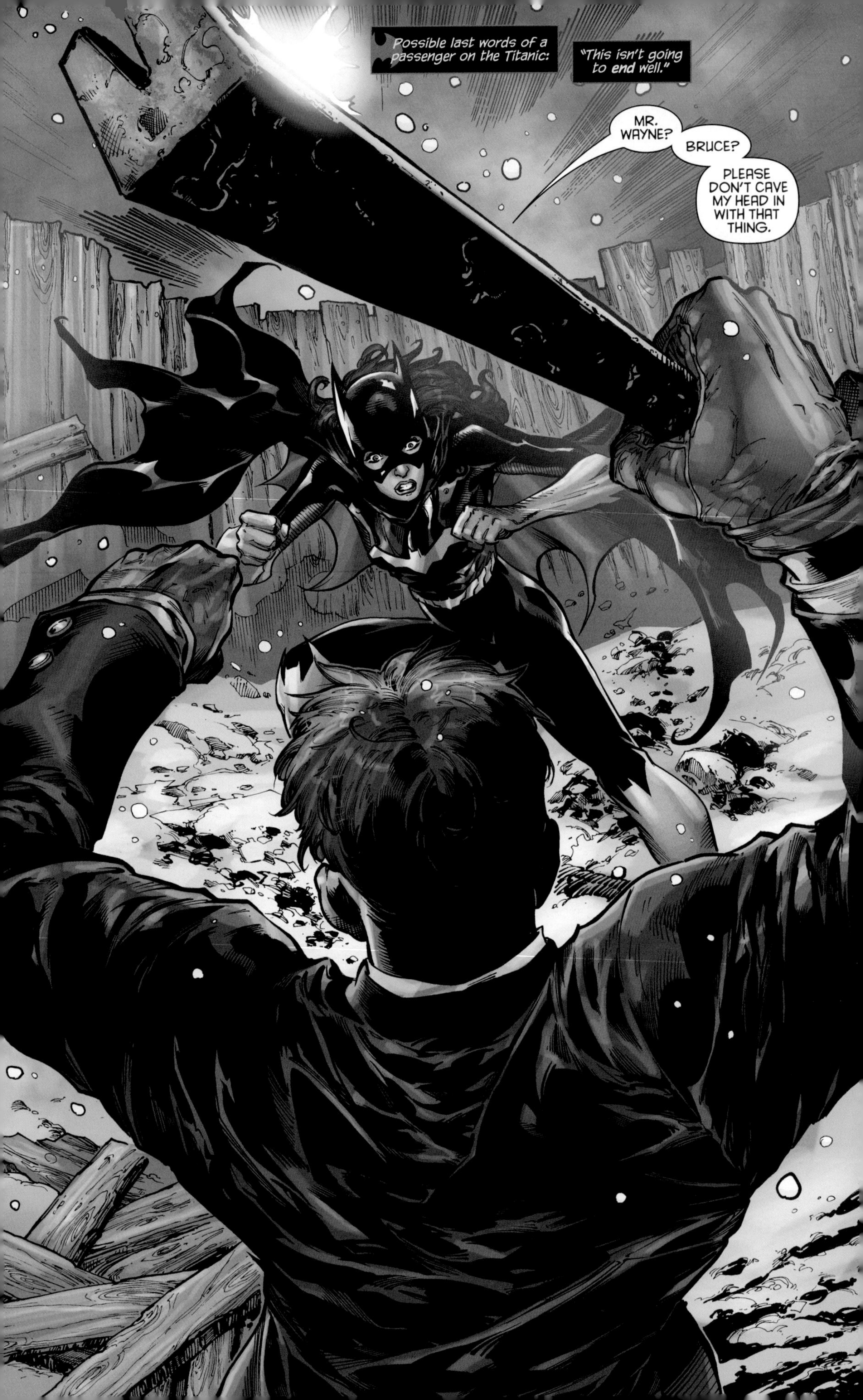
Possible last words of a passenger on the Titanic:
"This isn't going to end well."
MR. WAYNE?
BRUCE?
PLEASE DON'T CAVE MY HEAD IN WITH THAT THING.

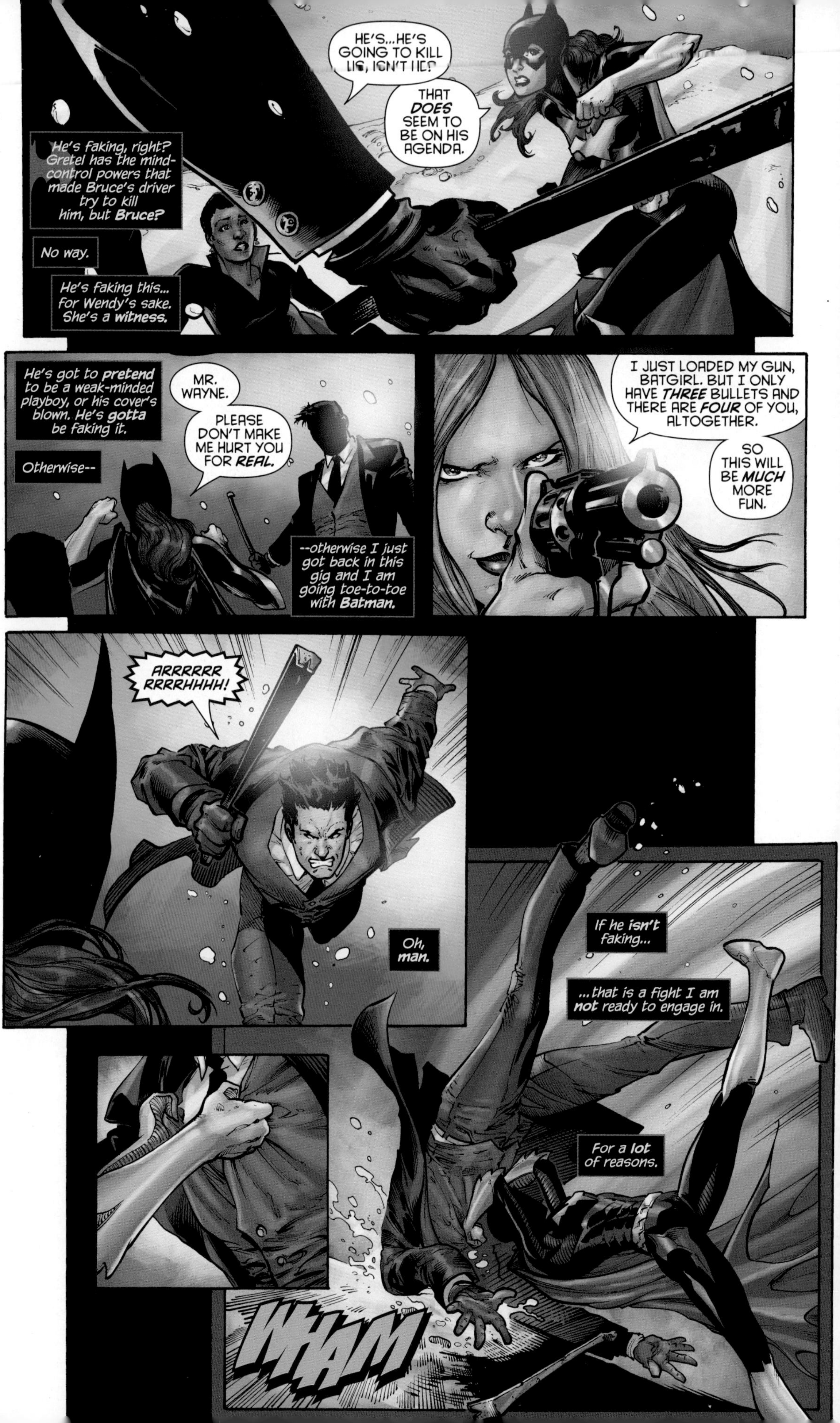
He's faking, right? Gretel has the mind-control powers that made Bruce's driver try to kill him, but Bruce?
HE'S...HE'S GOING TO KILL US, ISN'T HE?
THAT DOES SEEM TO BE ON HIS AGENDA.
No way.
He's faking this... for Wendy's sake. She's a witness.
He's got to pretend to be a weak-minded playboy, or his cover's blown. He's gotta be faking it.
MR. WAYNE.
PLEASE DON'T MAKE ME HURT YOU FOR REAL.
Otherwise--
--otherwise I just got back in this gig and I am going toe-to-toe with Batman.
I JUST LOADED MY GUN, BATGIRL. BUT I ONLY HAVE THREE BULLETS AND THERE ARE FOUR OF YOU, ALTOGETHER.
SO THIS WILL BE MUCH MORE FUN.
ARRRRRR RRRRHHHH!
Oh, man.
If he isn't faking...
...that is a fight I am not ready to engage in.
For a lot of reasons.
WHAM

DON'T MAKE ME THROW THIS, MR. WAYNE.

Concussion Batarang. It doesn't land *pretty*.

We weren't always close, Batman and I. Not always.

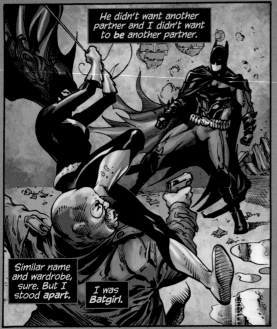

He didn't want another partner and I didn't want to *be* another partner.

Similar name and wardrobe, sure. But I stood *apart*.

I was Batgirl.

Then, on the worst night of my life, after being shot in the spine by the Joker...after losing the ability to walk...

...after a surgery that haunted my nightmares for a *year* after...

...he came to my hospital room.

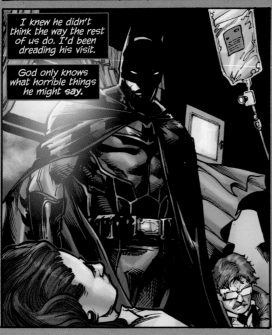

I knew he didn't think the way the rest of us do. I'd been dreading his visit.

God only knows what horrible things he might say.

"HOW DID YOU LET THIS *HAPPEN*, BARBARA?"

"DIDN'T I TRAIN YOU *BETTER* THAN THIS?"

"YOU SHOULD NEVER HAVE BEEN BATGIRL."

I actually thought he would say those things to me.

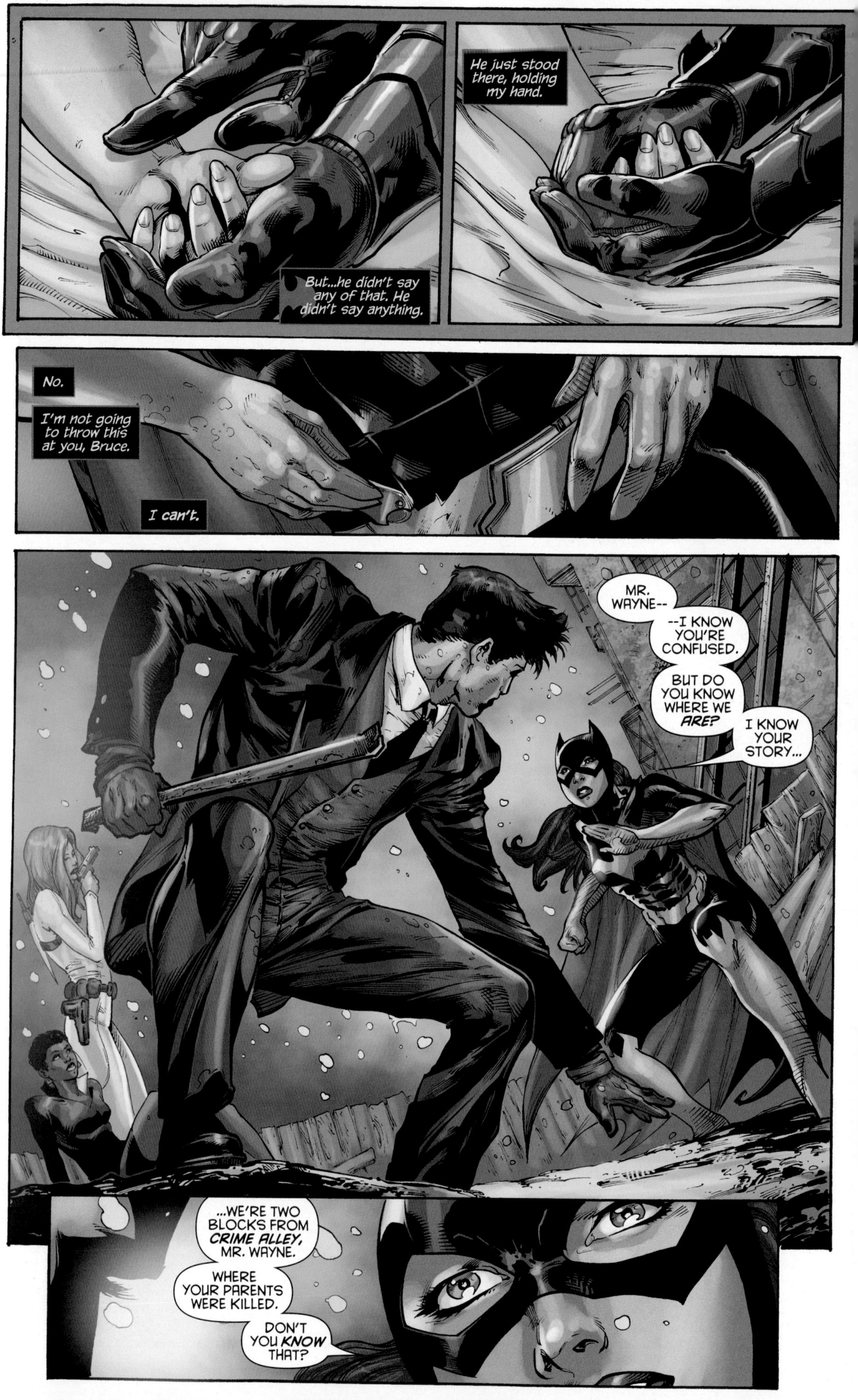
But...he didn't say any of that. He didn't say anything.
He just stood there, holding my hand.
No.
I'm not going to throw this at you, Bruce.
I can't.
MR. WAYNE--
--I KNOW YOU'RE CONFUSED.
BUT DO YOU KNOW WHERE WE ARE?
I KNOW YOUR STORY...
...WE'RE TWO BLOCKS FROM CRIME ALLEY, MR. WAYNE.
WHERE YOUR PARENTS WERE KILLED.
DON'T YOU KNOW THAT?

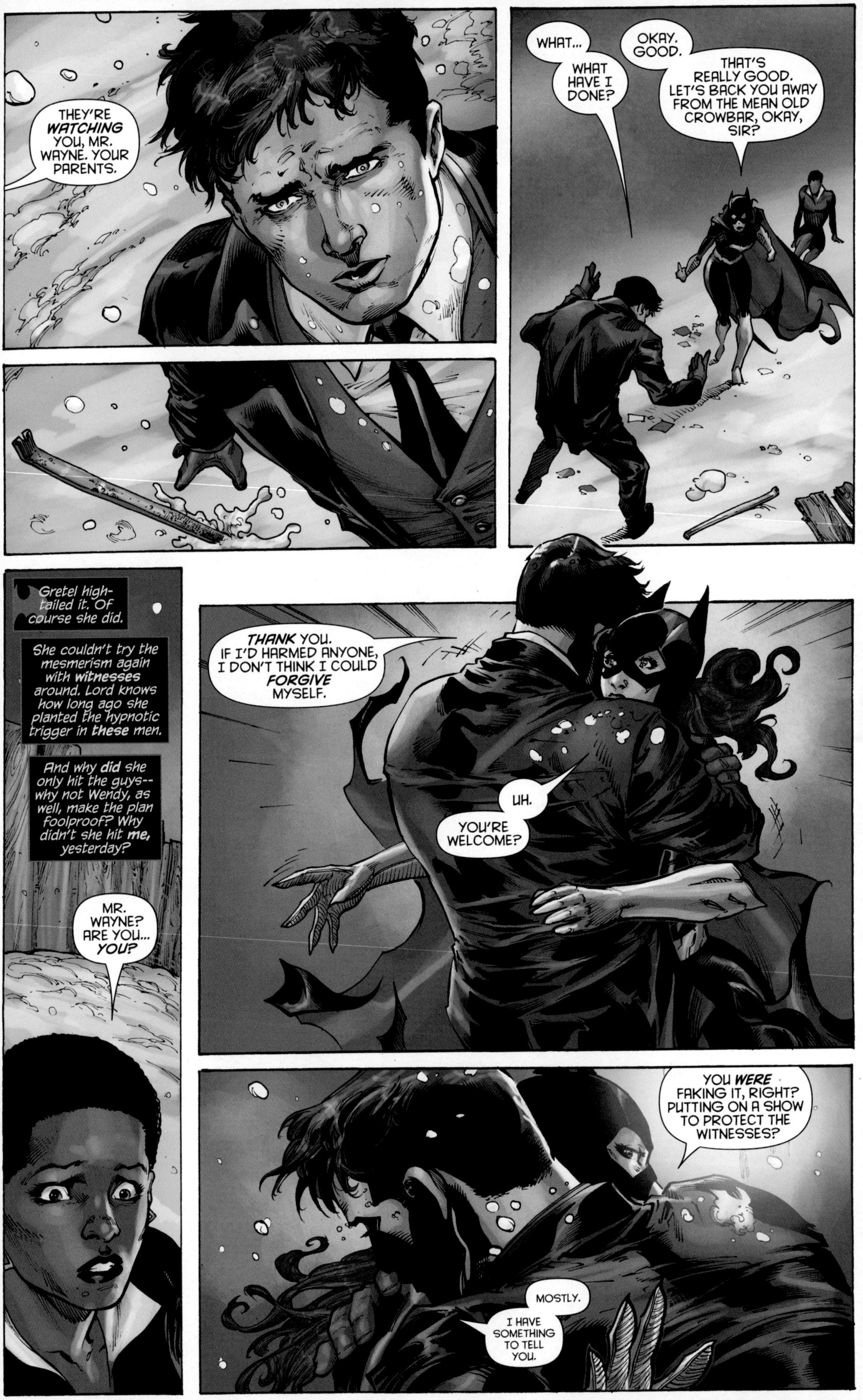

THEY'RE WATCHING YOU, MR. WAYNE. YOUR PARENTS.
WHAT...
WHAT HAVE I DONE?
OKAY. GOOD.
THAT'S REALLY GOOD. LET'S BACK YOU AWAY FROM THE MEAN OLD CROWBAR, OKAY, SIR?
Gretel high-tailed it. Of course she did.
She couldn't try the mesmerism again with witnesses around. Lord knows how long ago she planted the hypnotic trigger in these men.
And why did she only hit the guys--why not Wendy, as well, make the plan foolproof? Why didn't she hit me, yesterday?
THANK YOU. IF I'D HARMED ANYONE, I DON'T THINK I COULD FORGIVE MYSELF.
UH.
YOU'RE WELCOME?
MR. WAYNE? ARE YOU... YOU?
YOU WERE FAKING IT, RIGHT? PUTTING ON A SHOW TO PROTECT THE WITNESSES?
MOSTLY.
I HAVE SOMETHING TO TELL YOU.

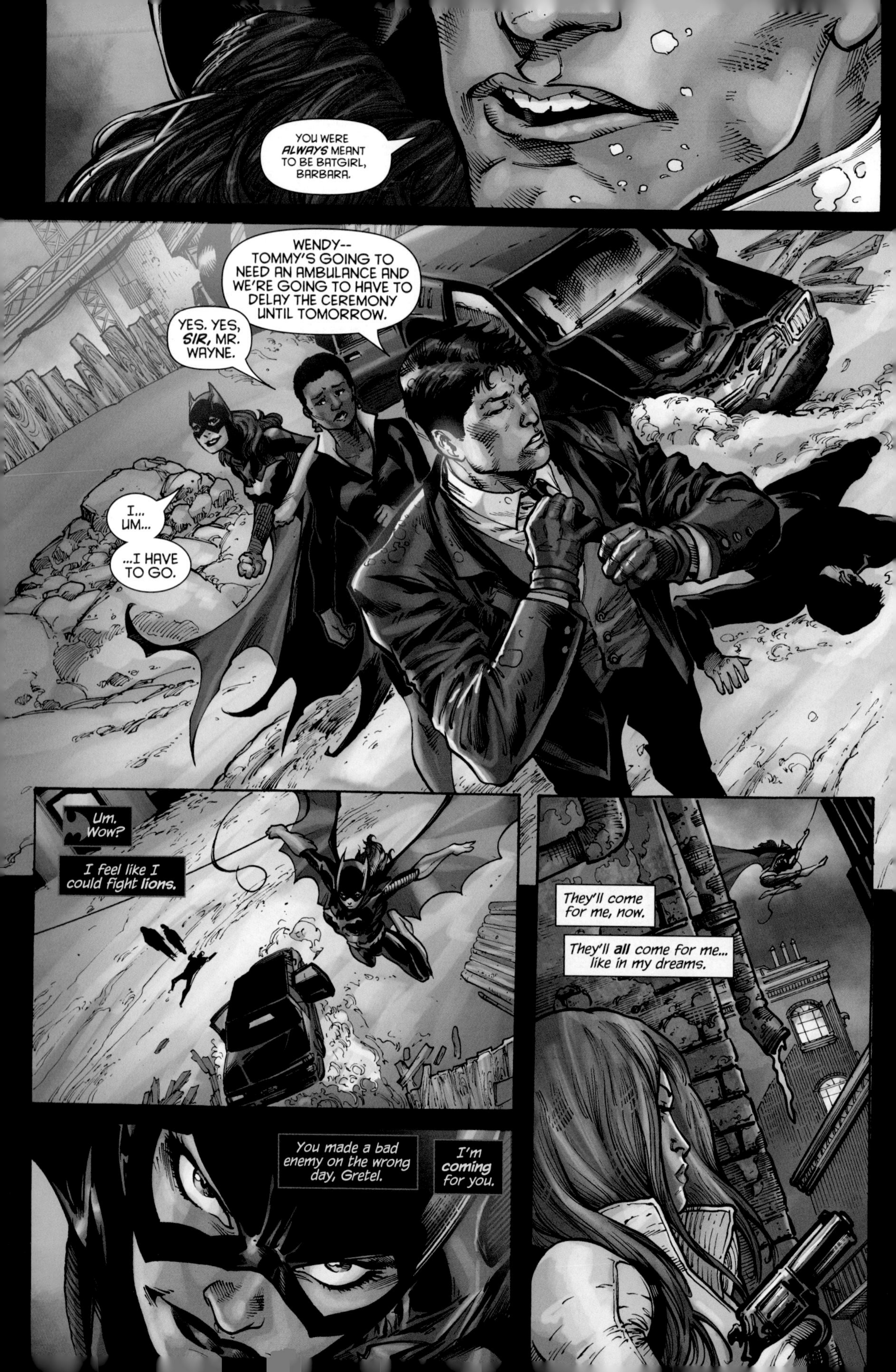

YOU WERE *ALWAYS* MEANT TO BE BATGIRL, BARBARA.
WENDY-- TOMMY'S GOING TO NEED AN AMBULANCE AND WE'RE GOING TO HAVE TO DELAY THE CEREMONY UNTIL TOMORROW.
YES. YES, *SIR*, MR. WAYNE.
I... UM...
...I HAVE TO GO.
Um. Wow?
I feel like I could fight ***lions.***
They'll come for me, now.
They'll ***all*** *come for me... like in my dreams.*
You made a bad enemy on the wrong day, Gretel.
I'm ***coming*** *for you.*

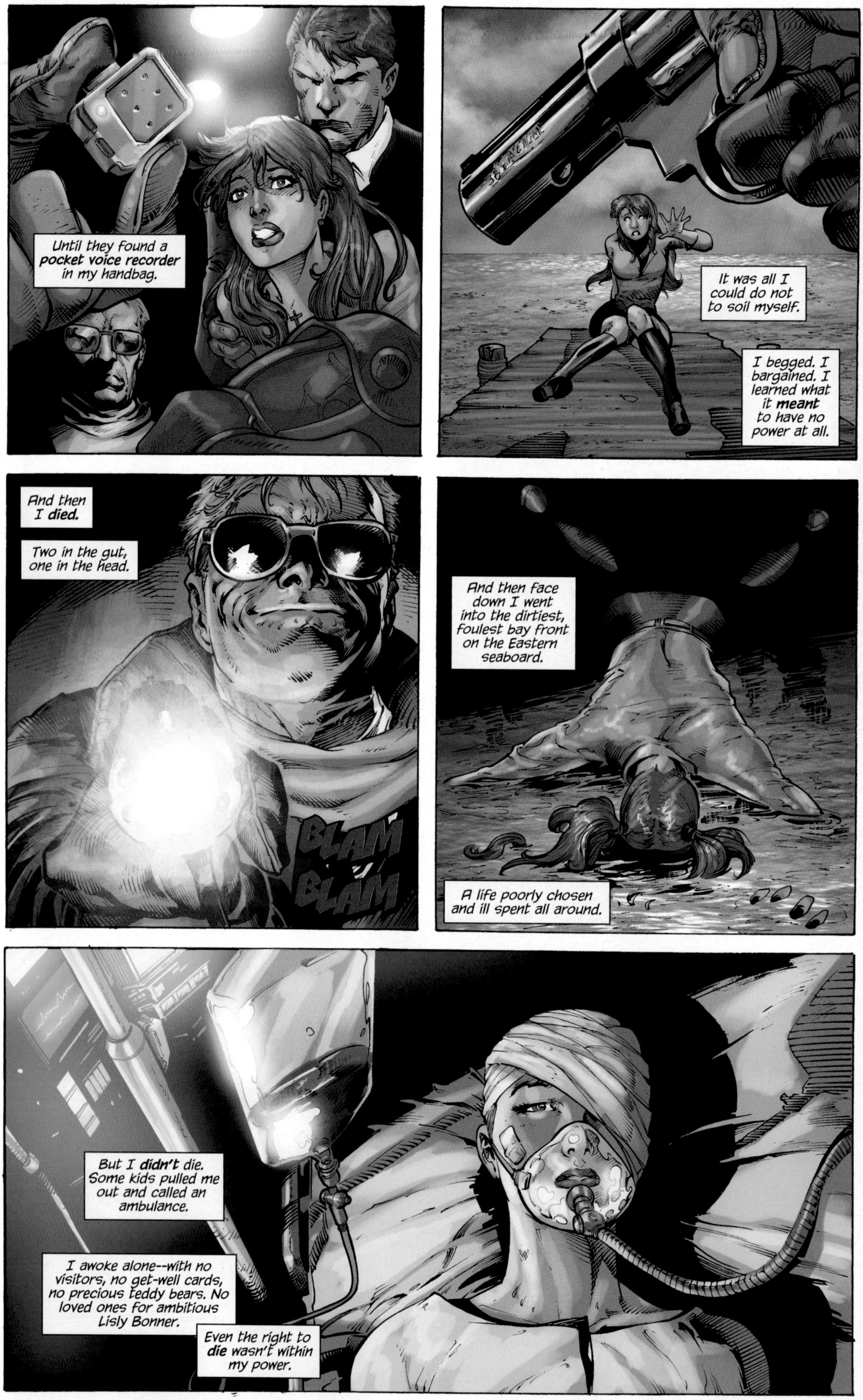
Until they found a pocket voice recorder in my handbag.
It was all I could do not to soil myself.
I begged. I bargained. I learned what it meant to have no power at all.
And then I died.
Two in the gut, one in the head.
BLAM BLAM
And then face down I went into the dirtiest, foulest bay front on the Eastern seaboard.
A life poorly chosen and ill spent all around.
But I didn't die. Some kids pulled me out and called an ambulance.
I awoke alone--with no visitors, no get-well cards, no precious teddy bears. No loved ones for ambitious Lisly Bonner.
Even the right to die wasn't within my power.

I...I MADE CRANBERRY-BANANA MUFFINS, THOSE ARE YOUR FAVORITES, RIGHT?

*I have things I want to say, like, "How would **you** know what I like?" and, "Please keep your sad little bribes out of my **face.**"*

I'M NOT HUNGRY.

*Instead I say something that **sounds** nicer, but is just as mean, in its way.*

OF COURSE, DEAR.

MOM.

HAVE YOU CALLED DAD...LET HIM KNOW YOU'RE IN TOWN?

NOT...NOT QUITE YET, BARBARA. SOON, I PROMISE.

Sure. Sure you will, Mom.

*I snuck two of the muffins. I'm not made of **stone.***

Gretel said she just reloaded, but that she only had three bullets.

*A .38 revolver, like she was holding, holds **six** bullets.*

*She's a hit man for hire, she said as much, and there's a clear **revenge** thing happening.*

Three bullets, from a .38 caliber revolver.

338.

GTHAM FLAME REPORTER LISLY BONNER SHOT--

CURRENTLY IN CRITICAL CONDITION

Reporter, three shots, from a .38 caliber pistol.

Boss Whittaker declared a "person of interest" in the shooting, but later set free for lack of evidence.

Hello, Gretel.

At some point, family is the life you choose.

Bruce paid for my medical treatments, anonymously.

He's not like Dad... he's never said he loves me.

*He's never **had** to.*

BRUCE. I'VE FOUND HER.

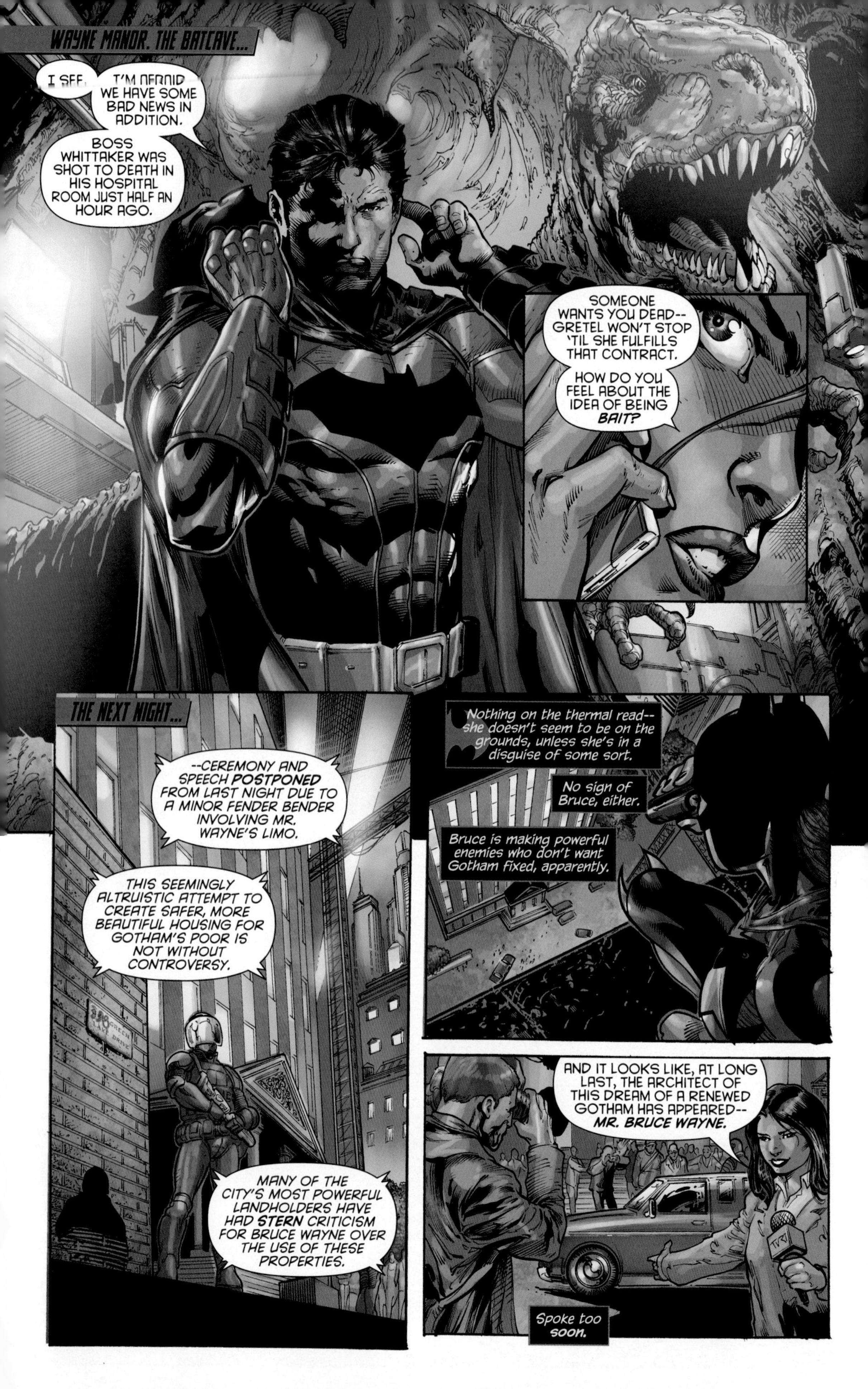

WAYNE MANOR. THE BATCAVE...
I SEE.
I'M AFRAID WE HAVE SOME BAD NEWS IN ADDITION.
BOSS WHITTAKER WAS SHOT TO DEATH IN HIS HOSPITAL ROOM JUST HALF AN HOUR AGO.
SOMEONE WANTS YOU DEAD--GRETEL WON'T STOP 'TIL SHE FULFILLS THAT CONTRACT.
HOW DO YOU FEEL ABOUT THE IDEA OF BEING BAIT?
THE NEXT NIGHT...
--CEREMONY AND SPEECH POSTPONED FROM LAST NIGHT DUE TO A MINOR FENDER BENDER INVOLVING MR. WAYNE'S LIMO.
THIS SEEMINGLY ALTRUISTIC ATTEMPT TO CREATE SAFER, MORE BEAUTIFUL HOUSING FOR GOTHAM'S POOR IS NOT WITHOUT CONTROVERSY.
MANY OF THE CITY'S MOST POWERFUL LANDHOLDERS HAVE HAD STERN CRITICISM FOR BRUCE WAYNE OVER THE USE OF THESE PROPERTIES.
Nothing on the thermal read--she doesn't seem to be on the grounds, unless she's in a disguise of some sort.
No sign of Bruce, either.
Bruce is making powerful enemies who don't want Gotham fixed, apparently.
AND IT LOOKS LIKE, AT LONG LAST, THE ARCHITECT OF THIS DREAM OF A RENEWED GOTHAM HAS APPEARED--MR. BRUCE WAYNE.
Spoke too soon.

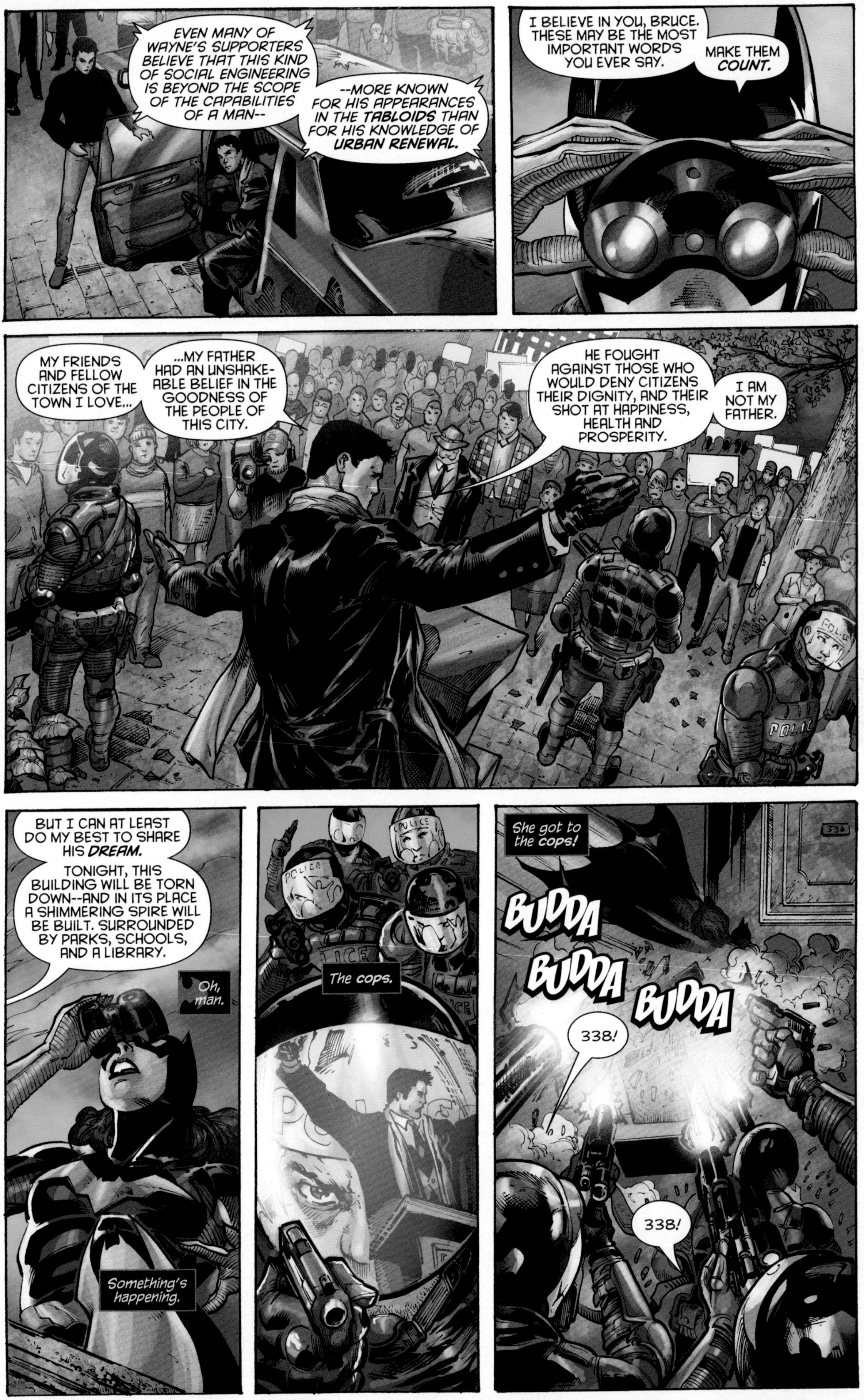
EVEN MANY OF WAYNE'S SUPPORTERS BELIEVE THAT THIS KIND OF SOCIAL ENGINEERING IS BEYOND THE SCOPE OF THE CAPABILITIES OF A MAN--
--MORE KNOWN FOR HIS APPEARANCES IN THE TABLOIDS THAN FOR HIS KNOWLEDGE OF URBAN RENEWAL.
I BELIEVE IN YOU, BRUCE. THESE MAY BE THE MOST IMPORTANT WORDS YOU EVER SAY.
MAKE THEM COUNT.
MY FRIENDS AND FELLOW CITIZENS OF THE TOWN I LOVE...
...MY FATHER HAD AN UNSHAKE-ABLE BELIEF IN THE GOODNESS OF THE PEOPLE OF THIS CITY.
HE FOUGHT AGAINST THOSE WHO WOULD DENY CITIZENS THEIR DIGNITY, AND THEIR SHOT AT HAPPINESS, HEALTH AND PROSPERITY.
I AM NOT MY FATHER.
BUT I CAN AT LEAST DO MY BEST TO SHARE HIS DREAM.
TONIGHT, THIS BUILDING WILL BE TORN DOWN--AND IN ITS PLACE A SHIMMERING SPIRE WILL BE BUILT. SURROUNDED BY PARKS, SCHOOLS, AND A LIBRARY.
Oh, man.
Something's happening.
The cops.
She got to the cops!
BUDDA
BUDDA
BUDDA
338!
338!

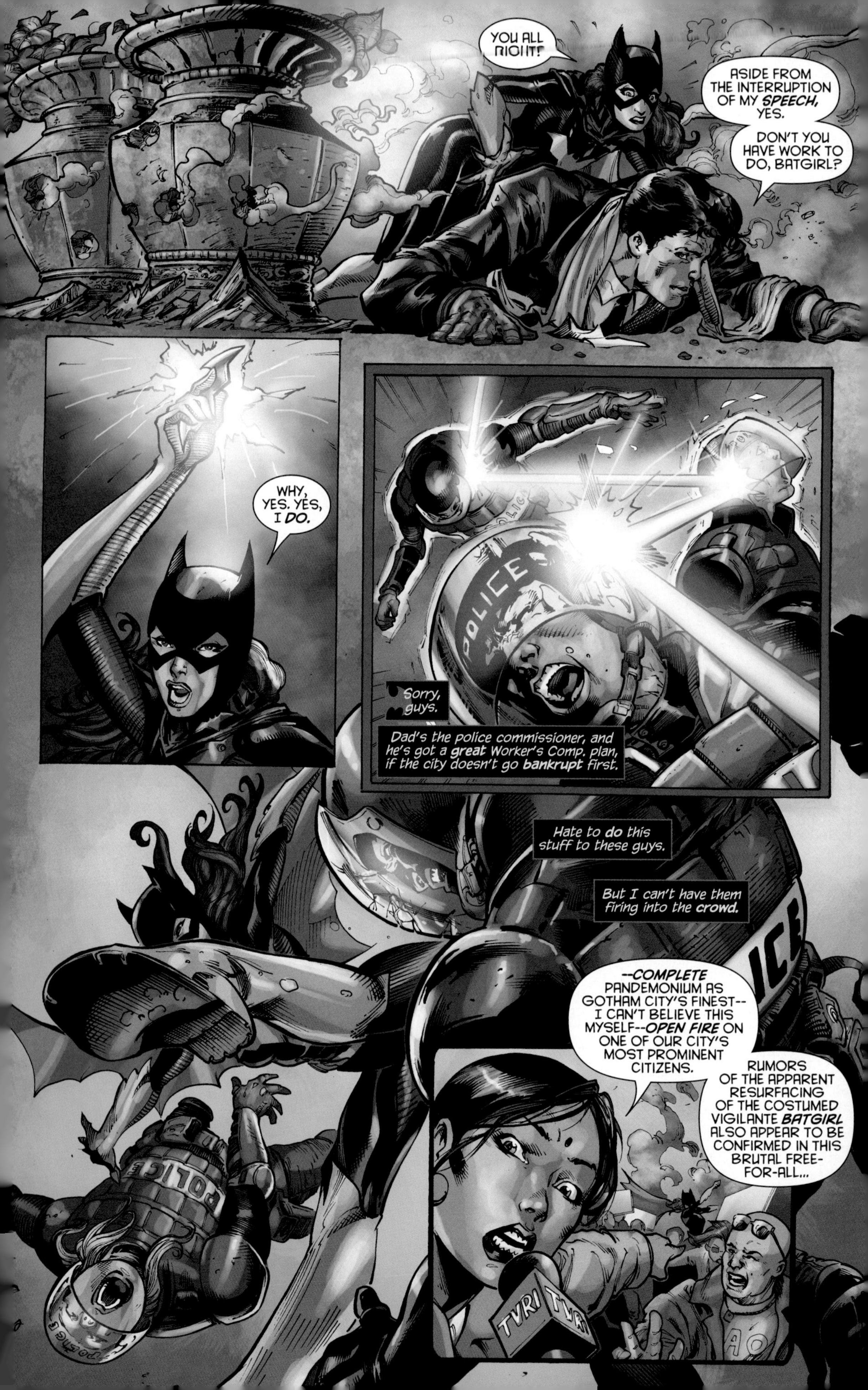

YOU ALL RIGHT?
ASIDE FROM THE INTERRUPTION OF MY SPEECH, YES.
DON'T YOU HAVE WORK TO DO, BATGIRL?
WHY, YES. YES, I DO.
Sorry, guys.
Dad's the police commissioner, and he's got a great Worker's Comp. plan, if the city doesn't go bankrupt first.
Hate to do this stuff to these guys.
But I can't have them firing into the crowd.
--COMPLETE PANDEMONIUM AS GOTHAM CITY'S FINEST--I CAN'T BELIEVE THIS MYSELF--OPEN FIRE ON ONE OF OUR CITY'S MOST PROMINENT CITIZENS.
RUMORS OF THE APPARENT RESURFACING OF THE COSTUMED VIGILANTE BATGIRL ALSO APPEAR TO BE CONFIRMED IN THIS BRUTAL FREE-FOR-ALL...

There she is! On the crane!

OH, *GREAT MEN OF GOTHAM.*

HEY!

WHAT *NOW?*

YOU ARE *UNDER ARREST,* BATGIRL.

ASSUME THE *POSITION.*

KRAK

EVERY *BAD* THING THAT'S HAPPENED IN THIS CITY LIES AT YOUR *FEET.* IT *FEEDS* YOU LIKE THE *DISEASED SOIL* THAT BEARS *POISON FRUIT.*

COME INTO MY *HOUSE* OF *CANDY* AND *DELIGHT* AND *BURN FOREVER!*

She's lost it. Can't let this go on another second.

YOU. MCKENNA.

LOOK, I'M *SORRY* ABOUT YOUR PARTNER. I COULDN'T *HELP* HIM.

BUT YOU HAVE *GOT* TO LET ME *STOP* THAT WOMAN ON THE *CRANE!*

LET THE *PROFESSIONALS* DO THAT, GIRL.

STAND BACK, BATMAN-- SHE'S AN *ACCESSORY!*

YOU CAN ARREST US *BOTH,* THEN--

--BUT *LATER.*

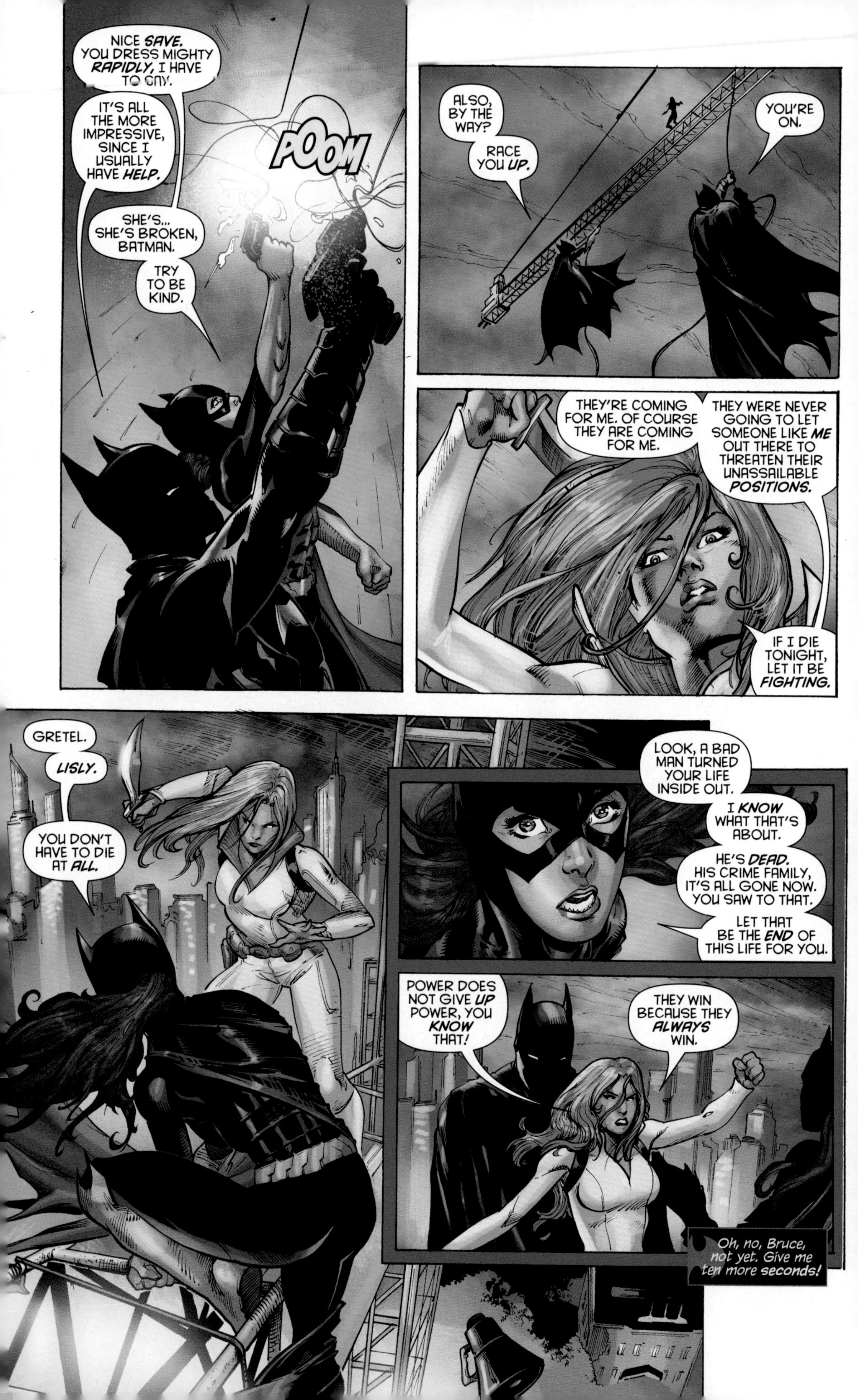
NICE SAVE. YOU DRESS MIGHTY RAPIDLY, I HAVE TO SAY.
IT'S ALL THE MORE IMPRESSIVE, SINCE I USUALLY HAVE HELP.
SHE'S... SHE'S BROKEN, BATMAN.
TRY TO BE KIND.
POOM
ALSO, BY THE WAY?
RACE YOU UP.
YOU'RE ON.
THEY'RE COMING FOR ME. OF COURSE THEY ARE COMING FOR ME.
THEY WERE NEVER GOING TO LET SOMEONE LIKE ME OUT THERE TO THREATEN THEIR UNASSAILABLE POSITIONS.
IF I DIE TONIGHT, LET IT BE FIGHTING.
GRETEL.
LISLY.
YOU DON'T HAVE TO DIE AT ALL.
LOOK, A BAD MAN TURNED YOUR LIFE INSIDE OUT.
I KNOW WHAT THAT'S ABOUT.
HE'S DEAD. HIS CRIME FAMILY, IT'S ALL GONE NOW. YOU SAW TO THAT.
LET THAT BE THE END OF THIS LIFE FOR YOU.
POWER DOES NOT GIVE UP POWER, YOU KNOW THAT!
THEY WIN BECAUSE THEY ALWAYS WIN.
Oh, no, Bruce, not yet. Give me ten more seconds!

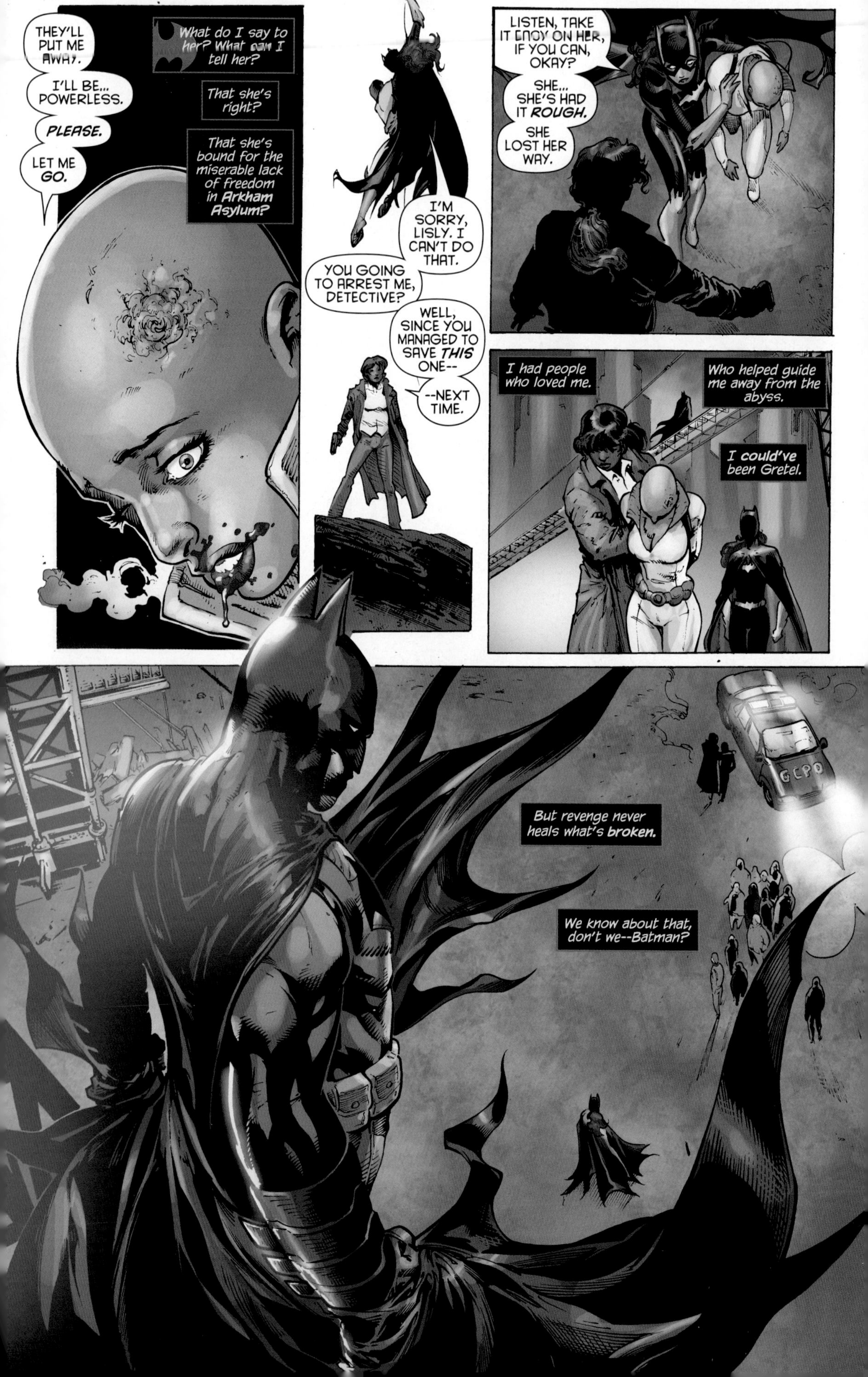

THEY'LL PUT ME AWAY.
I'LL BE... POWERLESS.
PLEASE.
LET ME GO.
What do I say to her? What can I tell her?
That she's right?
That she's bound for the miserable lack of freedom in Arkham Asylum?
I'M SORRY, LISLY. I CAN'T DO THAT.
YOU GOING TO ARREST ME, DETECTIVE?
WELL, SINCE YOU MANAGED TO SAVE THIS ONE--
--NEXT TIME.
LISTEN, TAKE IT EASY ON HER, IF YOU CAN, OKAY?
SHE... SHE'S HAD IT ROUGH.
SHE LOST HER WAY.
I had people who loved me.
Who helped guide me away from the abyss.
I could've been Gretel.
GCPD
But revenge never heals what's broken.
We know about that, don't we--Batman?

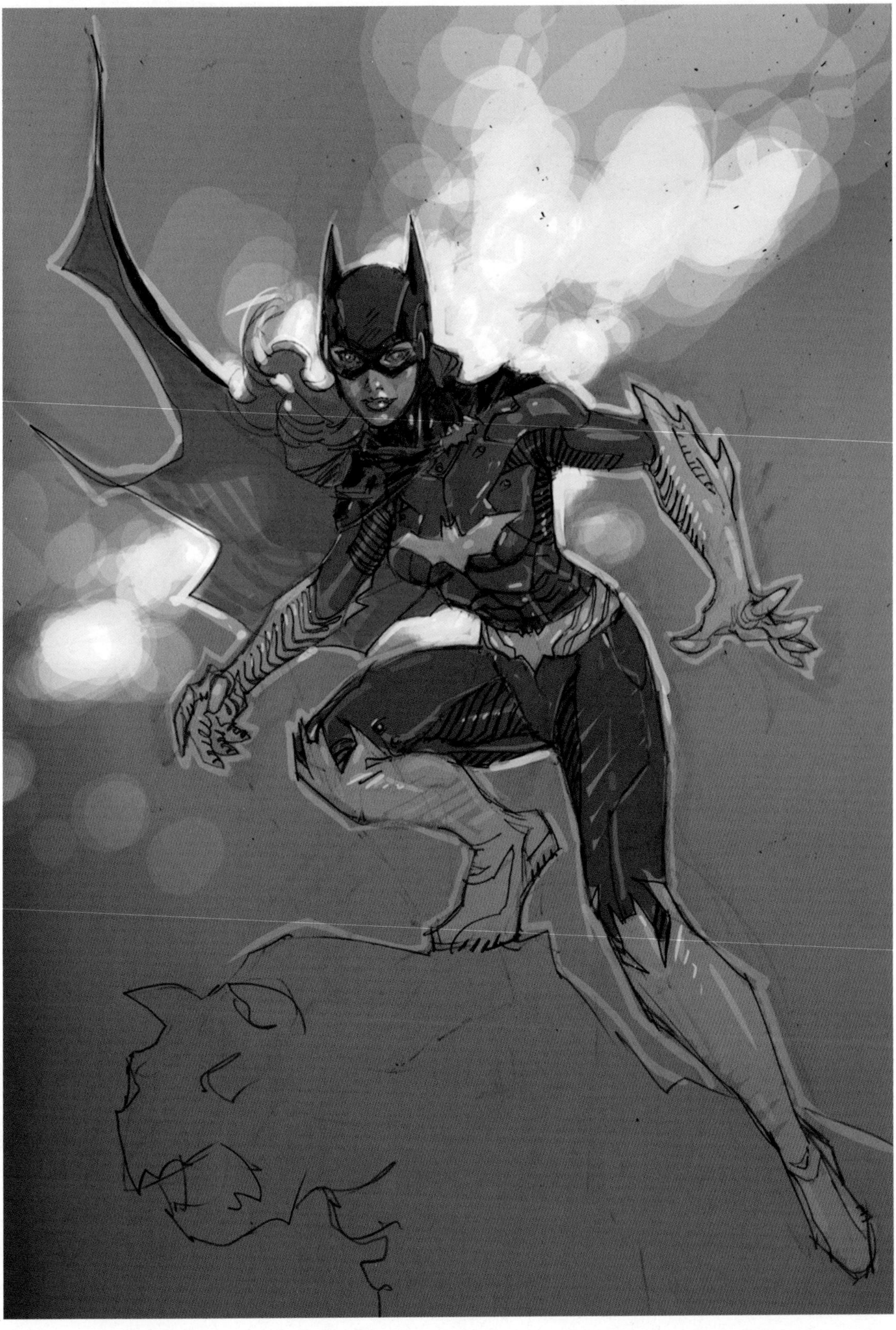

BATGIRL and MIRROR
CHARACTER DESIGNS BY ARDIAN SYAF

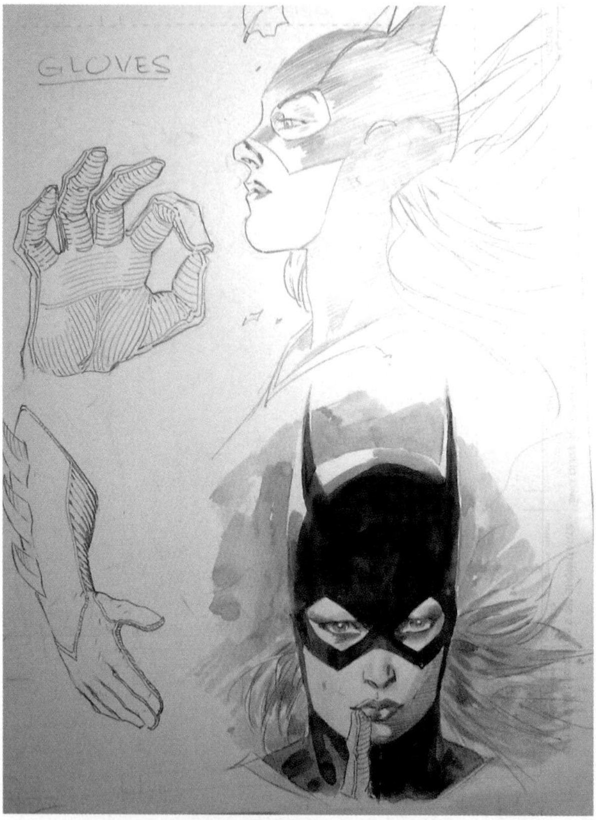
GLOVES

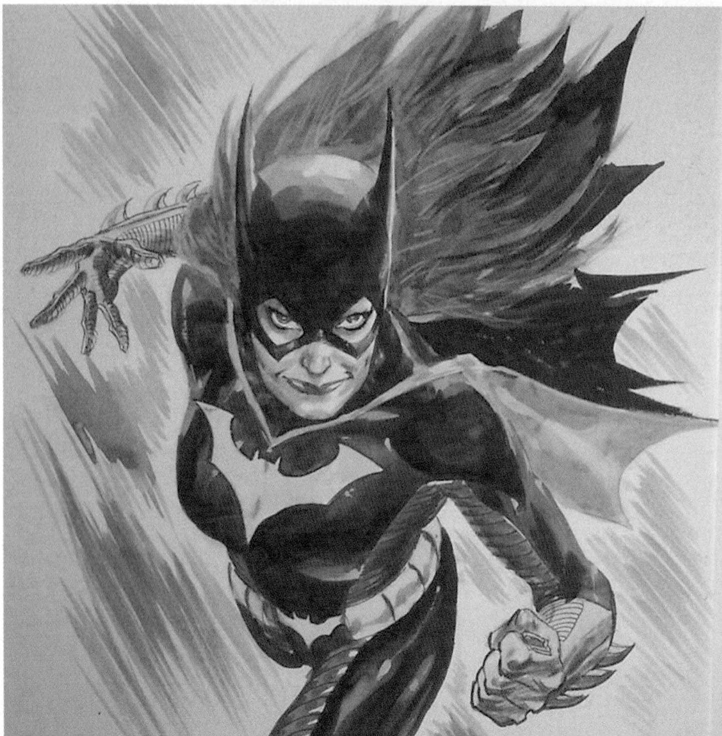

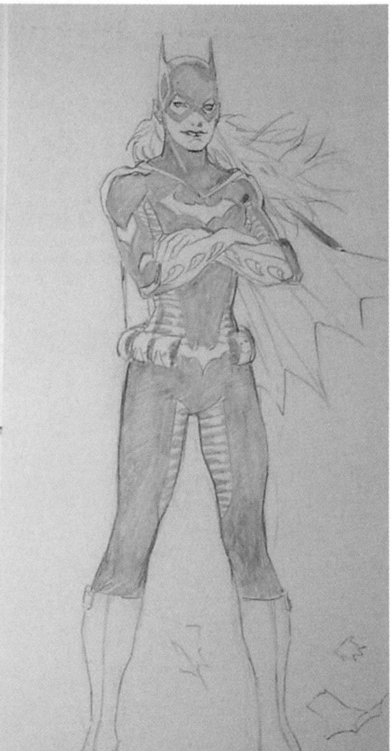

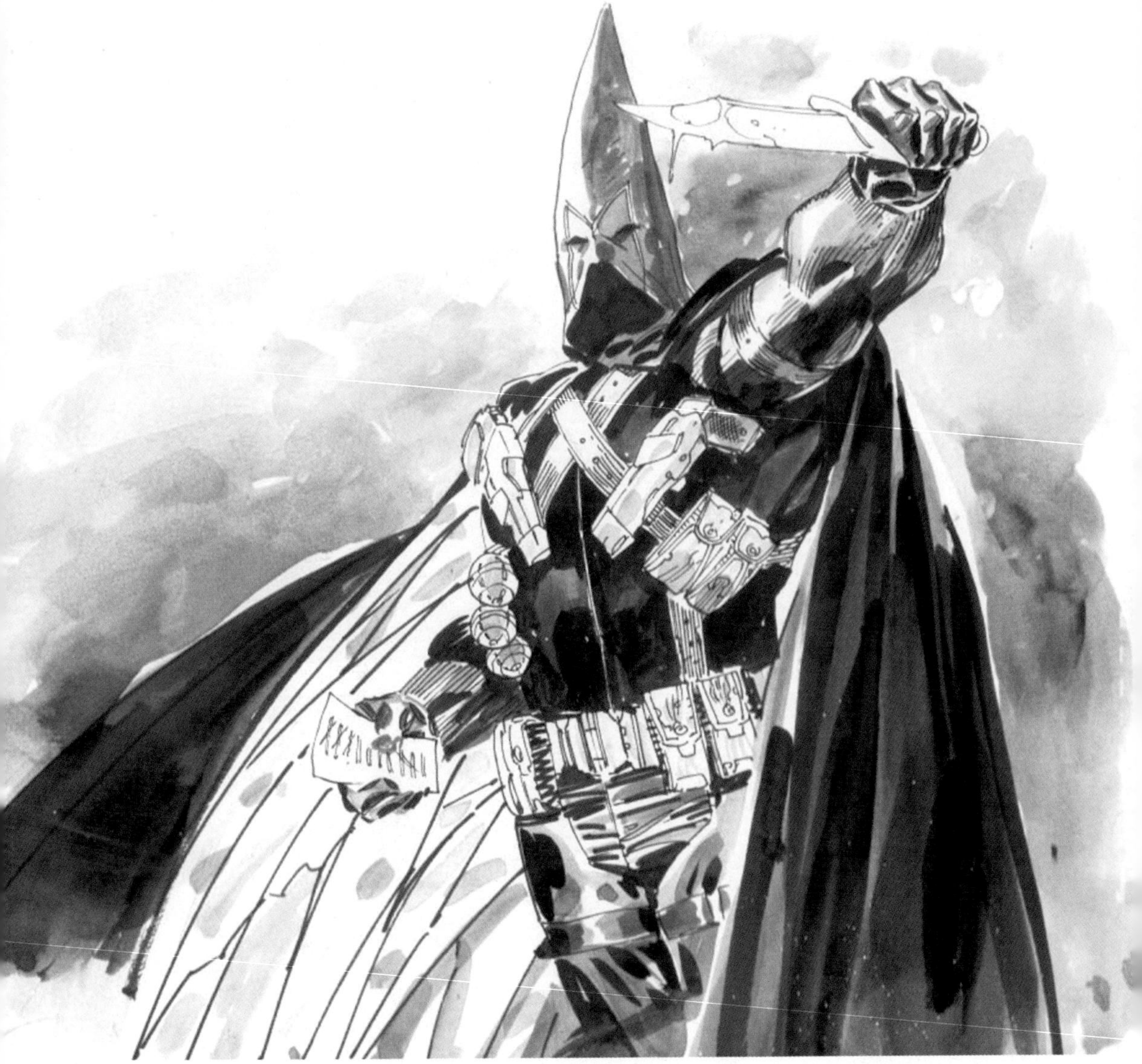

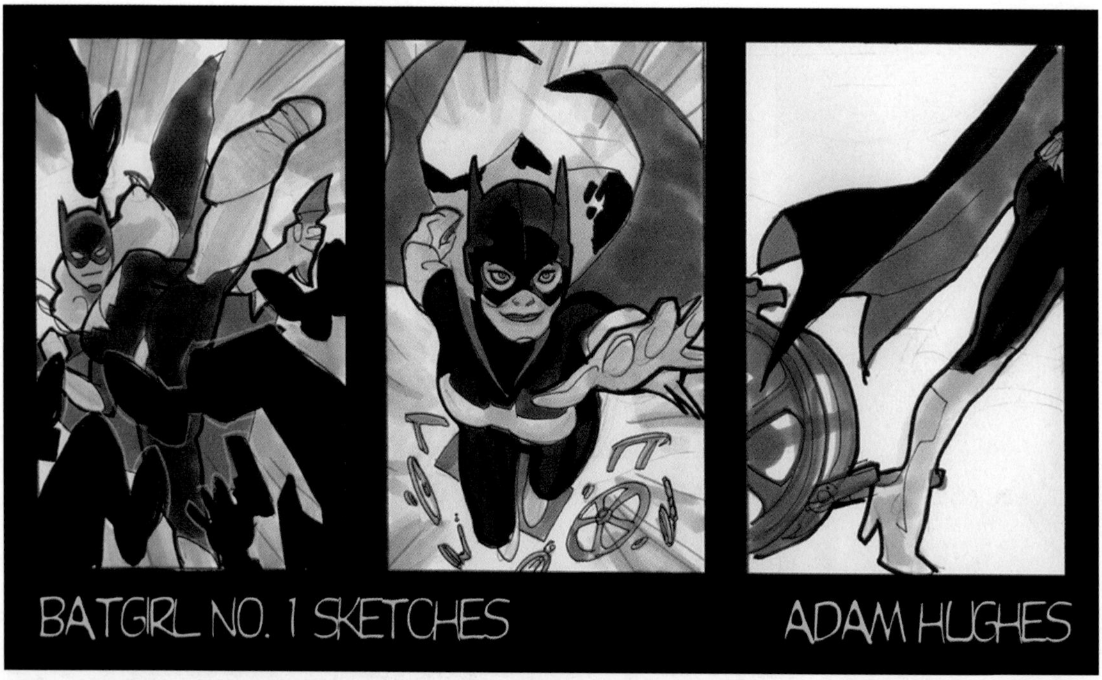
BATGIRL NO. 1 SKETCHES
ADAM HUGHES

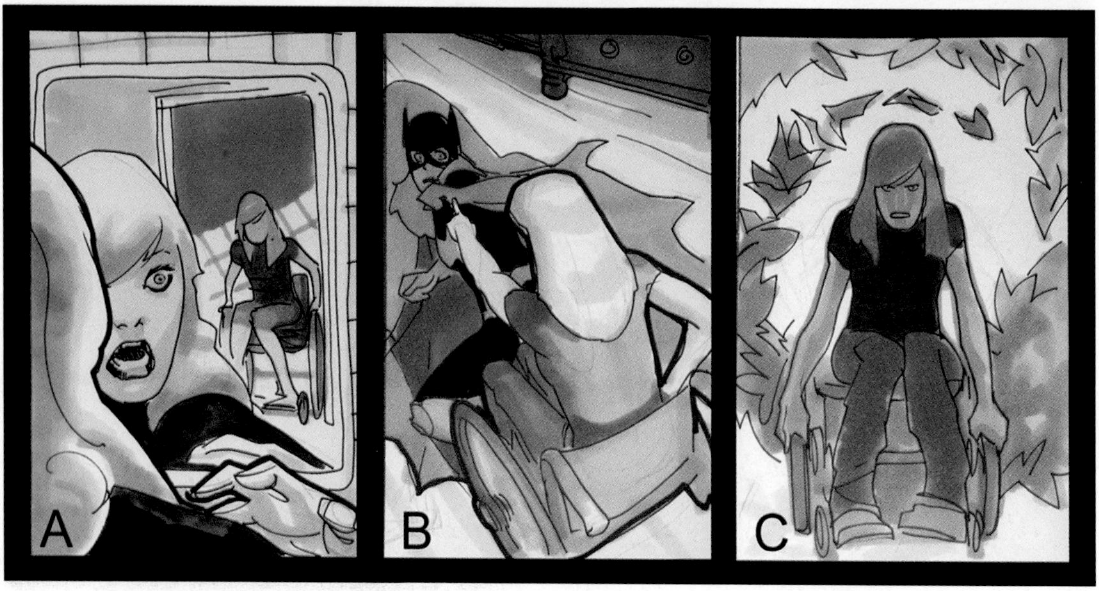
A
B
C

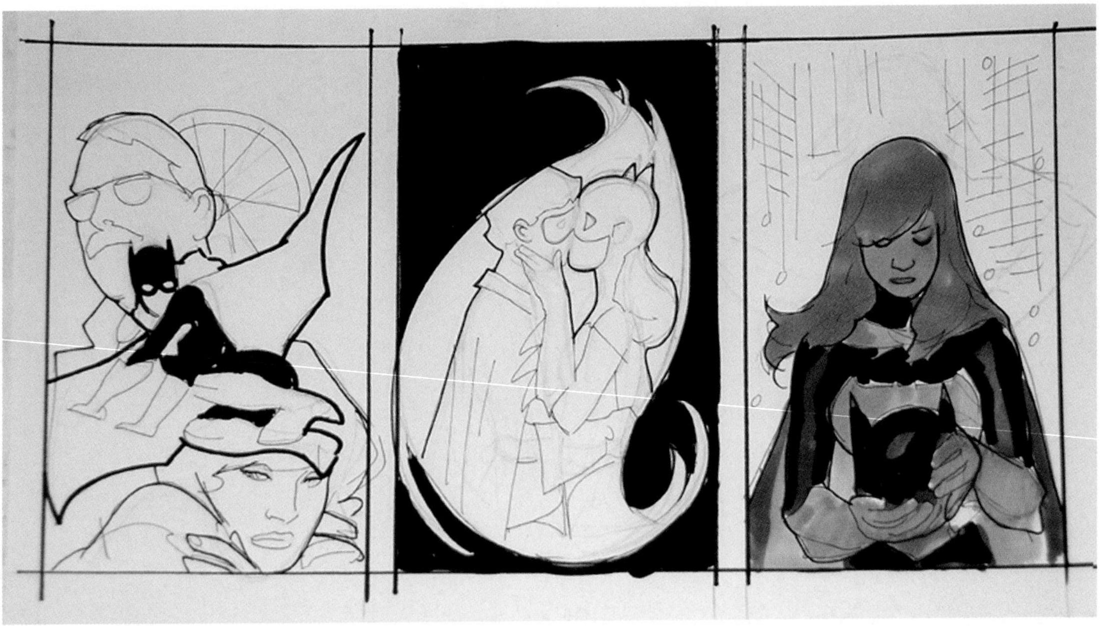

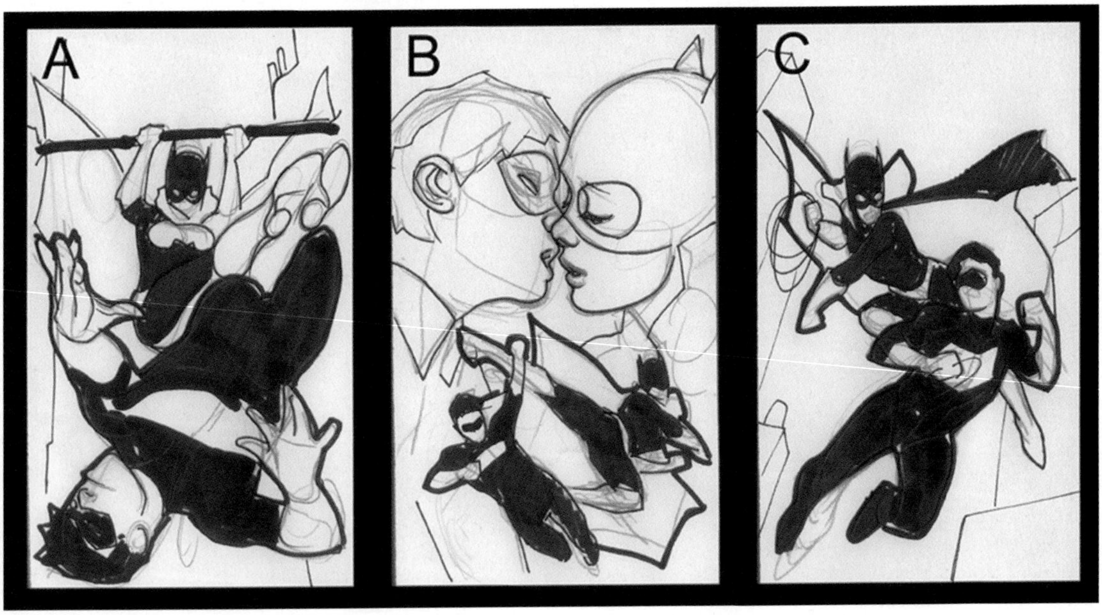
A
B
C

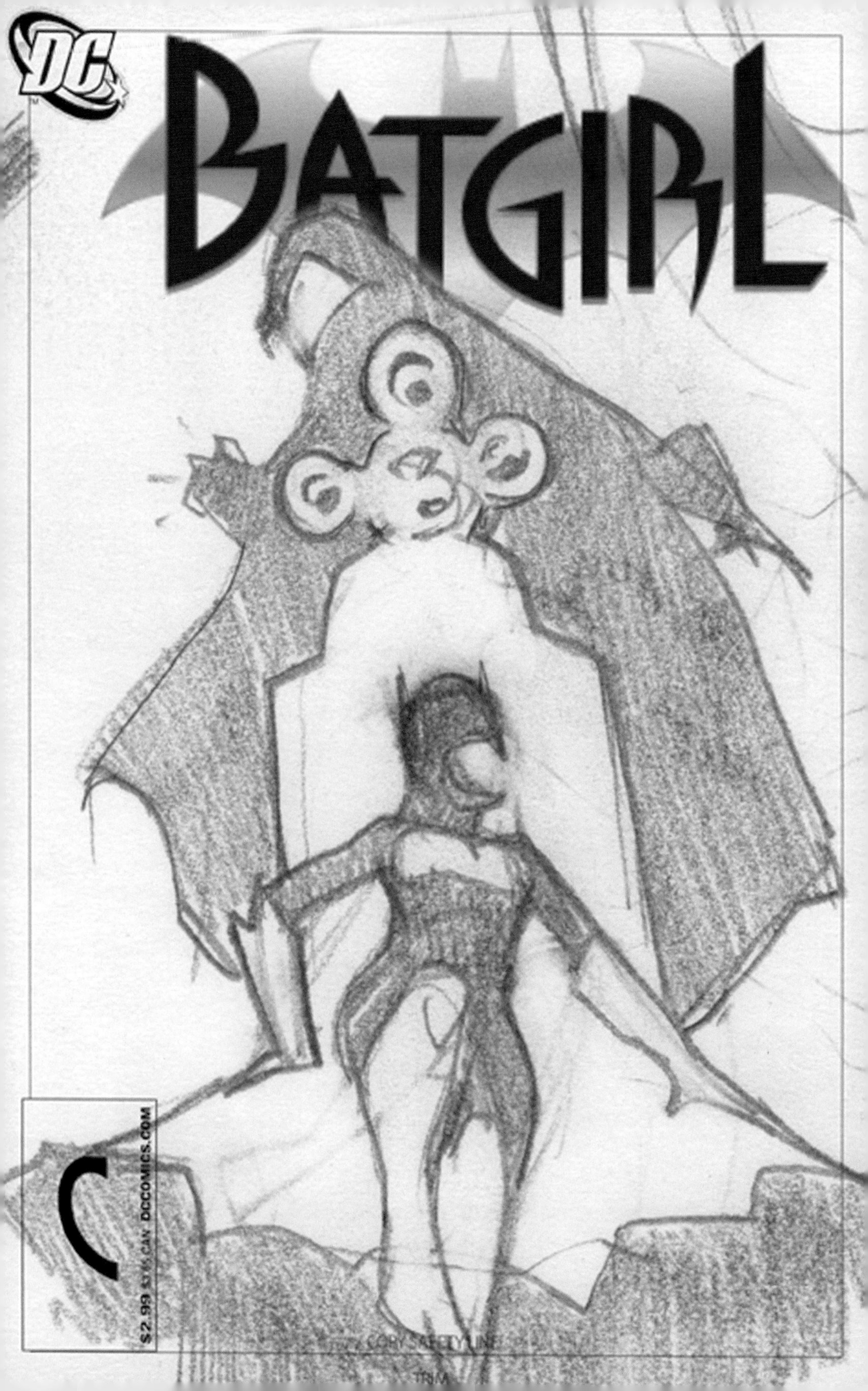
BATGIRL
$2.99 US/CAN DCCOMICS.COM
COPY SAFETY LINE
TRIM

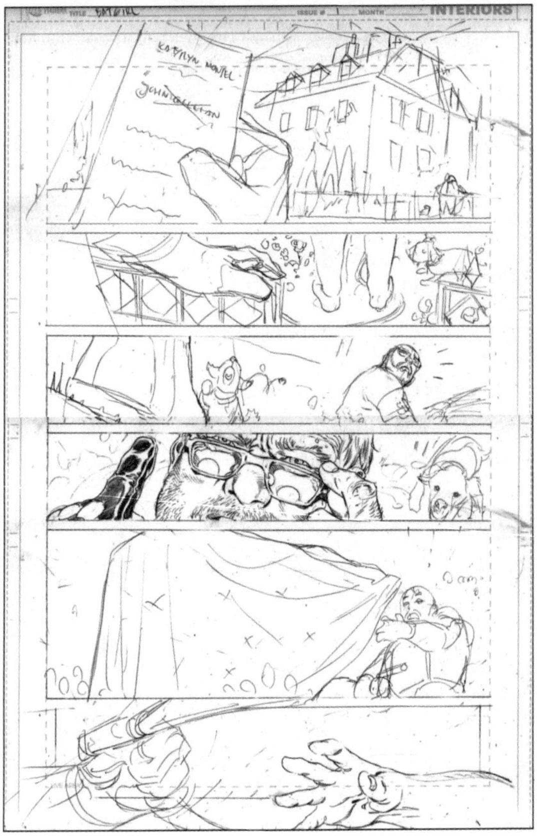
INTERIORS
KATRYN MONTEL

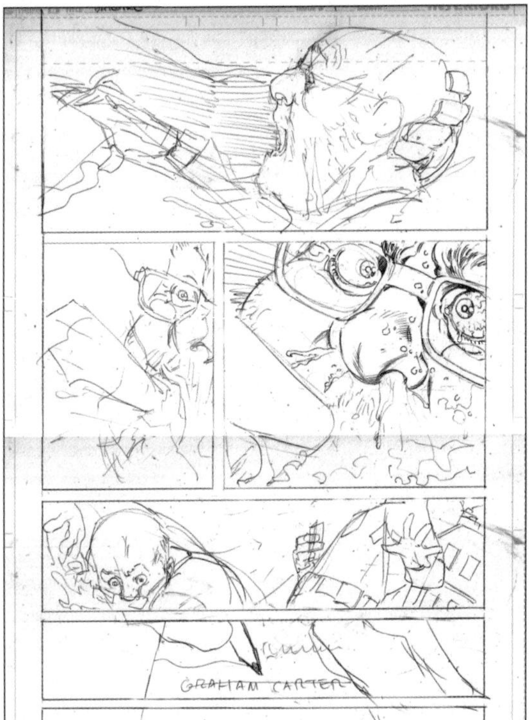
GRAHAM CARTER
BARBARA GORDON

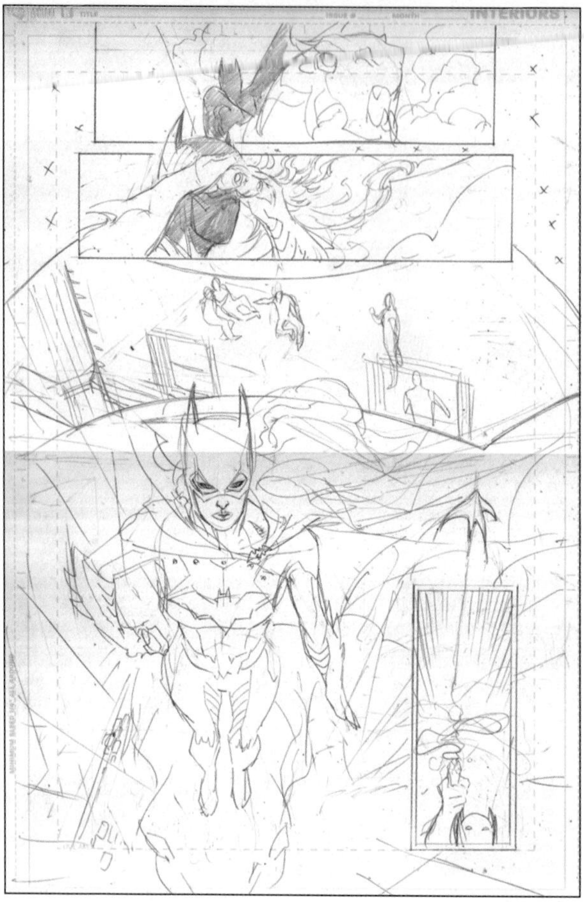
INTERIORS

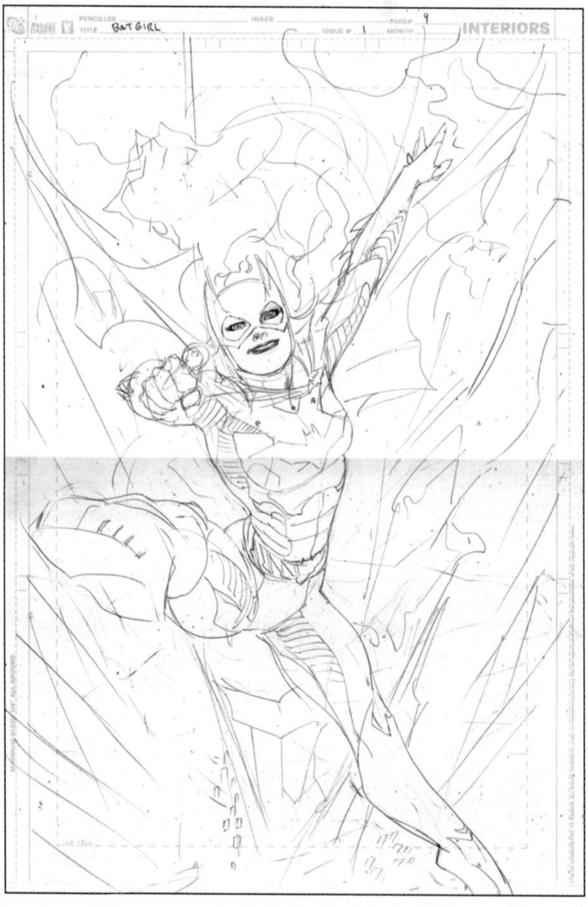
BATGIRL
1
4
INTERIORS